ANNA KONARZEWSKA graduated from the Institute of International Relations (Warsaw University) and the Polish-French Programme for European Studies SGH-SciencesPo (Warsaw School of Economics). She has an MA diploma in international political and economic relations and in economics. She is a doctoral candidate at the International Security Department (Warsaw School of Economics).

Her interests include economic and monetary integration within the European Union, development of the European Security and Defence Policy (including European defence industry), the history and culture of Scandinavian countries and Great Britain, their position in the EU and their attitude towards European integration.

She is a co-editor (with Professor K. Żukrowska) of the book *External Relations of the European Union – Determinants, Casual Trends and Areas* and the author of several publications in Polish (including *Swedish Model of Welfare State, Towards Common EU Policy in Defence Industry*) and English (*Political Interests and Financial Capabilities in View to the Enlargement, European Defence Agency as a Step Towards ESDP*).

Great Britain, Denmark and
Sweden versus the Economic
and Monetary Union

Great Britain, Denmark and Sweden versus the Economic and Monetary Union

Anna Konarzewska

ATHENA PRESS
LONDON

Contents

List of Figures

Introduction

The purpose for creating the European Community (EC) was clear and simple – to turn struggle and mutual destruction into peace, stability and prosperity. Over years the organisation has developed into a complex and broad framework for European cooperation. Starting from an integration of coal and steel industries, it has been gradually covering new sectors of economy, agriculture, social affairs, ecological matters and finally political relationships among European democracies. Furthermore, the features of cooperation have significantly changed. The six continental European countries started from being a free trade area, leading to a customs union and the single European market with common policies and the free flow of goods, services, labour and capital. Finally, one of two main goals of Europe has been reached, namely the creation of the European Economic and Monetary Union (EMU). The idea of European integration has proven to be a success, changing an age-old rivalry into friendship and partnership.[1]

Establishing the Economic and Monetary Union is a very controversial issue among the EU member states. Proponents of this historic undertaking emphasise that without it the single European market, created in 1993 by the Single European Act, would be distorted and fail to achieve its aspiration of unrestricted free trade between the EU member states. Objectively, economists agree that the EMU brings intensive competition across the European continent, thanks to nominal exchange rate stability, reduced transaction costs, greater price transparency, productivity and competitiveness as well as low and stable inflation. Nevertheless, only twelve out of fifteen EU member states joined the third stage of the Economic and Monetary Union. Three countries, namely the United Kingdom, Denmark and Sweden, have remained outside, arguing that such an extensive economic integration could be dangerous for their economy and sectors of industry. Moreover, their societies express a rather unwilling

---

[1] The second main goal of the organisation is to establish a political union.

attitude towards the whole process, underlining a possible loss of national sovereignty.

The United Kingdom of Great Britain and Northern Ireland, as well as Denmark, became legal members of the European Community on 1 January 1973. In the case of Sweden this momentous event took place twenty-two years later, on 1 January 1995.

The history of the British view on the European integration, and her relations with the other member states in that field, is rather controversial. The United Kingdom has always had her own vision, different from the other countries, of the integration business. Her opinion was usually justified by defending her national interests and a broad understanding of the raison d'être. According to common knowledge, Great Britain has never been in favour of deepening European integration and shifting national powers to the supranational level, preferring intergovernmental contacts among the European countries. Until now, Brits have been against shifting many fields of politics and the economy that are perceived as vital for maintaining Britain's position in the world to the European level of cooperation. The country has thus extraordinary rights and opt-out clauses in many cases, of which the one regarding entry to the third stage of the EMU is the most significant. Nevertheless, it is said that in the process of European integration, the United Kingdom has a special role to play, one that is significant and momentous.

Denmark decided to enter the EC mostly by virtue of the British application for a membership to the organisation. The United Kingdom, Germany and Sweden have been, and still remain, main Danish trading partners. Taking Denmark's size and dependency on international economic relations into account, it was a fully justified step. The incumbent Danish government perceived it to be profitable to join the organisation together with its main trade partner. Within the EC, Denmark has chosen to develop cooperation on an intergovernmental level, and worked mostly for transparency of the EU procedures, protection of the environment and stimulation of employment strategies in Europe. Even though the Danish government decided to participate in the EMU from the outset, Denmark is the best example of a country where the nation's opinion conflicts with political decisions approved by the government and the parliament. Both the Maastricht Treaty on

European Union in 1993 and EMU membership in 2000 were rejected in national referenda by the majority of Danish citizens, even though both issues had been supported by the political elites.

Sweden entered the European Union on 1 January 1995. For many years Swedish membership in the EC was not deliberated, since the country has traditionally participated in broad economic and trade relations with the whole world. Moreover, it has pursued the policy of neutrality and it perceived the process of European integration as threatening its established political course. Both factors contributed to its rather moderate attitude towards integration within the European continent. Yet, the country had signed many trade agreements and cooperated with the organisation on a regular economic and social basis before signing the accession treaty; but the cautious attitude survived. Sweden rebuffs not only economic integration within the Economic and Monetary Union, but it also disagrees on closer political collaboration.

The United Kingdom, Denmark and Sweden are the three EU member states which decided not to participate in the project of merging their national currencies into a single one – the euro. The three countries support close economic integration within the single European market, with common policies and free movement of goods and services, people and capital, but they are hostile to handing over their national monetary powers to the European Central Bank (ECB), which, according to the Maastricht Treaty, is responsible for conducting interest rate and exchange rate policies in the Eurozone. Despite the shared profits of EMU membership, opponents of the project underline mostly the loss of national sovereignty and the prospects of creating a federal United States of Europe. Moreover, they point out the inability of the ECB to pursue an integrated economic policy appropriate for all EMU members in regard to their monetary and fiscal conditions, which could prevent unexpected asymmetric shocks. Finally, the possibility of unifying taxes across the European Union is also underscored. Politicians, especially in Denmark and Sweden, are in favour of joining the EMU, while the people themselves, especially in the British Isles, consider the common currency to be a very dangerous threat to their sovereign existence in the world. Nevertheless, the three countries have close economic ties with the euro area, and therefore it would be appropriate for them to become members of the zone. It would intensify their economic integration because elimination of exchange rate risks would reduce uncertainty and costs in regard to trade and investment. Moreover, they would gain direct access to euro-financial markets with attractive investment and financing opportunities. However, the countries have stayed out of the EMU mainly for political reasons. Their politicians have announced the holding of referenda on the issue of entering the Eurozone but no date has been fixed so far.

This book is dedicated to examining the British, Danish and Swedish attitude to the European Economic and Monetary Union. The aim of the analysis is to show the specific features and dimensions of their stances on membership in the Eurozone. The thesis reveals the evolution of the standpoint of the countries towards the development of integration. The main interest is put on reasons for their cautious approach to the process of European integration itself as well as within the economic sectors. The motives for abstaining from the EMU membership, with any political and socio-economic consequences flowing from such a decision, are analysed.

The paper aims at presenting an objective picture and makes a critical review of British, Danish and Swedish attitudes towards the most recent European undertaking in the area of economic and monetary policies. Therefore it has a nation by nation construction. Thanks to this structure, it is possible to demonstrate the most divisive aspects of the approach of each country in the case of membership in the Eurozone. The main idea of the paper is to present and analyse historical, political and socio-economic determinants of the countries' reluctance towards the European Communities/European Union in general, with the main emphasis on reservations towards the EMU and the single currency – the euro. Furthermore, the author demonstrates the broad consequences for the countries in question derived from their non-participation in the EMU. The argument concentrates on profits and losses in the socio-economic and political performance of the countries, taking into account such factors as the political position in the European affairs, shifts in economic determinants and consequently, the general economic situation in international economic and financial affairs.

In section one, the history of economic integration is summarised and developed. The discussion is qualified by a theoretical overview of the process which led to establishment of the

Economic and Monetary Union. The research begins with characterisation of the Werner Plan in 1970, the Snake, the European Monetary System, the Delors Report, creation of the Single Market, and eventually, completing the European Economic and Monetary Union. The second section presents main points of the Maastricht Treaty, which was the most significant document in concluding the project. The main preconditions of a membership in the EMU according to the Treaty are described. In addition, institutional matters – the position of the European Central Bank and the European Board of Central Banks – are mentioned. On each stage, reactions of all countries in question are presented and interpreted critically. In section three, the examination moves on to the subject of political and economic consequences for each country based on their non-participation in the Eurozone. The main attitude of each country towards the process of European integration is characterised, with special emphasis on reactions to several economic solutions proposed by the organisation. Furthermore, the socio-economic and political impacts of abstaining from membership in the EMU on a country performance are described (e.g. interest rates and exchange rates, inflow of capital and foreign direct investments, and competitiveness towards EMU member states). In the conclusions section, future scenarios and solutions are drawn, and their possibility is examined.

I: Towards Economic and Monetary Union

The main goal of the European Communities according to Article 2 of the Treaty on the European Community is:

> ...by establishing a common market and an economic and monetary union and by implementing common policies (...), to promote a harmonious, balanced and sustainable development of economic activities, a high level of employment and of social protection, equality between men and women, sustainable and non-inflationary growth, a high level of protection and improvement of the quality of the environment, the raising of the standard of living and the quality of life and economic and social cohesion and solidarity among Member States.[1]

The above goal was supposed to be achieved by introduction of free flow of goods and services, workers, and capital as well as by the creation of common policies. The members of the European Communities developed their economic cooperation according to the theory of Bartholomew Balassa, who in 1953 presented five major stages of economic integration. Starting with the creation of a free trade area, countries should move towards a customs union, a common market, an economic union and last but not least, economic and monetary union. The process could be successfully concluded by an introduction of a political union.[2]

The member states of the European Communities followed the concept proposed by Bartholomew Balassa, launching common policies in the 1960s (first the Common Agriculture Policy, along with the Common Transport Policy and the Common Commercial Policy), the customs union in 1968 and the Common Market on 1

---

[1] 'Treaty establishing the European Community (Consolidated Version)', in *Dokumenty Europejskie*, edited by A. Przyborowska-Klimczak and E. Skrzydło-Tefelska, Lublin, 1999, vol. III, p.102.

[2] F. McDonald, 'Market integration in the European Union', in *European Economic Integration*, edited by F. McDonald and S. Dearden, Longman, 1999, p.34–35.

January 1993. The last phase, namely the creation of the European Economic and Monetary Union (EMU), was finished as the national currencies of the member states were replaced by the common currency – the euro – on 1 January 2002. Nevertheless, there are three countries which have taken no part in this momentous undertaking – the United Kingdom, Denmark and Sweden.

The United Kingdom has always supported economic integration, especially in terms of a free trade area followed by establishment of a single market. The arguments in favour were announced widely, relating mostly to the profits of the British economy, the process of restructuring national factories and companies, the increase of the competitiveness of British exports on both the European and world markets, as well as an inflow of the foreign investments. However, the British have been rather reserved concerning the idea of replacing the pound sterling with the euro. Both politicians and economists underline differing economic cycles in Great Britain and on the European continent, the relative weakness of the common currency in comparison to the pound sterling, the possibility of higher inflation rates and what comes next – the diminishing competitiveness of British exports. Moreover, there are also political reasons, especially concerning the defence of the national sovereignty, which could explain negative attitude towards the EMU in Britain.

In the case of Denmark and Sweden, the arguments for staying outside the Eurozone and the common currency are broadly the same as in the United Kingdom. Since entering the European Community, Denmark was in favour of environmental and social cooperation but against the creation of a common market and an economic and monetary union. The country had a strong position in international economic and financial relations, thanks to its dealing with the other Nordic countries, Great Britain and West Germany. Furthermore, any creation of an economic union with a single currency threatened not only the Danish economy but the national sovereignty of the country as well.[3]

1.   The Werner Plan

In 1957, six European countries (Germany, France, Belgium, the Netherlands, Luxembourg and Italy) signed the Treaty of Rome,

---

[3] K. Kołodziejczyk, *Geneza wspólnotowej waluty euro*, Warszawa, 2000, p.45.

establishing the European Economic Community (EEC). Nevertheless, the document contained only general provisions, which might have led to an economic and monetary union in the coming years. The reasons for such a cautious move were twofold. First, the Bretton Woods system was responsible for providing the international community with a high level of financial stability. Its effects were known by the stable international markets and long-lasting surpluses in the budgets of the EEC countries. Second, the failure to create the European political and military union in the 1950s demonstrated that the process of integration must be pursued cautiously.[4] The Treaty set up a Monetary Committee, which was responsible for reviewing national economic policies of the EEC member states together with their monetary and financial situation. General clauses on supranational economic cooperation were viewed as an obstacle to create even a framework of a closer monetary collaboration. Economists such as Stephen Frank Overturf judge that the additional reason for the failure of the process was lack of overlapping specific interests of the countries involved in the project, whose interplay could have developed a European economic policy.[5]

In the late 1950s and 1960s several proposals to tighten up the economic cooperation among the members of the European Communities were submitted. In 1962 the EEC Commission recommended establishing a supranational economic planning with:

> ...a committee of governors of member central banks, a common monetary policy with fixed rates of exchange between member states with very narrow limits on the variation allowed, a European reserve currency, a 'confrontation' of national budgets, and a continuation of the liberalisation of capital movements.[6]

However, there were countries in the organisation that were not in favour of the creation of a European common economic and financial policy, especially West Germany and France.[7]

---

[4] In 1950 a proposition to create the European Defence Community was submitted but the French National Assembly rejected it in 1954.

[5] S. F. Overturf, *Money and European Union*, London, 2000, p.4.

[6] Ibid., p.5.

[7] West Germany supported economic and political relations with the United States, especially their liberalising dimension. The fear of uncontrolled inflation explained

Applications for a membership from Great Britain, Ireland, Denmark and Norway in 1961 posed another difficulty for formulating conditions of a common monetary policy. However, the EEC Commission managed to establish the Committee of Governors of the Central Banks of the EEC, a Budgetary Policy Committee and a Medium-term Economic Policy Committee, whose role consisted of consultations on the monetary and exchange rates changes.

The next step towards the more advanced economic cooperation within the EEC was the first Barre Plan, submitted in 1969. The Plan consisted of two elements. The first one called for regular consultations in the field of national economic policies. The second one suggested launching a common financial aid system by offering loans for each member state in times of an economic crisis or serious budgetary turbulences. Nonetheless, the Plan was not warmly welcomed until the Hague Summit in December 1969, which was a milestone in the European integration as a whole. It was organised following the shifts of power in two most important members of the ECC. The French president, Georges Pompidou, who replaced General de Gaulle, showed much more inclination towards the process of economic and monetary integration. So did the German chancellor, Willy Brandt. With their leadership the other four countries followed the initiatives and the Hague Summit decided on several noteworthy issues, e.g. the accession negotiations with Great Britain, Ireland, Denmark and Norway were reopened, and the foundations for the political cooperation were established. The great mass of consultations was devoted to the creation of a monetary and economic union, and the heads of state and governments agreed to prepare a detailed plan for the gradual creation of such a union. The successful outcome of European integration in the 1960s, the favourable state of the international economy as well as the signs of weakness shown by the Bretton Woods system, are perceived to be the main reasons for the acceleration of the process. However, there were two groups in the European Council that had their own suggestions on the subject. According to the 'monetarists' from France, Belgium and

---

the rest. The French president, Charles de Gaulle, expressed his negative attitude towards supranational cooperation several times. To read more see S. F. Overturf, [2000], p.5.

Luxembourg, the first step on the way to an economic and monetary union should have consisted of fixing exchange rates and introducing a single currency, followed by the necessary adjustments in individual national economic policies. Contrary to the above views, the group of the 'economists' from West Germany, the Netherlands and Italy, postulated coordination of the most important aspects of economic policy such as inflation, budget deficit, public debt, and then heading for monetary integration.[8] The European Council wanted to reconcile both groups and appointed Pierre Werner, the Prime Minister and Finance Minister of Luxembourg, to be a chairman of the Committee, whose task was to draw up a consociational plan for an economic and monetary union. However, the Committee was not able to set up common practices regarding how to achieve the goal, and split up into two groups again. Fortunately, in the end, agreement between monetarists and economists on future economic integration was accomplished.

In October 1970, the Werner Committee presented a consistent report,[9] which included opinions of both the 'economists' and the 'monetarists', and offered a compromise acceptable for all. It decided that creation of the European Economic and Monetary Union would be pursued simultaneously ('parallelism') in three stages during a 10-year period. However, the Werner Report pointed out the prerequisites for the first stage of the process only. They consisted of:

> '...total and irreversible mutual convertibility free from fluctuations in rates and with immutable parity rates, or preferably they will be replaced by a sole Community currency', a centralised control over money and credit, a unified capital market, strong control over public financing at the Community level, and increased regional and structural policies.[10]

---

[8] France was very concerned about fixed exchange rates, which had a twofold meaning. First, they would contribute into the Common Agriculture Policy (CAP) that benefited France, and they would provide Europe with 'monetary personality' versus the US dollar. On the contrary, Germans preferred to start with coordination of the national economic policies, which might have brought stable economic growth and controlled inflation. To read more, see S. F. Overturf, [2000], p.9–13.

[9] The original text of the Werner Report see S. F. Overturf, [2000], p.185–207.

[10] K. Dyson, K. Featherstone, *The Road to Maastricht. Negotiating Economic and Monetary Union*, Oxford, 1999, p.108–109.

It was clear that the project envisaged transferring part of the national sovereignty on the supranational level, especially to a special unit responsible for the economic policy as well as to a Community system of central banks. Consequently, a political union would become necessary, and in the long run it would be impossible to do without it. Furthermore, the final step would be a creation of a Community single currency. The European Council managed to decide on the beginning of the first stage according to the provisions of the Committee. Additionally, the European Fund of Monetary Cooperation to coordinate funds for mutual support ('pooling of reserves'), and a body based on the US Federal Reserve System model to keep and manage ECC reserves, were to be established.[11]

The Werner Report was a significant document, and it laid the foundations for the future creation of the Economic and Monetary Union. The authors accepted the need to reinforce cooperation in both economic and monetary policies, taking further steps simultaneously. The Werner Report also made some striking points, which were important to realise while launching the process, especially the need for transferring national sovereignty and part of state powers onto the supranational level. It is however important to emphasise that West Germany, in accordance with France, proposed the 'safeguard clause', which established the possibility of withdrawing support for the monetary obligations if the progress on the field of converging the economic and monetary policies of the member states was not sufficient. It meant that the second stage was not introduced automatically but according to the level of economic coordination, and with the consent of all countries. Any member could resign from participating in the further steps of the union if its national interests were endangered. This clause is compared with the 'opting-out' clauses, which allow current members (the United Kingdom and Denmark) to stay outside the third stage of the EMU.[12]

The Werner Report set out an ambitious plan to establish a monetary and economic union among the European countries which decided to follow its requirements and commenced the strenuous process of creating advanced economic cooperation at

---

[11] K. Kołodziejczyk, [2000], p.21–22.

[12] Ibid., p.24.

the supranational level. Nevertheless, the internal opposition chaired by France reappeared. The French were mainly concerned about transferring national sovereignty to a supranational body created by the EEC.

> France refused to consider any binding agreement on final transfer of powers, a revision of the Treaty of Rome, the creation of new economic and monetary institutions, or new powers for the European Parliament.[13]

In the meantime the international monetary problems of 1971–1973 (oil crises) emerged and caused tensions in the exchange rates of main international currencies. Therefore, the member states of the European Communities sacrificed the idea of economic integration, while reacting differently to the economic turbulences appearing on the national scene. Then the oil crisis of 1973 occurred. It worsened the divergence between the economic policies of the EEC members and weakened support for any proposal for European integration in general, and economic and monetary union in particular.[14]

The United Kingdom as well as Denmark could not express their opinions on the Werner Plan as they were still in the process of negotiating future membership in the European Communities. However, British politicians were fairly satisfied with the outcome, bearing in mind their negative attitude towards any proposals which went beyond intergovernmental cooperation. The same was applicable to Denmark, which had strong economic and trade ties with the Nordic countries and Great Britain.[15]

2.   The European Monetary System

The internal turmoil in the European Communities at the beginning of the 1970s, as well as international events mentioned above, prevented the project proposed in the Werner Report from progressing. However, in April 1972 the Basel Agreement was

---

[13] S. F. Overturf, [2000], p.15.

[14] J. Muns, 'From the Werner Plan to the Euro or the History of the Long March Toward European Monetary Union', in *Spain and the Euro: Risks and Opportunities*, edited by J. Muns, Barcelona, 1997, p.13.

[15] D. Heathcoat-Amory, 'Single European Currency. Why the United Kingdom must say "No"', European Commission Economic Paper, July 1994, no.108, p.2–3.

reached among the central banks, according to which the 'snake in the tunnel' was created. It functioned outside the formal EC institutions. Moreover, five non-members – the United Kingdom, Ireland, Denmark, Norway and Sweden – entered the system. The European states succeeded in narrowing down the margins of fluctuations between the exchange rates of their national currencies to ±2.25%. Moreover, the ECC national currencies were allowed to float within the wider tunnel established by the International Monetary Fund. The agreement consisted also of requirements for short-term credit.[16] Great Britain did not oppose the idea, albeit she managed to keep the pound in the system only until June 1972 because of speculative pressures and a deficit on the balance of payments.[17] In addition, the negative effects of the oil crisis of the 1973 as well as the Labour Prime Minister James Callaghan's opposing view on a fixed exchange rates system prevented the pound from returning to the snake.[18] His decision was strongly attacked by the Conservative Party and its leader Margaret Thatcher, who talked about 'a sad day for Europe'. According to her view, Great Britain would benefit from the membership in the snake, especially in terms of reaching a stability of finances disturbed during the oil crisis.[19]

Denmark had to leave the snake as well, although it soon re-entered it and remained within the system until 1977, together with West Germany, the Netherlands, Luxembourg, Belgium and Norway.[20] Nevertheless, the currencies split into weak and strong ones; the former consisted of those of Germany, the Netherlands

---

[16] *Unia Europejska. Podręcznik akademicki*, edited by L. Ciamaga, E. Latoszek, K. Michałowska-Gorywoda, L. Oręziak, E. Teichmann, Warszawa, 1999, p.213–228; A. Moravcsik, *The Choice for Europe. Social Purpose and State Power from Messina to Maastricht*, Cornell University Press, 1998, p.293–294.

[17] The EEC member states were influenced by the oil crisis differently – in Great Britain the unemployment rate increased up to 5%, and inflation up to 24%, while in Germany it amounted to 5%, which made it difficult to reach economic convergence.

[18] A. Gamble, 'The European Issue in British Politics', in *Britain For and Against Europe. British Politics and the Question of European Integration*, edited by D. Baker and D. Seawright, Oxford, 1998, p.20.

[19] A. Moravcsik, [1998], p.282–283.

[20] Norway refused to join the European Communities but decided to stay in the snake as an associate member (the same was applicable to Sweden). R. Matera, *Integracja ekonomiczna krajów nordyckich*, Toruń, 2001, p.17.

and Norway, the latter being the French, Belgian and Danish ones. The weak-currency countries attempted to avoid unilateral devaluation against the German mark, using external financing and capital controls, which proved to be ineffective. As a result, the German mark ruled in the system, but it was a limited system, nonetheless.[21]

The existence of the snake was complicated primarily because of the international obstacles influencing the economic situation of the ECC members, namely the oil crisis, together with disorders of the US dollar and the Bretton Woods system.[22] On the other hand, internal barriers to an economic and monetary integration, created mostly by France, remained vivid. The individual situation of each member state and its particular ways to overcome economic difficulties predominated and barred convergence of national economic policies from appearing. The discussions on the subject in question were reduced to establishment of a European Monetary Cooperation Fund in 1973 and a Regional Fund in 1975. However, with the French exit from the snake the process of European integration slowed down, not to be reopened until the late 1970s.

During the 1970s some proposals targeted on deepening an economic integration in the Communities were submitted,[23] but the European Council took the historic step of constructing the European Monetary System (EMS) in December 1978. The decision was based on the suggestions of Roy Jenkins, a president of the EEC Commission, which were presented in 1977. Jenkins realised that only tight cooperation of main actors could be beneficial and enable the European Communities to launch a monetary union. His project was focused on methods of bringing down inflation rates, and was addressed to those countries which had such difficulties, mainly West Germany, Great Britain, France and Italy. Its main idea was to reinforce the snake and bring non-snake EEC member countries back into the system. Jenkins found the views of monetarists and economists (on ends and means respectively) complementary and suggested they should be bound together. Moreover, he outlined those functions which could be

---

[21] A. Moravcsik, [1998], p.294–295.

[22] About the oil crisis of 1973 and its international effects read: S. F. Overturf, [2000], p.17–19; K. Kołodziejczyk, [2000], p.24–30.

[23] To read about details of the proposals see S. F. Overturf, [2000], p.24–25.

best performed on the supranational level, leaving the rest for a state to cope with on the national level. Consequently, the best results of each would be achieved. In such a way problems with high unemployment rates, inflation and regional imbalances could be conquered and decreased.[24] Moreover, in 1977 the MacDougall Report was published. It emphasised the need for fiscal federalism at the European level to compensate asymmetric shocks once monetary independence was lost. It estimated that an EEC budget of at least 5% of European GDP was needed for carrying out this job.[25]

The main aim of the European Monetary System (EMS) was an establishment of 'an area of monetary stability in Europe'.[26] Under the decision of the Council of Ministers the EMS began to operate on 13 March 1979, as an agreement between the participating members' central banks. The system consisted of three elements, namely the Exchange Rate Mechanism (ERM), credit mechanism and the definition of the European Currency Unit (ECU), which was based on the value of all national currencies of the EEC member states counted proportionally to their economic value and status in the European Communities (according to the value of the GDP of each member and its share in the Community trade). The Exchange Rate Mechanism was meant to keep the fluctuations of exchange rates of the national currencies within the margins of ±2.25% (for Italy the margins were widened up to ±6%), and its most important feature was the parity grid, which showed the central rates between each pair of member states that could be modified within the noted margins. Last but not least, EMS comprised the credit mechanism, which obliged the participating central banks of participants to intervene in the financial market if the margin of monetary fluctuations reached the border of ±15%.[27]

Great Britain participated in preparatory meetings of the EMS but her attitude towards the Plan was rather negative and she opted out in the first phase. All the EEC member states except the United

---

[24] To read more about Jenkins's propositions see S. F. Overturf, [2000], p.26–28.

[25] B. Eichengreen, 'Saving Europe's Automatic Stabilisers', in *The Impact of the Euro*, edited by M. Baimbridge, B. Burkitt, P. Whyman, London, 2000, p.87.

[26] J. Muns, [1997], p.13.

[27] K. Kołodziejczyk, [2000], p.31–40; L. Oręziak, *Euro. Nowy Pieniądz*, Warszawa, 1999, p.18–20; N. Healey, 'Macroeconomic policy coordination', in F. McDonald and S. Dearden, [1999], p.82–86.

Kingdom joined all aspects of the EMS. Britain was not included in the ERM, an essential part of the whole undertaking. The reasons for such a move were numerous and complex. In the United Kingdom the market was strongly believed to be the best determinant of the equilibrium exchange rate. Moreover, the anti-inflation economic policy in Britain was focused on controlling the money supply (through depreciation, as Great Britain was a weak-currency country) contrary to the European countries, which were dedicated to exchange rates targets. Accordingly, the British took a global view, and regarded stability to be more international (and therefore reached within the International Monetary Fund, IMF) than the European matter. The reason for such an approach was caused by the fact that a great many of Britain's trade partners originated in non-European continents. Moreover, Great Britain pursued distinctive international economic interests. Until the late 1970s the pound sterling was still the world's second reserve currency and hence, the sterling balances held by foreign banks exposed the currency to any fall in Britain's balance-of-payments position, and to short-term swings on the foreign exchange markets. Furthermore, the British economic cycle resembled more that of the United States than that of the European continent. 'This asymmetry was probably the result of the pattern of wider international trade relations and also of a similarity in the structures of the British and US capital markets.'[28] In conclusion, economic convergence of the United Kingdom with the EEC member states was very difficult to manage.[29]

In 1979 the Conservative Party gained power in Westminster and gave great support for the creation of a single market. However, the new British government was adamantly against introducing the EMS, stressing British insularity and the traditional defence of national interests. The British politicians regarded the new activity as a way of competing with the US dollar, which could have dangerous results. Additionally, they had a broader worldview, paying more attention to the international solutions which occurred within the IMF. Finally, the United Kingdom underscored that the system could fail to meet the expectations of its founders. And even though it might succeed, it would not be

---

[28] K. Dyson, K. Featherstone, [1999], p.538.

[29] Ibid., p.538.

able to diminish difficulties linked with the high inflation rates.[30] On the other hand, Great Britain realised that in political terms it should have joined the EMS so that her position in the European Community would be enforced, and the situation of the organisation itself would be more favourable in international economic and financial relations.[31] Nevertheless, the attitude of the British companies and financial institutions toward the EMS was negative. The Confederation of British Industry (CBI) stressed the miserable situation of the British economy. It regarded floating exchange rates as profitable for the competitiveness of British industry. Moreover, the CBI recognised the helpful role of the floating exchange rates for decreasing interest rates and raising the prices of export goods, which could make a considerable contribution to the British budget, thus having an impact on the inflation rate. For the CBI, the best solution for the British economy was to depreciate the pound in relation to the European currencies and the US dollar. In that sense, opponents of the British membership in the EMS emphasised that the system could contribute to create an asymmetry between weak (e.g. the pound sterling) and strong currencies (e.g. the German mark). In other words, rocketing inflation, which might occur, would force the British government to put restrictions on public expenditure, which consequently would cause a slowdown in economic and financial reforms as well as a decrease in economic growth. On the other hand, supporters of the EMS pointed out that the membership would be the best way for combating inflation and introducing budget discipline.[32] In the end, the argument of inflationary inclinations in the British economy and the possibility of cutting down the budget spendings by £2 billion prevailed. The Callaghan government published a 'Green Paper on the European Monetary System', where it was stressed that the possible profits for the British economy from participating in the system would be noticed only when the European Community provided it with financial transfers, which could protect it from declining economic growth,

---

[30] K. Kołodziejczyk, [2000], p.33.

[31] Great Britain knew that her membership in the EMS would have been appreciated by the other EEC members but she wanted something in return, namely reforming the CAP, increasing transfers from the European Fund of Regional Development, and alteration of the rules of the common budget. K. Kołodziejczyk, [2000], p.35.

[32] A. Moravcsik, [1998], p.275–278.

and negative shifts in the capital and workforce as well as inflation. Indeed, the new government's official position displayed a notable lack of enthusiasm. An initial government meeting on 17 October 1979 was dedicated to discussing possible entry to the EMS, but it concluded that this might happen only in the medium term. It was not regarded as a priority or as a pressing issue.[33] In consequence, the Prime Minister announced that the United Kingdom would not participate in the EMS; but he stipulated that the country could join the system as a legal member if inflation was under control and the system itself brought positive results. He repeated a well-known British saying about 'joining when the time is right', even though there were appealing arguments which indicated that entry would be justified.[34]

The United Kingdom entered the ERM in 1985, scarred by the second oil crisis in 1979 as well as having lost profits from the oil resources of the North Sea in 1981. The pound was allowed to fluctuate within the margins of ±6%. However, financial difficulties made Britain leave the system a couple of months later. At the Madrid Summit in June 1989, consensus between Great Britain and her partners was reached. The pound sterling would have entered the ERM if a single market had been completed, capital liberalisation implemented, and the financial sector opened. Needless to say, participation in the ERM was being traded for the establishment of a complete free trade area. The then Chancellor of the Exchequer, John Major, understood that full membership in the EMS was the best option left for Britain. Targeting on a domestic inflation rate had been discredited by the performance of the British economy, and the ERM could become a means of last resort for the Thatcher government. Therefore the Chancellor sought to convince Margaret Thatcher that there was no alternative to entry.[35] In short, the United Kingdom re-entered the system in 1990, but the collapse of the sterling exchange rate on 16 September 1992 (Black Wednesday) made her never join the EMS again.[36]

---

[33] K. Dyson, K. Featherstone, [1999], p.543–544.

[34] K. Kołodziejczyk, [2000], p.36.

[35] K. Dyson, K. Featherstone, [1999], p.549–552.

[36] It is, however, worth stressing that the United Kingdom, although being outside the ERM, pursued a policy like being inside the mechanism as far as an exchange rate and an inflation target were concerned. H. Young, *This Blessed Plot. Britain and Europe from Churchill to Blair*, London, 1999, p.365–367 and p.437–441.

The Danish case was slightly different. As the country was a member of the snake it was interested in the EMS and insisted on the continued existence of economic rules similar to those of the snake. Denmark believed that it could help in strengthening the European currencies as well as in contributing to a greater stabilisation of the financial market, weakening the position of the German mark and more specifically, would decrease the high unemployment rate in the country. 'In the Bretton Woods period from 1948 to 1973, in which the Danish krone was tied to the US dollar, the currency was only adjusted twice, both times simultaneously with the devaluation of the British pound in 1949 and 1967, which could largely be explained in terms of the dependence of Danish export on the British market at the time.' The oil crises in the 1970s stimulated Denmark to launch several devaluations. Nevertheless, at the beginning of the 1980s it was known that this kind of policy could not permanently develop Danish competitiveness and thus the country's hopes for growth and employment, since after the devaluations wages and prices began to become equal. When the conservative/liberal parties came to power at the beginning of the 1980s, a fixed exchange rate policy within the ERM became a key element in Danish economic policy. [37]

The EMS is said to have been an experiment which was likely to produce consolidation in terms of European financial relations. It also had considerable success in retaining the EEC national currencies within an area of relative stability, which has had beneficial effects on intra-community trade and on the economic activity of participating countries. Furthermore, discipline in exchange rates forced the convergence of inflation rates. The enhanced cooperation between the EEC members in establishing economic policies compatible with the mechanism for fixed parities incorporated in the EMS was important as well. Summing up, despite its problems and limitations, the System was a very useful instrument in reinforcing the process of integration within the European Communities. Without this initial period it would have been unrealistic to put the process for an economic and monetary union in Europe into practice. [38]

---

[37] K. Skjalm, 'On the Outside... Denmark and the Euro', Danish Institute of International Affairs, DUPI Report no.2000/8, p.26–27.
[38] J. Muns, [1997], p.13–14.

3.   The Delors Report

In 1985 the EEC Commission published a 'White Paper' suggesting that a European economic area without borders and a common market should be created. It was likely to be achieved by removing various fiscal, technical and physical restrictions, which put barriers on the flow of goods, services, workers and capital. Therefore the EC Commission called for organising an intergovernmental conference (IGC) of the EEC members in order to pursue certain amendments to the EEC foundation treaties. All the member states apart from Great Britain and Denmark supported the idea of arranging the conference. The United Kingdom was in favour of a single market, which would stimulate four free flows, but she resisted both entering the EMS and creating an economic and monetary union. By 1985, with strong support from British industry and financial interests in the City of London, the British government had introduced and implemented many reforms suggested in the White Paper, including service deregulation, capital liberalisation (as early as in 1979), and simplification of customs procedures, whilst demanding their application at the European level. On the other hand, the Prime Minister, Margaret Thatcher, tried to avoid any institutional change, as well as introducing qualified majority voting (QMV), which might lead to its extension on environmental and social issues. Nor did she support formalisation of the monetary cooperation. In June 1984, Margaret Thatcher published the paper entitled 'Europe: the Future' in which she outlined the government's vision for Europe, emphasising liberalisation of the internal market, particularly in services, and removing all economic barriers, with a deadline of 1990. The Prime Minister, Margaret Thatcher, said that:

> ...another good reason for staying in [Europe] is the effect that there would be on investment and jobs if we were to pull out. Obviously, quite a number of multinational companies will prefer to invest in Europe rather than here, if we are not a member of the Common Market.[39]

Denmark completely opposed the idea of commencing an ICG to negotiate formal changes in the foundation treaties related to an

---

[39] 'Europe – The Future', HM Government, *Journal of Common Market Studies*, vol. 23, no. 1/1984, p. 78.

establishment of the QMV on internal market issues. Together with the United Kingdom and Greece, Denmark supported reiteration of the voluntary and informal steps to encourage majority voting in such cases. Denmark was especially afraid that the QMV might force it to lower its environmental, safety and social standards. Hence, it wanted to protect its extensive system of economic regulation. The Danish efforts preventing the ICG from being held were all in vain, and the conference started in October 1985. The politicians tried to keep as many issues as possible on intergovernmental level.[40]

Nonetheless, the IGC took place and its most striking outcome was the Single European Act (SEA), which came into force on 1 July 1987. In the preamble, against British wishes, it was written that preparations aimed at establishing a European monetary union would be continued. The Prime Minister, Margaret Thatcher, approved the above sentence because she had gained another concession from the other member states in return. It said that the United Kingdom would be able to veto all proposals connected with the monetary integration within the European Communities in the future.[41] It was a fact that later on, the Prime Minister herself, as well as her ministers, paid little attention to this reference in the Single European Act confirming that establishing an economic and monetary union was a Community goal. Kenneth Dyson and Kevin Featherstone conclude that:

> ...this reference was judged to be no more than the relatively meaningless declaratory politics in which the EC often indulged. The Thatcher government had rejected any necessary link between the establishment of the single European market and a single currency.[42]

The SEA established the separate title, namely 'The European Monetary Union', which contained legal provisions to establishing a common market (the deadline was fixed at 31 December 1992) with free movement of goods, services, workers and capital among the EEC member states. The elimination of cross-border restrictions on providing capital services was a great success of the document. The deregulation comprised investment services and

---

[40] A. Moravcsik, [1998], p.440–441; F. Overturf, [2000], p.61–63 and 66–67.

[41] A. Moravcsik, [1998], p.365–366.

[42] K. Dyson, K. Featherstone, [1999], p.602–603.

insurance as well. The free capital mobility (with better allocation of resources) might have an impact on the functioning of the EMS, leading to more positive attitude of the EEC member states towards currency union. Furthermore, removal of capital controls contributed to enhancing shifts from exchange rate to interest rate fluctuations within the EMS, adjusting the latter in all member states and eliminating speculative flows of capital in Europe.[43]

The EEC member states realised very soon that introducing the four freedoms and creation of the common market would need to move forward in terms of economic integration as well as launching a common currency. The system of the fixed, though adjustable, exchange rates imposed by the EMS, made it impossible to pursue national economic and monetary policies without close coordination among the member countries. Nevertheless, it seemed to serve German economy best, forcing weak currencies to adjust more, which was strongly opposed by France. Therefore, at the Hanover Summit in June 1988, a committee headed by Jacques Delors, the then president of the EEC Commission, was established to prepare a plan for further European integration. The members of the committee comprised governors of the EEC central banks as well as a group of independent experts.

The Delors Report was presented in April 1989.[44] It referred simultaneously to an economic and monetary union. The former should consist of four elements: a single market with free flow of goods, services, labour and capital; the competition policy and other measures established to reinforce the mechanisms of the single market; common policies aimed at structural change together with regional development and structural aid; and coordination of macroeconomic policies including obligatory rules of budgetary policy. For its own part, a monetary union included the three elements – full and irreversible convertibility of currencies; complete liberalisation of capital transactions, and full integration of banking and financial markets, as well as elimination of fluctuation margins in exchange rates by introducing irrevocable parities between currencies.

The Report did not mention a single currency, although it said

---

[43] To read about details of the financial deregulation within the EEC see F. Overturf, [2000], p.62–65. To read about the Single European Act see A. Moravcsik, [1998], p.364–368.

[44] For the original text of the Delors Report see F. Overturf, [2000], p.209–240.

that for political reasons a monetary union would be 'a natural and desirable' step forward so that transaction costs would be eliminated. It did however suggest the creation of a new monetary institution, a European System of Central Banks (ESCB), which would be an autonomous mechanism to control monetary policy and exchange rates. Decisions would be taken by the ESCB Council and implemented by the national central banks. On the other hand, there was no need for a separate economic institution. According to the Report, currently existing institutions would be vested with broader competencies.[45]

Ultimately, the document announced that while creation of an economic and monetary union was a profound process, which should be taken in three stages, the process as such should be regarded as one. Hence, the decision to enter on the first stage would be a decision on involvement in the whole process. The first step towards a union focused on preparing the next one, including several actions within the existing institutional framework. During the first stage, all currencies of the EEC member states were to join the EMS. Likewise, a committee of central bank governors would be established to coordinate monetary policies, especially budgetary policy and financial market integration. At last, the single market would be fully completed. The second stage would consist of activities leading to the final creation of an economic and monetary union. The new institutional framework with the ESCB would appear after successful alteration of the existing foundation treaties (therefore the intergovernmental conference should take place at the beginning of the first stage). Additionally, pooling of reserves and narrowing fluctuation margins would be conducted.[46] The final stage would complete the process: exchange rates would become irrevocably linked, and the transfer of powers needed for the union would be concluded. Monetary policy would be transferred to the ESCB where official reserves would be pooled and managed. Finally, 'the changeover to the single currency would take place during this stage'.[47]

The first institutional reaction to the Delors Report came at the Madrid Summit in June 1989. The United Kingdom showed the

---

[45] J. Muns, [1997], p.15–17.

[46] Pooling of reserves was not achieved until May 2003.

[47] D. Heathcoat-Amory, [1994], p.8–9.

greatest level of concern out of the other eleven member states. She was sceptical towards an economic union and transferring powers to the supranational level, especially in connection with losing part of her national sovereignty. Britain's negative attitude was presented in two governmental statements. First, in Bruges in 1988 the Prime Minister, Margaret Thatcher, spoke about the meaning of the national countries in the EEC. In January 1989 the Chancellor of Exchequer, Nigel Lawson, expressed his anxiety that the creation of an economic and monetary union was a preparatory step towards a political union, which the United Kingdom could not approve.[48] Nonetheless, the British, being afraid of political isolation, agreed on IGC proposals in the Delors Report.

Denmark showed a very cautious attitude towards the Delors Report as well. She was afraid of losing the ability to take independent economic and political decisions. For Denmark it was not necessary to coordinate economic and monetary policies, nor to create a common market, because it was deeply immersed in economic and financial international relations, especially with the Nordic countries. According to the Social Democratic Party, which ruled in Denmark at that time, establishing a common market and pursuing preparations towards closer economic integration would threaten Danish political sovereignty and jeopardise cooperation within the Nordic Council. Therefore Denmark preferred to develop collaboration in fields of environmental and social policy. It also criticised the Delors Report for not giving precise economic details desired in the second and third stages of a union. For Denmark, the worst passage was connected with automatic agreement on the whole process while deciding on the first phase.[49] Nevertheless, the heads of state and government accepted the Delors Report and decided to begin the first stage of economic and monetary union on 1 July 1990.[50]

Differences between the United Kingdom and the majority of the other member countries of the European Communities, as well as the problems in Eastern Europe, which attracted German attention, impacted on the fact that preparations to an economic and monetary union lost their priority. German unification caused alarm

---

[48] L. Oręziak, [1999], p.16.

[49] K. Kołodziejczyk, [2000], p.58.

[50] J. Muns, [1997], p.17.

among the EEC member states, including Great Britain, France, the Netherlands, Belgium and Denmark. With its number of citizens, large area, growing GDP and borders with the Central and Eastern European countries, Germany might grow into the most powerful country in Europe and in the European Communities. Therefore, especially for the French politicians, tight integration of Germany into the Western European structure seemed to be the only satisfactory strategy. Andrew Moravcsik says that, 'without French fears of a united Germany, Maastricht would not have happened'.[51] It was, however, very traditional thinking, since in reality the German state was already strongly integrated and controlled. But 'the German threat' was a good explanation for the continuing of a plan for economic and monetary union.

4.   Intergovernmental Conference at Maastricht

After the Madrid Summit in June 1989, preparations for the coming IGC were made. Meanwhile, the member states pursued fierce discussions on the future shape of any economic and monetary union. During almost two years of negotiations, many subjective and individual plans were put forth. In March 1990 the EC Commission submitted the 'Working Document', known also as 'Economic and Monetary Union: the Economic Rationale and Design of the System', in which draft proposals towards a new treaty were made. The propositions were accelerated in the 'Final Proposal', published in August 1990, after the first stage of the union had begun. In this paper it was written that the second phase would start on 1 January 1994, and after successfully agreeing on the rights of a new monetary institution.

The debate before and during the IGC, which started in December 1990, circled around detailed provisions for the functioning of the future economic and monetary union. There were seven main issues which caught the attention of the major players, namely Germany, France and the United Kingdom. The first problem was connected with the creation of a body responsible for monetary policy and establishment of the union. In line with draft proposals, a federal council, comprising of the central banks'

---

[51] A. Moravcsik, [1998], p.380. To read more about the German position in Europe at the beginning of the 1990s see F. Overturf, [2000], p.89–92.

governors, and a board implementing current decisions on monetary policy would be shaped. Control over state budgets was left in the hands of national states, but it should follow two main rules. It was strictly forbidden to finance public debt deficit through increased money supply as well as to utilise access to international capital. Furthermore, a country with financial problems could not be left alone either by the EEC as a whole nor the other member states. Also, coordination and close convergence of economic policies was determined by the strong German stance over the issue. The regional and structural aid for less developed countries was also underlined. The external relations in terms of external exchange rate decisions were associated with the Monetary Committee, which consisted of officials from the central banks and finance ministries.

Besides, stages to create the union were another matter to be discussed during the IGC. In the 'Final Proposal' the EC Commission suggested dividing the process into three phases, as the Delors Report had recommended. The second stage was supposed to start on 1 January 1993, but in the discussions the EC member states postponed it for a year until 1 January 1994. Finally, the EEC countries decided to revise the foundation treaties and to sign a completely new document where the structure, as well as the institutional and operational conditions of an economic and monetary union, would be envisaged.[52]

During the negotiation period, the United Kingdom realised that creation of a common market would involve establishing supranational institutions which would participate in preparations for an economy and monetary union. Subsequently, it was necessary to introduce social allowances for workers to diminish the negative aspects of the imposed economic reforms. Moreover, shifting the powers to the EC Commission, the Council of Ministers and the European Parliament was unavoidable. Margaret Thatcher was afraid of agreeing on such a move because for her it was strictly connected with approval for an introduction of a single currency in years to come. Furthermore, it would mean transferring fiscal competences to a European body, which in consequence might have caused a loss of control over the British economy by

---

[52] To read about the debate before and during the EC Intergovernmental Conference at the beginning of the 1990s see F. Overturf, [2000], p.89–103.

the national authorities. This was, however, a false argument, since even until now the fiscal policy remains within national economic bodies of the EU member states. Nevertheless, the Prime Minister repeated several times that the policy conducted by the European Communities 'was more socialist and interventionist than the British economy', and therefore all significant industrial reforms on the British Isles might be discontinued if the United Kingdom joined the economic union.[53]

According to the British view, only the first phase recommended by the Delors Report should be implemented. In November 1989 the United Kingdom presented her own evolutionary project of an economic and monetary union based on 'competing currencies', whereby the currencies of all member states would be legal tender in every EEC country. The plan was based on precondition that existing national currencies of the EEC member states might compete for usage by consumers, firms, and institutions. Adherently, a common market, which should contribute to expanded competitiveness of the national currencies exposed to higher and lower inflation rates, was to be established. In particular, a single market in financial services and capital liberalisation would enable an effective competition among currencies and reduce transaction costs and exchange risk, resulting in choosing low-inflation currencies by consumers and companies. By virtue of this advantage, national monetary policies would also be obliged to compete in launching their anti-inflationary credentials. Furthermore, the country with the most credible anti-inflation stance would obtain the greatest benefit in terms of the lowest interest rates. Nevertheless, the other EEC member states refused to accept the project. Critics showed the negative elements of the scheme, pointing out that the system of competition could also become a system of chaos – even monetary crisis – mostly to ordinary consumers. 'On the other hand, if differences of national inflation rates remained low, the usage of foreign currencies at home might remain low. This would defeat part of the purpose of the scheme.'[54]

The defeat of the Plan of 'competing currencies' encouraged the

---

[53] A. Moravcsik, [1998], p.417.

[54] To read more see K. Kołodziejczyk, [2000], p.59–60; H. Young, [1999], p.364–365; K. Dyson, K. Featherstone, [1999], p.617.

United Kingdom to work on an economic union even harder than before. In June 1990 the Chancellor of Exchequer, John Major, suggested a plan of a 'parallel currency' for the second stage of a monetary union, which encompassed a 'strong ECU' with a parallel 'thirteenth currency' issued by a European Monetary Fund, to be a legal tender existing next to the ECU based on the basket of national currencies. In this way, the greater monetary convergence achieved would lead towards a union, though in a non-defined future. The plan included a market-driven approach preferred by the British. Nevertheless, it was rejected as well.[55] The main reason for such an outcome was connected with endeavours to overcome the power of the German mark, which was obvious for inter alia the French and Italian governments. Both systems – of 'competing currencies' and of a 'parallel currency' – would leave the German Central Bank and the German mark leading. Hence, 'the concerns of European states about dependency on Germany were not addressed by the British proposals. On the other hand, German politicians and economists were afraid of the lack of monetary discipline in the British alternatives.'[56] The German Central Bank found them technically imperfect. Other anxieties focused on the possible effects on inflation, control of the money supply, and coordination of monetary policy, which might have resulted from adoption of British proposals.[57]

In that situation, it was obvious for the United Kingdom that the process of creation of an economic and monetary union would not be stopped. John Major, who replaced Margaret Thatcher as the Prime Minister in November 1990, was more open to economic integration within the European Communities. He did not refuse to join the project proposed in the Delors Committee explicitly, but he kept on pointing out British domestic difficulties, focusing on low competitiveness and high inflation. However, he realised that British exclusion from the commenced project would mean a lowering of the British position in financial and economic international relations. It is worth mentioning that 70% of the British industrial and financial institutions associated with the City of London supported economic integration; but on the other hand

---

[55] A. Moravcsik, [1998], p.440–441; F. Overturf, [2000], p.96–97.

[56] K. Dyson, K. Featherstone, [1999], p.614.

[57] Ibid., p.614.

they expressed uncertainty in connection with fixed exchange rates and the independence of central banks.[58]

Therefore, the United Kingdom insisted throughout 1991 that, although it might fulfil all conditions necessary to enter the final stage of an economic and monetary union, it would not accept any pressure to join. The member states thus reached a consensus composed of three rules: no single country could oppose the formation of a union by those countries, which fulfilled the necessary conditions ('no veto'); no country which successfully fulfilled conditions for joining the third stage of the EMU could be excluded ('no arbitrary exclusion'); no country could be obliged to participate in the third phase of economic and monetary union, even if it fulfilled the conditions ('no coercion').[59]

During the negotiations of the IGC, Denmark supported Great Britain in many of her statements. Accordingly, it was against the establishment of a strict timetable leading to the formal economic integration. Likewise, the Danish as well as the British politicians considered the convergence criteria proposed by Germany as necessary for domestic monetary discipline. Finally, Denmark demanded the general opt-out clause, which would enable it to decide on the participation in an economic and monetary union. Nevertheless, the other member states, led by the Germans, succeeded in persuading Denmark to abandon its position, leaving the United Kingdom alone in opposition.[60]

In sum, the Plan for an economic and monetary union was established in Maastricht and developed further, even though the United Kingdom was very sceptical towards it and Denmark had its own reservations.

---

[58] It is the British government that is responsible for UK monetary policy, and the Bank of England is not fully independent from the national authorities. To read more see F. Fries, *Spór o Europę*, Warszawa, 1998, p.350–351.

[59] J. Muns, [1997], p.18–19.

[60] A. Moravcsik, [1998], p.440–441; F. Overturf, [2000], p.416–417 and p.439–442.

II: European Economic and Monetary Union

Creation of an economic and monetary union had been a primary goal of the EEC member states since they established European Community in the 1950s. For many years, the debate between the federalists and the functionalists on the correct approach towards such an undertaking had continued.[1] Nevertheless, the difficult economic condition of European industrial affairs after the Second World War, turbulences in the international economy and finances in the 1970s, as well as a lack of the political will of the countries in question, resulted in a low speed for the whole process. Even though attempts to integrate economic and monetary policies were introduced, difficulties in their completion arose as the member states kept on refusing to accept them, either because of a lack of internal will to delegate sovereign rights on exchange rates to an international body, or because of external problems. The Werner Plan, the snake and the European Monetary System were brave endeavours on the way towards the Economic and Monetary Union, albeit they must have entailed a lot of pressures and mutual reluctance. It did however, lead to coordination of the exchange rate policy, limiting the power to use devaluation as a tool in trade relations. Germany and France, despite minor differences in their position towards economic integration, were allied on the issue and struggled for its fulfilment. The United Kingdom opposed closer economic integration beyond creation of a single European market, and tried to block all efforts of the other EEC member states to establish an economic and monetary union.

The Treaty on European Union signed in Maastricht in February 1992 enabled the EEC countries to integrate closely in

---

[1] The group of *federalists* wanted to unify the continent of Europe first and afterwards pursue common economic and monetary integration. On the other hand, the *functionalists* called for sectoral integration before establishing any economic union. To read more, see I. Popiuk-Rysińska, *Unia Europejska – geneza, kształt, konsekwencje integracji*, Warszawa, 1998, p.8–11.

economic terms. It introduced the Economic and Monetary Union and suggested the Plan for its realisation. The Economic and Monetary Union involved 'irrevocably locked currencies' for those which qualified. The transition period was divided into three parts and was to start automatically in 1999, even though there would be few countries to become members. During the 1990s an independent European Central Bank was formed and started to operate according to the rules formulated and implemented by a transition organ – the European Monetary Institute. Political control was kept only over external exchange rates with the third countries.

Great Britain, together with Denmark, managed to win the opting-out clauses according to which they could not be forced to enter the third stage of the Economic and Monetary Union, namely launching the common European currency – the euro. The euro began to be used in economic and financial transactions on 1 January 1999. Likewise, it became legal tender in the participating countries of the European Union on 1 January 2002. The United Kingdom, Denmark and Sweden did not decide to be part of the project and up till now they have stayed outside the Eurozone.

1.   Treaty on European Union

The Treaty on European Union contained the 'road map' for creating an economic and monetary union by introducing dates for achieving different stages of monetary integration, which were afterwards followed in practice.

The intergovernmental conference was opened in December 1990 in Rome. It was continued during the year of 1991, to be finally concluded at the meeting in Maastricht in December 1991. The Treaty on European Union was signed on 7 February 1992.[2] Ratification of the document by the respective parliaments was to take place throughout 1992, with a draft provision to come into force on 1 January 1993. However, the ratification process was longer and more complicated than expected and it was finally accomplished in November 1993.

---

[2] The Treaty was signed even though the Danish delegation underscored possible problems with its ratification at home. Denmark emphasised mostly that the Treaty contained provisions too complicated to be explained clearly to citizens. To read more, see A. Moravcsik, [1998], s. 449.

Negotiations during the IGC were difficult and complex. Needless to say, they required an inclination to compromise. The Treaty on European Union in its final form was based on the Delors Report to a large extent. First and foremost, it adhered to the creation of a common currency introduced in 1999 at the latest. Joining the economic and monetary union would be possible for a country after meeting several economic criteria, known as the *convergence criteria*. The European Central Bank would be exclusively responsible for the monetary policy, while policy regarding exchange rates would be vested in the European Council. The member states would be independently in charge of the fiscal policy. And last but not least, there was an option for any country to remain outside the economic and monetary union (an option which was taken up by Great Britain and Denmark).[3]

1.1 THREE STAGES OF EUROPEAN ECONOMIC AND MONETARY UNION

The Treaty on European Union, as noted above, launched three stages of creation of the Economic and Monetary Union. However, it was impossible to begin the process of creating such a union without first signing the Single European Act and the establishment of the single European market offering four freedoms, among which the free flow of capital was the most important. Concluding, stages noted in the Treaty on European Union could not have started without this so-called preliminary stage.

The first stage of the creation of an economic and monetary union started on 1 July 1990, and consequently the Treaty underlined the need of continuing the process of eliminating existing capital controls and any other obstacles to the unconditional flow of capital. Common rules on competition, taxation, and other means of governmental intrusion on the market were to be eliminated. The coordination of the economic policies was introduced, and the member states were obliged to avoid excessive deficits. The process of creating independent central banks began.

The Maastricht Treaty established the second stage on the way to the EMU. It was supposed to be commenced on 1 January 1994. The European Monetary Institute, which consisted of the governors

---

[3] J. Muns, [1997], p.20–21.

of the national central banks with an independent president created by the governments, was to be established. It was supposed to be a transition institution, and its main function was to prepare the creation of the European Central Bank. Additionally, it was responsible for controlling the EMS, coordination among the central banks in terms of monetary policy (and creation of the common monetary policy on the third stage), as well as putting down the rules for the central banks within the ESCB.[4]

Consequently, the third stage was deemed to begin when the future single currency was irrevocably fixed. The European Council was supposed to receive special reports from the European Monetary Institute and the European Commission in which the requested convergence was to be summarised. Based on information provided, the Council was obliged to formulate a decision about which countries had successfully managed to meet the necessary economic criteria by that time. It also concluded on entering the third stage of preparations to the Economic and Monetary Union, which should happen not later than 31 December 1996. Nevertheless, in case no decision was made before the date mentioned, the Treaty specified that the third stage would start irrevocably on 1 January 1999, if an earlier date were not introduced. In such a situation, in 1998, the European Council was obliged to decide on future members who met the convergence criteria, and establish a fully independent European Central Bank (ECB) within a European System of Central Banks (ESCB), which comprised the central banks of the member states. Great attention was given to both institutions to maintaining price stability and supporting the economic policies of the European Union. The ECB would be in charge of controlling monetary instruments. The tangible example of this was a prerequisite that the ECB would not fund national budget deficits. The ESCB would have to monitor the situation and prevent member states from running excessive deficits, using methods of surveillance and recommendations. However, the best device for protection against budget deficits was a fine for those who did not obey the rule. The monetary policy was defined as setting up:

---

[4] N. Healey, [1999], p.109–110; P. Arestis, M. Sawyer, 'The Deflationary Consequences of the Single Currency', in M. Baimbridge, B. Burkitt, P. Whyman, [2000], p.146.

...the intermediate monetary objectives, key interest rates and the supply of reserves of the ESCB (…), and establishing the necessary guidelines for their implementation.[5]

The Council would be also responsible for setting external exchange rates and participation in any external exchange rates regime setting.[6]

1.2. CONDITIONS OF THE EMU MEMBERSHIP

In the Maastricht Treaty it was stressed that joining the economic and monetary union would be possible only if a country fulfilled several economic criteria, as well as technical requirements written in the Treaty. Article 109j (Article 121 of the Treaty of Nice) established four convergence criteria according to the stance of the German government and the German Central Bank.

The convergence criteria could be divided into two groups – the fiscal and monetary ones. The former group included two elements – first, the budget deficit should not exceed 3% of the GDP ratio of a member state, and should not be greater than 60% of government debt to GDP ratio; and second, membership in the EMS, and observing the fluctuation margins established by the ERM for at least 2 years before examination. Moreover, any member state ought to abstain from devaluating its currency's bilateral central rate against any other member currency on its own initiative within 2 years. The monetary group consisted of price stability and long-term interest rates. It was underlined that a member state was stable in terms of prices if its inflation rate was not higher than 1.5% of the three best performing member states measured by an appropriate consumer price index. In the case of long-term interest rates, they could be 2% higher in comparison to the three best performing member states, over the period of one year. The measure was to include interest rates on long-term government bonds or comparable securities.[7]

---

[5] S. F. Overturf, [2000], p.106.

[6] On the organisation and responsibilities of the European Central Bank and the European System of Central Banks see S. F. Overturf, [2000], p.105–106.

[7] On arguments on the convergence criteria see S. F. Overturf, [2000], p.109–113; N. Healey, [1999], 110–113. In 1997 the Annexed Protocol was attached to the Treaty of Amsterdam. It sustained a requirement of 3% for the ratio of the planned or actual budget deficit as well as allowing 60% for the ratio of government debt.

The most important obstacle in the creation of the EMU was the relationship between the countries which were to be selected and those which remained outside the project, known as 'ins' and 'outs'. The problem ultimately depended on the economic importance of those excluded. Countries forming the core of a common currency were concerned to establish a certain relationship between their currencies and the currencies of the 'outs'. Otherwise, the latter might take advantage of the situation and undergo competitive devaluations. As a result, it was suggested that the single currency and the other currency, which remained outside, should be linked by the Exchange Rate Mechanism 2 (EMR2) proposed by the European Council at the meeting in Dublin in December 1996. Fundamentally, it was decided that a new exchange rate mechanism would be established, based on the central exchange rates of the currencies remaining outside the third stage of the EMU in relation to the single currency. The levels of fluctuation were not specified, but the decision to widen the margins of exchange rate fluctuations up to ±15% was taken in Amsterdam in 1997.[8]

1.3 BRITISH AND DANISH COMMENTS ON THE MAASTRICHT TREATY

John Major, the new British Prime Minister, was not against the European Community as such but opposed plans for committing the United Kingdom to the Economic and Monetary Union described in the Maastricht Treaty. He came to the Netherlands with a strong conviction for fighting for an 'opt-out' clause, enabling Britain to remain outside the EMU.

The British politicians criticised the convergence criteria. The Foreign Secretary, Douglas Hurd, resisted the restricting fiscal deficits proposed by Germany saying it could lead to 'a fitness club, which would keep everyone underweight for ever'.[9] The United Kingdom was also against fixing a strict plan for creation of the economic union, and accordingly opposed any commitment to the creation of an ECB. Furthermore, the British also voted against any regulations which would impose an obligation to join the Exchange Rate Mechanism 2. Finally, the government wanted to

---

[8] J. Muns, [1997], p.34–35.
[9] A. Moravcsik, [1998], p.425.

maintain its general rights of national sovereignty in relation to both economic and monetary policy. It rejected any 'parallelism' between a commitment to monetary integration and an acceptance of fiscal coordination at the supranational level. In that context, British negotiators opposed limiting national autonomy on excessive deficits. They argued against any regulations constraining participants regarding the extent and management of their budget deficits. Moreover, it was believed that there ought not to have been any financial sanctions imposed on those governments that failed to follow the convergence requirements. With respect to monetary policy, the British managed to uphold national regulations on it. Their government also argued that member states should still be able to possess foreign exchange reserves, and it raised a great deal of objections to the transfer of management or ownership of foreign exchange reserves to a new Community institution. Finally, the British were concerned to protect their national sovereignty against any increased power for the European institutions. They postulated that any decision on an economic and monetary union related to the economic policy coordination should be made by the Council of Ministers.[10]

However, in the end, the Prime Minister neither questioned any of the convergence criteria, nor did he prevent the Treaty from being signed. Likewise, he supported Germany in its struggle to prevent the European Monetary Institute (EMI) from having any control over the monetary policy as a separate council of the central banks was established. Unfortunately, London lost in the battle against Frankfurt am Main over a seat of the European Central Bank.[11]

The British industrial institutions warmly welcomed the final agreement reached by the Prime Minister, John Major. He was proclaimed to have won 'game, set, and match' for Britain.[12] In other words, Major's triumph in Maastricht, combined with his role in the Gulf War, enhanced his reputation on the international stage. Nevertheless, the Prime Minister's vision of a European economic and monetary union is said to lack clear principles and foresight.[13]

---

[10] K. Dyson, K. Featherstone, [1999], p.664–667.

[11] A. Moravcsik, [1998], p.441–446.

[12] Quotation in K. Dyson, K. Featherstone, [1999], p.645.

[13] Ibid., p.647.

However, Great Britain was exempted from those common policies, which could jeopardise British competitiveness and her financial interests (social policy). On the other hand, the door to the economic and monetary union remained open, thanks to the opting-out clause.

The opting-out clause is said to give freedom, but it must be mentioned that it also imposed some constraints. The Protocol on the opting-out clause states that successful ratification of the Maastricht Treaty did not automatically mean that the United Kingdom would participate in the third stage of the Economic and Monetary Union. However, Britain could not block remaining countries from continuing the project. So long as a decision to enter was not made, British monetary policy would remain subject to national law, and the Bank of England need not be made independent. But, outside the third stage, the United Kingdom would have no rights to participate in setting rules for the countries involved (e.g. management of a single currency; the counter-inflation policy of the ECB). The Protocol provides that the European Council was to decide on a possible British membership by qualified majority voting. Such a decision would follow a recommendation from the European Commission, following consultation with the European Parliament. The Protocol recognises that Great Britain will keep her right to move to the third stage provided only that it satisfies the necessary conditions. The Council would decide on whether the conditions written in the Maastricht Treaty were met. It is interesting to see what Kenneth Dyson and Kevin Featherstone argue:

> No doubt a British decision to end its exclusion would be welcomed. But in the deferred, subjective and political judgement by the Council there were inherent risks that the bargaining between Great Britain and the rest might involve other conditions being asked of the latecomer.[14]

Denmark caused much fewer problems during the IGC negotiations than the United Kingdom. In the Danish government's *Memorandum*, published on 4 October 1990, it was stressed that

---

[14] Ibid., p.662.

...the main task of the coming IGC must be to adapt and strengthen the Community in such a way that it is enabled to play a central role in European and international affairs. The Community must be strengthened, so that it becomes the foundation for the political and economic unity of all of Europe (...), because the Community [is], due to its structure and construction, the best instrument to include the other European countries in broad and binding cooperation. [15]

The document was positive about a plan for the creation of an economic and monetary union, and strengthening the European Political Cooperation on the basis of consensus, but excluded a common defence and defence policy cooperation. Furthermore, new areas of European collaboration, such as environmental and social questions with increasing use of majority decisions, were suggested. But the general policy line still favoured intergovernmental integration.

In 1991 the country presented the broad inter-party agreement on the Danish stance for the Intergovernmental Conference in Maastricht, the so-called 'Danish Memorandum on IGC'. The document emphasised that closer economic and monetary integration was necessary to obtain the full economic benefits of the Economic and Monetary Union, especially exchange rate stability, growth and employment. The Memorandum favoured a rapid transition to the final stage, keeping the second stage as short as possible. Moreover, the document considered it natural that the primary objective of the monetary policy of the European Central Bank would be price stability, while the Ecofin should take care of other objectives in setting economic policy, including growth and employment. It also suggested that the objective of full employment should be 'expressly included among the higher principles of the Community', and consequently the Ecofin should be strengthened, which would also facilitate its necessary coordination with the ECB.

On the foreign exchange rate policy towards third countries, the Memorandum endeavoured to assure the Ecofin Council of its necessary influence and hence suggested that it ought to take decisions concerning formal exchange rate arrangements, including

---

[15] H. Larsen, 'British and Danish European Policies on the 1990s: A Discourse Approach', *European Journal of International Relations*, London, 1999, vol. 5(4), p.464–465.

realignment of central parities and the size of fluctuation bands. On the other hand, the ECB should be responsible for the daily performance of the EU exchange rate policy. Inclusion of the EU Council in the monetary decisions was important for the Danes, and therefore they proposed establishing regular meetings between the chairman of the Ecofin Council and the ECB.

Finally, in the area of fiscal and budgetary policy, the Memorandum was strictly against the Ecofin being able to take legally binding decisions on a member state's 'budget surplus or deficit or its revenue and expenditure, just as distribution policy must remain a national matter. Anything else would be unacceptable to the national parliaments'.[16] Multilateral surveillance and EEC members' pressure was regarded sufficient to maintain budgetary discipline.

At the IGC, Denmark often stood against its alliance with Germany, to which it traditionally had belonged. 'Apart from an ill-fated proposal to narrow the bands of exchange rate fluctuations in the second stage, Denmark kept a low profile throughout the negotiations on an economic and monetary union.'[17] This became clear in the final round of the IGC when the British government pressed for a general opting-out clause on the third stage of the EMU to be included in the Maastricht Treaty. All other EU member states, except Denmark, rejected this agreement, arguing that it would undermine the credibility of the whole process if there were no clear and irrevocable promise to complete the process of creating the European Economic and Monetary Union supported by all members. In this view, frustrations amongst the British over how the Danish delegation was pursuing the opt-out goal were unjust. Great Britain felt the Danes were being too careless in the drafting of an opt-out, but they were even more ready to accept an individual solution. The Danish delegation was not particularly keen on closer supranational monetary and fiscal cooperation, but it simply did not want the same protocol as the United Kingdom.[18]

Another problem occurred when it came to ratification of the Maastricht Treaty. Despite positive prognoses about the ratification by the Danish parliament in May 1992, the Danes rejected the

---

[16] K. Skjalm, [2000], p.7–8.

[17] K. Dyson, K. Featherstone, [1999], p.658.

[18] Ibid., p.658.

Treaty in the referendum on its ratification, which was held on 2 June 1992.[19] As the Treaty was to be ratified by all member countries without exception, the Danish 'no' was a severe reversal of hopes for a progress towards the Economic and Monetary Union. The reason for such a move were various and complex. At the centre of the debate in Denmark were such elements as losing control over the national currency, higher interest rates and higher unemployment caused by membership in the EMS, and linking the monetary policy to the German one. Moreover, the Danes were concerned about losing national identity to the big countries and 'strong and potentially even arrogant European institutions',[20] which would not have any respect for such a small country as Denmark. For the Danish nation, steps to sacrifice their interests in fisheries, their social welfare state, environmental policy and common European defence system were impossible to agree upon.

The result of the Danish referendum encouraged the United Kingdom to hold back on her ratification procedures. The ratification process in Britain was extremely laborious. Prime Minister John Major had to confront an alliance of the opposition Labour Party and the 'euro-sceptical' wing of his own party, encouraged by Margaret Thatcher. Consequently, the British politicians decided to wait for a resolution of the situation in Denmark. On 30 September 1992, the Danish government issued the memorandum entitled 'Denmark in Europe'. It emphasised that:

> ...the Danish 'no' to the EC-Union on 2 June 1992 was an expression of the fact that a majority of the Danes do not want the united states of Europe. However, it was not a 'no' to EC membership or European co-operation (...). Europe needs committed co-operation and the European Communities are the natural framework for such a co-operation (...). Denmark shall not be isolated but play an active role in the future development of Europe. A national compromise constitutes, at the same time, the point of departure for a new discussion within the population about a more European policy directed towards the future (...). Denmark must therefore in relation to the aim of a union (...) make clear that co-operation within the EC

---

[19] Out of 175 members of the Danish parliament, 130 voted for the Treaty in comparison to 25 against and 20 absent on the day of voting. During the referendum, the percentage of citizens in favour of the Treaty was 49.3 and against, 50.7. To read more see K. Kołodziejczyk, [2000], p.68.

[20] S. F. Overturf, [2000], p.118.

> consists of states (…) who have freely decided to exercise certain of
> their competences in common (…). [This] has as its obvious base
> that Denmark is an independent state.[21]

The hardened position of both the United Kingdom and Denmark forced the other member states to renegotiate the Treaty on European Union at the meeting in Edinburgh in December 1992, even though such a move had not been foreseen before.[22] Denmark, according to its wishes expressed in the Memorandum, was granted a protocol giving it an opting-out clause, which enabled it not to join the third stage of the EMU.[23] Denmark could decide, by itself, if and when it entered the Eurozone. With the noted concession, the Danes held a second referendum on 18 May 1993, which this time resulted with 'yes' for the ratification of the Treaty on the European Union.[24] Such a result changed the British attitude towards the Treaty, which was finally ratified in Britain on 21 June 1993.

In the meantime, financial problems within the EMS occurred and forced members to lower the interest rates and devalue their currencies. The failure to comply with this challenge led to 'Black Wednesday' (16 September 1992), when the British pound and Italian lira, even though they were not a target of heavy speculative attacks, could not keep the margin of the required exchange rate fluctuation band, because of tensions on exchange rates in the neighbouring countries and the reunification of the two German states. As a result they dropped out of the system. The turmoil lasted till the second half of 1993, but it was successfully overcome in the end. Nevertheless, the pound sterling remained outside the EMS, never to enter it again.[25]

After agreeing on the Maastricht Treaty, Denmark started to

---

[21] H. Larsen, [1999], p.465–466.

[22] Such a stance was reinforced twice – on the meeting in Oslo on 4 June 1992, and in Lisbon on 26–27 June 1992. To read more see K. Kołodziejczyk, [2000], p.68.

[23] The protocol also enabled Denmark to refuse to participate in the military structures of the European Union, in cooperation in asylum and immigration policies, as well as in the project of the European citizenship. To read more see J. Muns, [1997], p.22.

[24] In the referendum 56.7% of voting citizens accepted the Treaty while 43.3% rejected it. To read more see D. Leonard, *Przewodnik po Unii Europejskiej*, Warszawa, 1998, p.150.

[25] To read more on the problems within the European Monetary System in 1992–1993, see S. F. Overturf, [2000], p.120–121.

introduce the National Convergence Programme, whose main goal was to fulfil convergence criteria in order to enter the European Economic and Monetary Union. The necessary reforms changing status of the National Central Bank (Danmarks Nationalbank) were pursued. It became more independent from the political authorities, especially the government. The average inflation rate was in accordance with the EU average.[26]

2.   Introduction of the Single Currency

Introduction of the common currency was supposed to serve as a splendid finalisation of the long process of creating the Economic and Monetary Union. The Treaty on European Union did not mention the exact date of the introduction of a single currency. Therefore, having agreed on it, the member states commenced preparations for the last phase of this historic project. This included decisions on a detailed schedule and the name of a new currency, as well as adhering to the informational campaign focused on the citizens. In May 1994, a special working group headed by Cees Maas was appointed to participate in the technical preparations for the introduction of the new currency, what was supposed to be based on four points: credibility, simplicity, flexibility, and not causing too high costs.

In April 1995 the European Commission presented a separate document entitled the 'Green Paper on the Methods of Transition to the Single Currency', which confirmed decisions taken in Maastricht. Having presented the complete scenario of the preparations, as well as defining all problems which might occur during the process, the European Commission aimed at diminishing social and economic anxiety towards a single currency. The main attention was drawn to the fulfilment of the convergence criteria, together with a three-phase scenario for the introduction of a new currency. Phase A was worked around preparations towards the Economic and Monetary Union, with setting up a date for currency conversion, designating countries which performed well in terms of the economic criteria, and establishing a European Monetary Institute (EMI). In Phase B a single currency was supposed to start functioning in economic and financial transactions and serve as

---

[26] R. Matera, [2001], p.180–181.

accounting currency. The irrevocable exchange rates were to be established, and the ECB and the ESCB had to start conducting economic and monetary policies. Finally, Phase C had to conclude the process of conversion towards the new single currency (still known as the ECU) with its entering into circulation.[27]

In November 1995 the European Monetary Institute published the report 'The Process of Change to the Single Currency' on the preparations towards the final step of the EMU, which coincided to a great extent with the European Commission's document. These papers served as the basis for the decision taken by the European Council in Madrid in December 1995. The European Council confirmed its strong aspiration to create the Economic and Monetary Union. During the negotiations, a name for the new currency – 'euro' – was approved. In addition, a schedule for its introduction in the coming years was submitted. It mostly repeated the division into three stages proposed in the 'Green Paper'. The provisions for Phase A were approved unchanged. The starting date for Phase B was decided on 1 January 1999. The last Phase was to begin on 1 January 2002, and last till the end of June 2002. During this short period all national currencies were to be withdrawn from circulation on the market. On 1 July 2002 the euro was to become the only legal tender among the members of the EMU.[28]

At the next summit in Dublin in 1996, definition of the regulatory, organisational and logistical framework for the third phase was approved, together with the legislation and operational regulations of the European Central Bank and the European System of Central Banks. The member states also decided on relationships between participants and non-participants in the Economic and Monetary Union. The main goal was to prepare a list of countries which fulfilled the convergence criteria and could join the Union. During this time all necessary legislative measures to initiate the third phase were formulated (e.g. measures related to the monetary policy with the single currency as well as economic and financial sectors were prepared). During that phase the European Monetary Institute was changed into the European Central Bank, and the European System of Central Banks was created. Paradoxically, in the report of the German Central Bank submitted to the Chancellor,

---

[27] K. Kołodziejczyk, [2000], p.90–93.
[28] Ibid., p.96.

Helmut Kohl, on 27 March 1998, only five countries fulfilled the convergence criteria and could be members of the EMU without restrictions: Finland, Luxembourg and Ireland, as well as the United Kingdom and Denmark, two countries unwilling to join the European project.[29]

As mentioned above, the second stage began on 1 January 1999, and its main objective was fixing the irreversible exchange rates. The ECU-basket ceased to exist and the euro became the legal tender in non-cash transactions. The legislation relating to the euro came into force and was implemented (e.g. monetary policy was conducted only in euros; the euro became a unit of accounting for the central banks; national public debts were issued in euros). The Stability and Growth Pact, agreed on Germany's request in Dublin in December 1996, came into force. Its main aim is to guarantee budgetary discipline, and it foresees strict fines for exceeding budget deficit of more than 3% of GDP.[30]

The third and last phase began on 1 January 2002, when euro notes and coins entered into circulation and national currencies started to be withdrawn. Additionally, all monetary assets were converted into euros. The process was planned to end on 30 June 2002, when all the national currencies of the twelve participating EU member states ceased to be legal tender. They were replaced by the euro on 28 February 2002.[31]

---

[29] L. Oręziak, [1999], p.42–43.

[30] J. Muns, [1997], p.34.

[31] To read more about the creation of European Monetary Union in the 1990s, see J. Muns, [1997], p.27–33; L. Oręziak, [1999], p.27–34, 48–67 and 76–84.

III: Reasons for Non-participation in the Economic and Monetary Union

The United Kingdom, Denmark and Sweden have remained outside the third stage of the Economic and Monetary Union. They present different reasons in explaining their unwilling attitude towards this major European undertaking. Their motives could be divided into four groups, namely historical, political, economic and socio-cultural. Moreover, the factors which characterise British, Danish and Swedish special status in the European Union, and hence their reluctance towards the EMU, could be internal as well as external. Out of the four aforementioned groups, historical and political reasons strictly apply to certain countries, while economic and social causes are applicable to three of the cases examined. Therefore, the main reservations towards integration within the European Union in general will be mentioned first. Afterwards, specific arguments pro and contra participation in the Eurozone will be summarised.

The United Kingdom has supported economic integration within the European Communities, especially in terms of introduction of a free trade area, which resulted in the creation of a European common market. British politicians argued that such economic changes would be profitable for the British economy. They underlined the significant contribution of economic collaboration in restructuring British industry, increasing its competitiveness in the international economy, and in percentage of foreign direct investments (FDI) coming on the British Isles. In the meantime, Britain has exercised a strong veto over the issue of merging the pound with the euro. British politicians and economists have pointed out different economic cycles between the United Kingdom and the continental countries, the weakness of the common currency in comparison to the pound,[1] the danger of

---

[1] A weak euro is not the case anymore, but its current increase in value could be easily diminished. It was caused by problems of the US dollar and a decreased level of confidence in the American currency (consequences of the terrorist attack on 11

increasing inflation in Britain and the diminishing competitiveness of British exports. In the 1980s and 1990s, Britain's negative attitude towards the European Economic and Monetary Union also had strong political background, which was connected with fighting to defend British sovereignty. On the other hand, in 1997, the Labour Party won the general election and took over power from the Conservative Party. The new Prime Minister, Tony Blair, announced arrangements towards pursuing adequate economic reforms which would prepare the United Kingdom to enter the third stage of the EMU.

Denmark applied for membership in the European Communities twice in 1961 and 1967, together with the United Kingdom, Norway and Ireland. Nevertheless, on both occasions the French President, Charles de Gaulle, exercised France's veto over possible British membership, and in consequence none of the candidates pursued negotiations any further. Denmark did not wish to enter the organisation without the United Kingdom, and only after concluding the accession negotiations on the EEC Summit in the Hague in December 1969, did Denmark become a member of the organisation, together with Ireland and Great Britain.

Since joining the Economic European Community new areas of policy have been brought under the influence of the supranational power of the European Communities. Since 1973, Denmark has worked for transparency in the EEC decision-making process. It supported inclusion of high environmental standards in all regulations and it promoted policy on stimulating creation of new working posts on the European continent. Moreover, the Danish government also conducted an active policy on such issues as consumer protection and work environment standards, many of which could be easily found in the Danish welfare state.[2] However, even though the Danish population has always regarded the European Community/European Union as an excellent forum for

---

September 2001, financial scandals in the leading American IT companies, and the outbreak of the war with Iraq) as well as the US economic slowdown. It helped the euro to deliver its most sustained recovery yet, but on the other hand there are serious economic problems within the Eurozone regarding fiscal discipline introduced by the Growth and Stability Pact, which influence mostly the biggest euro-economy – Germany. M. Atkinson, 'Euro Turns the Corner', in the *Guardian*, 5 December 2002.

[2] H. Larsen, [1999], p.467.

economic cooperation, it has been reluctant to accept any closer integration, especially in political terms. As a result, the Maastricht Treaty of 1992, with its chapters on increased supranational collaboration, was only accepted during the second referendum in 1993. This positive result was a consequence of obtaining the Edinburgh Agreement in December 1992, which allows Denmark to maintain opt-outs in four areas of the EU cooperation. It includes reservation from entering the final phase of the European Economic and Monetary Union and replacing the Danish krone with the single currency; abstaining from the security and defence cooperation as well as from an extension of the legal cooperation from the third EU pillar (mostly in relation to asylum and immigration policies) and union citizenship.[3]

There is still an active debate in Denmark concerning the advantages and disadvantages of the opt-outs established by the Agreement, and their impact on the political and socio-economic position of Denmark in international relations. The economic reasons for abstaining from the Eurozone resemble the British ones, namely different economic cycles, weakness of the common currency, danger of increasing inflation and unemployment rates. The parties such as the Socialist People's Party (*Socialistisk Folkeparti*) and the Unity List (*Enhedslisten*) on the left, together with the Danish People's Party (*Dansk Folkeparti*) on the right, oppose further integration, while all the others support the idea of entering into economic and monetary union or participating in closer political cooperation.

Last but not least, for many years Sweden has been regarded as one of the most stable of Europe's industrialised and affluent countries. Lee Miles argues that 'the historical development of Sweden has been intertwined with that of the European continent'.[4] Nevertheless, the process of European integration poses a lot of challenges for Sweden, causing reservations and a cautious approach towards creation of the EMU. The reason for that is the fact that during the last two centuries Sweden remained on the edge of the European affairs. Stig Hadenius says that:

---

[3] The EU Information Centre in Denmark, www.eu-oplysningen.dk

[4] L. Miles, *Sweden and European Integration*, Ashgate, 1997, p.9.

...international issues did not play a major role in Swedish politics before World War II. Sweden tried to influence events as much as possible through the League of Nations, but it was not an active participant in the international politics power game.[5]

Since the nineteenth century the country tried to modernise its economy and sectors of industry so as to be well prepared to respond to international challenges rather than participate in military conflicts among European powers. Moreover, Sweden did not take part in either world war, and during the Cold War tried to be neutral in order to maintain peaceful relations with members of two opposing blocs. Nevertheless, changes in the geopolitical and socio-economic situation in Europe at the beginning of the 1990s contributed to the alteration of Swedish attitudes towards the process of European integration. It resulted in a successful ending of the accession negotiations to the organisation and finally becoming a full member on 1 January 1995. But the careful attitude has not been abandoned, especially among the Swedish population, for whom the European Union is just a bureaucratic organisation whose existence fails to bring positive effects. Furthermore, a significant group of citizens believe that their country could do well in international relations without being a member of the European Union. In consequence, Sweden is still an awkward partner, which is convinced of its self-sufficiency and whose prosperity could be well preserved on its own.

1. Historical and Geographical Reasons

In the British attitude towards Europe and the process of European integration there are two major factors which have a strong impact on continuing policy on the international scene: her geographical location, alongside her colonial and imperial past.

Geographical features, namely being an island, situated on the fringe of northern Europe, influenced British expansion on the seas in the past.[6] Hence, her maritime traditions shaped the British political position in international relations. In the sixteenth century

---

[5] S. Hadenius, *Swedish Politics During the 20th Century*, Swedish Institute, Stockholm, 1999, p.55.

[6] Britain's supremacy on the seas was first established by her defeating the Spanish Armada in 1588.

the country created an imperial, global policy, namely the policy of 'balance of power'. According to David Hume, 'balance of power' meant that the British role was concerned with creating positive conditions on the European continent so that the balance between continental countries could be maintained, thus failing to threaten the United Kingdom. In such circumstances, Great Britain would be able to improve her international policy. Nevertheless, such a policy did not require a direct influence and presence in European affairs but it could be limited to diplomatic interventions.[7]

Nevertheless, it is a false impression that the Brits have resisted deeper involvement in European affairs. In fact, the other European countries were Britain's natural enemies in terms of colonial expansion (especially France, Spain and Portugal). Therefore the United Kingdom must have been interested in developments of any situation which took place in Europe so as to prevent it from affecting the country seriously. Accordingly, British politicians balanced their views between her imperial interests and European policy.[8]

Likewise, Britain's imperial position in international affairs, which stemmed from her maritime legacy, was reinforced in the seventeenth century with developments in knowledge and science, economics and finance, together with the beginning of the era of industrial relations. Thanks to the colonial expansion, the United Kingdom obtained international position and influence which could be maintained until the mid-twentieth century. Accordingly, after World War II the United Kingdom was convinced of the need to preserve her special relations with her former colonies and dependent territories. The reasons for such a policy were twofold. First, Britain wanted to import goods from her former colonies on more competitive conditions than the world prices; and second, colonies created a safe market for the British articles. These mostly economic reasons contributed to Britain's cautious attitude towards the European continent and its integration policy.

In the case of Denmark's historical reasons for restraining from the Eurozone, it is worth mentioning that it is the best example of a country where the opinion of the nation conflicts with political

---

[7] To read more see F. Gołembski, *Polityka zagraniczna Wielkiej Brytanii*, Warszawa, 2001, p.11–12.

[8] Ibid., p.13–15.

decisions approved by governments and parliaments. So far it has happened twice, when Danes rejected the Treaty on European Union, and in 2000 in the referendum on EMU membership. Because of the complexity of the process of European integration, it seems to be natural and justified that different social groups oppose its certain aspects. Nevertheless, in Denmark, on both occasions, it was particularly appalling to domestic politicians as well as for EU officials that a majority of the society was against the main elements of integration on the European continent.[9] In this light, the main reservations over Danish membership in the European Community, and especially in the Economic and Monetary Union, pointed out by Johnny Laursen, are based on such factors as the domestic policy interplay, the economic condition of the country, especially problems of reconciling the welfare state full employment policies with closer European alignment; and finally, Scandinavian relations and the precarious balance between the Nordic alliance and Europe.[10]

Immediately after World War II, Denmark was not actively present in the process of European political or economic integration. The country benefited from US financial help (the Marshall Plan) and participated in cooperation within the OEEC (and later in the OECD) but its main goal was to establish flourishing relationships with the Nordic countries as well as with the United Kingdom, its main trading partner. However, Denmark always wanted to create a free trade area in Europe, and therefore continental initiatives to coordinate industrial and later agricultural sectors of the economy was warmly welcomed in Denmark. The Kingdom of Denmark has been a well-known importer of farm goods for many years since the mid-nineteenth century. During that time Danish potatoes, milk and sugar were common products in

---

[9] However, it seems that the Danish example was warmly welcomed by other European nations. During the referendum in Ireland in 2001, the majority of Irish voters rejected the Treaty of Nice, explaining that its regulations could substantially influence their neutrality. It is another example that shows how European societies are not properly informed about the process of European integration, and in consequence support for supranational solutions is decreasing. This could impose obstacles on further integration within the EU.

[10] J. Laursen, 'Historical Studies of Denmark's Policy towards European Integration. Old and new Frontiers, 1945–1980', in *Made in Denmark*, edited by J. Laursen, H. D. Høyer, K.E. Jørgensen, publication of the Jean Monet Center, University of Aarhus, http://www.jmc.au.dk/Made_in_Denmark.pdf.

European markets. Furthermore, the United Kingdom and Germany were, and still are, the main importers of Danish dairy products. Having strong political and economic links with those main European economies, it was natural for Denmark to start accession negotiations with the European Community, together with Great Britain, Ireland and Norway in 1961.[11] Otherwise it could have led to serious economic and financial turmoil on the domestic market.

Nevertheless, negative opinion on the enlargement of the European Community and on participation by the four northern countries by the French president, Charles de Gaulle, in 1963, put a stop to Danish endeavours to join the organisation. Denmark was disappointed by the unfriendly attitude of the main European countries, so it decided to introduce and develop other integrating projects, namely the Nordic customs union in 1947–1959 and the Nordic Economic Union, known as NORDEK in 1960–1971. Moreover, in 1959, together with the United Kingdom, Sweden, Finland and Norway, Denmark established intergovernmental cooperation within the European Free Trade Area (EFTA).[12] In the meantime, Denmark, Sweden and Norway, had established a political intergovernmental organisation, the Nordic Council,[13] as well as an economic consultative forum with the United Kingdom, Uniscan, to discuss the socio-economic situation and develop mutual trade relationships.[14] Denmark, together with the United Kingdom, fiercely tried to fulfil membership requirements and join the European Community. Again, the main reasons for such an attitude were the Common Agriculture Policy, with its protectionist tools and subventions, as well as a plan to create a single European market with no barriers for trade and the flow of goods, services,

---

[11] Denmark could not become a founding member of the European Community as it was supposed to launch and develop the security and defence policy, which for Denmark was attributed with the United States and NATO. Furthermore, Denmark pursued an active neutral policy and therefore did not want to be involved in European military affairs. The situation changed when the idea of creating the European Defence Policy collapsed. To read more see T. Cieślak, *Zarys historii najnowszej krajów skandynawskich*, Warszawa, 1978, p.437–493.

[12] To read more about EFTA see J. Ruszkowski, E. Górnicz, M. Żurek, *Leksykon integracji eruopejskiej*, Warszawa, 1998, p.40–41.

[13] Finland did not participate in this initiative since it pursued a policy of neutrality caused by close proximity to the Soviet Union. The situation changed in the mid-1950s and Finland became a member of the Nordic Union in 1955.

[14] To read more about the Uniscan initiative see L. Miles, [1997], p.63.

workers and capital. Robert Matera emphasises that membership of the EEC would have been a great opportunity not only for Danish agriculture and farmers but for its industry as well. In other case, trade barriers and customs, in the event of staying outside the organisation, would be disastrous for Denmark, especially because of its strong economic ties with the United Kingdom.[15]

It must be emphasised, however, that Denmark and Britain alike were always in favour of European economic integration in terms of free trade and the four free flows. Even though at the beginning of the post-war period Denmark was indifferent towards integrating propositions, it changed its attitude at the beginning of the 1950s. It was even criticised by the other Nordic states, mainly Sweden, for pursuing 'open door' policy on membership in the EEC, which favoured joining the European organisation instead of developing Nordic economic integration.[16]

Sweden is a country whose economic performance is based on its economic and trade ties with Europe and hence it cannot be isolated from the continent. Nevertheless, for many years of the post-war period, Sweden has faced a twofold dilemma concerning the European integration. On the one hand, it was necessary for Sweden to maintain close trade relations with the continental Europe in order to maintain its access to the European markets and thus pay for an expensive welfare state. However, there was also a political dimension, concentrating on securing Swedish principles of independence and neutrality. Leading Swedish politicians were suspicious about a future framework and the final shape of the integration process. The major Swedish concern related to a transfer of national sovereignty to a supranational level, which as a result could violate its neutrality doctrine. Sweden did not want to be involved in any kind of international organisation which could abuse its traditional foreign policy 'of non-alignment in peacetime and neutrality at the wartime'. Hence, up till the 1980s the Swedish governments tried to merge conceptions of national sovereignty and neutrality with its economic relations with Europe. During this decade, Swedish attitude towards the European Communities underwent substantial changes, and eventually the country gained full membership in the organisation on 1 January 1995.

---

[15] R. Matera, [2001], p.165.
[16] L. Miles, [1997], p.63.

Nevertheless, its reluctant attitude remained alive, and as a consequence, Sweden is rather cautious towards proposals addressed to the EU member states.

It is hard to compare Sweden and the two previous countries, the United Kingdom and Denmark, especially because the latter have been members of the organisation for more than 30 years, while in the case of Sweden it is a term of ten years only. However, there are certain elements of European integration, in particular the issue of political integration, and the creation of a European Security and Defence Policy (ESDP), as well as the European Economic and Monetary Union which cause hot debate in Sweden. Membership in the third stage of EMU is very controversial and causes different opinions among political elites and economists, as well as the public.

For centuries Swedish political stability and economic prosperity has been, and continues to be, strictly linked with trade and economic relations with the rest of the European continent. Foreign trade is essential for Swedish development and affluence. It helped to transform Sweden into an economic power during the legacy of King Gustavus Adolphus (d. 1632) 'when the country rose from the ranks of the peripheral minor powers to become (...) a European Great Power'.[17] At that time Sweden developed its skills in securing foreign capital and military supplies from abroad; however, it was obvious that this emerging prosperity could only be maintained if political relations with Europe were properly shaped and sheltered. As an old member of the Hanseatic region, Sweden had previously established close relations with Germany, Denmark and other countries in the Baltic region. Additionally, at the beginning of the nineteenth century it started to cooperate with Great Britain, especially in trade and industrial relations, which contributed to the modernisation and industrialisation of Swedish manufacturing sectors.[18]

The Swedish economy has steadily become an open economy based on international relations, not only with European countries but the whole world as well. According to Stig Hadenius, there

---

[17] Ibid., p.3.

[18] In the mid-nineteenth century not more than 15% of the Swedish population lived in towns, and almost 70% were occupied with agriculture. At that time Sweden introduced modern achievements of new technology such as steam-powered engines, paper and pulp industries, and new inventions in telecommunication.

were three fundamental factors which transformed Sweden into an industrialised modern nation-state. First, Swedish industrialisation was linked to the continuing internationalisation of trade, since the increase in production was strictly linked to an overseas demand. Second, modern railroad networks were developed, which led to low transport costs and contributed to establishing firm links between regions, which before had been ignored. And last but not least, an increased number of births provided new companies and factories with a steady inflow of new labour. It is worth mentioning that the Swedish government has consequently promoted a high level of education within its citizens, which has helped to create and build up a knowledge-based economy.[19]

The factors mentioned above contributed to restructuring Swedish industry, agriculture and other sectors of national economy. In the twentieth century the country thrived, even though in political terms it remained outside 'big politics'. Although pursuing the policy of neutrality, Sweden was still present in international economic and financial relations, steadily capturing new trade partners and new markets to sell its high-standard products. On the other hand, Sweden has always been regarded as an attractive country for business, especially because of its well-educated and highly motivated workforce, high technological development and openness towards foreign investment, together with stable economic and political conditions. Over many decades, Sweden learnt how to operate alone in the highly perilous economic conditions of the global economy and therefore, being such a prosperous country, Sweden is afraid that membership in the third stage of the EMU could damage its position in international affairs.

2.   Political Reasons

Political reasons for non-participation in the third stage of the EMU are usually focused on the issue of sovereignty. Therefore opponents of participating in the Eurozone usually present the 'sovereignty argument', saying that replacing a national currency with the euro would deprive Britain, Denmark or Sweden of their nationality and autonomy. It is true that a national currency is one of tangible examples of a country's sovereignty and contributes to

---

[19] S. Hadenius, [1999], p.9–10.

its divergence from other countries in the world. However, nowadays it is very difficult to find a country that is completely autonomous in international relations. There are certain limitations upon sovereignty in the field of economic and foreign policy, which are mainly due to the increased interdependence of the modern world.

> Interdependence is a fact of life – in trade, in diplomacy, and in the fight against crime. Nowadays sovereignty means that people and their parliaments or other governing institutions can do all that a government can possibly do within a territory, within the constraints set by international treaties, law codes and linkages within markets. [20]

In that context, arguments that membership in the EMU reduces national sovereignty could be rejected because sovereignty is not total any more in the era of globalization and growing interdependencies among countries. Modern countries have actually already lost most of their economic and fiscal independence by virtue of globalisation of money markets and the development of computer, telecommunication and information (CTI) systems, or due to voluntary restrictions imposed by international treaties such as membership in NATO, the United Nations and the World Trade Organisation (WTO). Markets, not national governments, determine the value of national currencies and the level of interest rates now. In the modern world, the money markets are much more powerful than national authorities, as was illustrated very well by British expulsion from the ERM in 1992.

> That was perhaps the most brutal illustration of how a national government can find itself reduced to impotence. [21]

Moreover, national sovereignty must be shaped by international realities of the time. In the nineteenth century, each state operated within the system of the balance of power, which contributed to maintaining an international order. Consequently, there were constraints on domestic, foreign and economic policies, and there

---

[20] E. Heath, 'Sovereignty in the Modern World', in M. Baimbridge, B. Burkitt, P. Whyman, [2000], p.204.

[21] Ibid., p.207.

was a functioning system of fully-fledged sovereign states. However, that period ended after World War II:

> …when growing interdependencies challenged old ideas of sovereignty and national power. The challenge countries are now facing is to use their sovereignty not for some narrow outdated nationalistic purpose, but in the interests of their citizens.[22]

In the case of the United Kingdom the most appealing example of a 'sovereignty argument' is Margaret Thatcher's speech, which she presented in September 1988 in Bruges. The Prime Minister underlined necessity to sustain cultural and national features of each EU member state. The speech began with strong support for the European integration, reconsidering the historical role of the United Kingdom on the continent. It was said:

> Britain does not dream of some cosy, isolated existence on the fringes of the European Community. Our destiny is in Europe, as a part of the Community (…). That is not to say that our future lies only in Europe (…). The European Community is one manifestation of that European identity. But it is not the only one (…). In that sense working more closely together does not require power to be centralised in Brussels or decisions to be taken by the appointed bureaucracy. We have successfully rolled back the frontiers of the state in Britain, only to see them re-imposed at a European level, with a European super-state exercising a new dominance from Brussels.[23]

In Denmark the issue of sovereignty is also very much quoted while talking about joining the Eurozone. There is a certain understanding of a notion of 'state' and 'nation' in Denmark, which influence Danish attitude towards the continental integration. In political terms, the state is strongly connected with the notion of 'welfare state' and the main features of the Danish state are understood as welfare state features. This has made the state potentially sensitive to the process of European integration, which gradually included more political and socio-economic areas. The attitude towards creating and enhancing a free trade area has generally been positive. The right-wing coalition government in the

---

[22] Ibid., p.208–209.
[23] S. George, [1991], p.60–62.

1980s, for example, strongly supported the internal market introduced in the Single European Act. But it also wanted guarantees for protection of workers' safety. Second, the equivalent element of the state unity has been the 'rule of the people'. The core of the nation is 'the people', while parliament and government only present and fulfil people's will. The nation has strong cultural and ethnic features, which cause a high degree of overlapping between state, nation and society.[24]

2.1. THE UNITED KINGDOM

During 30 years of British membership in the European Community/European Union, political reasons for a rather negative attitude to European integration in the United Kingdom have been exposed to continuous change. They modified the structure of fundamental motives for the British behaviour and grounds for her decisions on European matters, frequently erasing old-fashioned reasoning and replacing it with new causes for the 'British special status'.

The external political reasons consisted of special relations with the United States, the role of the North Atlantic Treaty Organisation in securing peace in Europe after World War II, and British relations with the Commonwealth. The victory in 1945 enhanced a sense of 'uniqueness' regarding the British place in Europe and the rest of the world. The wartime alliance with the US gave the United Kingdom a strategic belief in the primacy of Atlanticism in her foreign policy. The Anglo-American relationship was 'special' because no other European nation had anything similar in relation to Washington. Accordingly 'Europe' was of lesser importance to Britain than either the US or the Commonwealth.[25]

Such attitudes not only induced a sense of separation from the rest of Europe but also an overestimation of Britain's international standing. As Jean Monet said, 'It was the price of victory – the illusion that you could maintain what you had, without any change.'[26]

Furthermore, Great Britain regarded intergovernmental organisations as the most acceptable method for maintaining security in the world. According to British politicians, the United

---

[24] H. Larsen, [1999], p.459–460.

[25] K. Dyson, K. Featherstone, [1999], p.558–559.

[26] Ibid., p.558.

Nations Security Council, where the United Kingdom has been a permanent member, and the United Nations itself, as well as the Council of Europe, had a special role of keeping peaceful relations within the international community. Moreover, Britain was one of a few nuclear powers, which in the system of balanced power, established after World War II, were the most dominant.[27] Looking back over the past centuries, she was also one of the great powers which had influenced international relations and situations in the world for many years. Hence British politicians, namely the Prime Minister, Winston Churchill, announced the theory of three concentric circles, according to which British foreign policy should be interdependent: complying relations with the US, the Commonwealth and finally with Europe. The Prime Minister foresaw only a supportive role for the United Kingdom in the emerging process of integration on the European continent. Furthermore, he underlined that Great Britain could not join a new organisation because it had a special mediating role among the countries belonging to each circle.[28] It is an example of global reasoning in the political, economic and military sense for which Great Britain is famous, and for that reason she argued that the European Community would create new divisions in the world. Consequently, it was more important for the Brits to fight against communism than to integrate with Europe.[29]

However, the other European countries and even the United Stated failed to encompass such global interpretations in their foreign policies. British historians say that after World War II:

> Britain has lost the Empire and not yet found a role. The attempt to play a separate role (...) was based on a special relationship with the United States, a role based on being the head of the Commonwealth, which had no political structure or unity or strength. This role was about to be played out.[30]

For the British, the creation of the EC and growing European

---

[27] The decision to develop the nuclear potential in the United Kingdom was taken by Winston Churchill at the beginning of the 1950s.

[28] S. George, *Britain and European Integration since 1945*, Oxford, 1991, p.50–51.

[29] The outbreak of the Korean War in 1950 caused removal of the British observers who took part in the European conference which prepared the Paris Treaty on the Steel and Coal Community.

[30] D. Austin, *The Commonwealth and Britain*, London, 1988, p.29–30.

market represented a unique offer, which the country needed to grasp to preserve the political and socio-economic interests she had around the world. Moving closer to EC membership was caused mostly by a reassessment of British economic interests in the light of the importance of having access to the growing European market. Nevertheless, changes in the international economy, mostly interdependent open markets, again forced Britain to think 'global' rather than just 'European'. Globalisation demanded open markets, and to reach this goal, existing nation-states had to be transformed into more open entities. Consequently,

> 'Thatcherism' in the 1980s suggested that 'Europeanism' was outdated, and slow in adjusting to the demands of global competition. Thus, the Economic and Monetary Union was seen as stemming from an ill-conceived notion of building regional blocs against the competitive and liberal logic of globalisation.[31]

Another set of grounds for not participating in the European Communities and, later on, disagreeing on deepening cooperation on the European level, was denoted as 'internal political reasons'. The United Kingdom has a different political system, which can be characterised by the following elements: monarchy, majority electoral system (first past the post), and a two-chamber Parliament where the upper chamber (the House of Lords) is the representation of citizens who have a title of nobility, and is not subjected to popular vote. Moreover, Parliament has a special status within the British political system, i.e. there exists the principle of the sovereignty of Parliament in two aspects. Hugh Gaitskel I said that, 'Parliament should be the sole law making agency and that the exercise of its will should be unfettered'[32] and parliamentary sovereignty is a crucial element in the British relations with Europe. 'The self-referential power of parliament, together with the executive it produces, is seen as absolute and beyond external control.'[33] And last but not least, British politicians underline differences between the Anglo-Saxon system of law and the Continental one, which may cause problems in obeying the European rules adopted mostly in accordance to the latter.

---

[31] K. Dyson, K. Featherstone, [1999], p.559.

[32] E. Heath, [2000], p.205.

[33] H. Larsen, [1999], p.460.

2.2. DENMARK

The unique Danish position in European affairs derived from it being a small state and its dual role in the European integration process since 1945. It is a well-known fact that since the eighteenth century, countries of the northern hemisphere have coordinated their policies as well as cooperating with one another on different political and socio-economic fields. Consequently, a historically based knowledge of the political mechanisms of Nordic cooperation and its comparison with modes of European integration would considerably help to understand better the relationship between Scandinavia and Europe, together with existing cross-currents in those relationships.

The Danish attitude towards the process of European integration is also influenced by close links between internal and European politics, which has a significant impact on general understanding of European affairs in Denmark. The European policy in Denmark has been profoundly interwoven with domestic politics.[34] Even though EU membership and its consequences are also a controversial issue in other countries, especially in Great Britain, in Denmark it has virtually become an integral part of internal politics, which could be exemplified by many referenda on EC affairs. However, European affairs contribute to domestic affairs also as a tactical factor in the process of political bargaining and in the struggle for dominance between the main socio-economic and interests.

One of the political arguments of Euro-sceptics considers the common currency to trigger much deeper integration within the monetary and fiscal national policies, and that consequently it tends towards strict political integration. Membership in the third stage of the EMU would therefore not only put Denmark on an irreversible way towards a federal Europe but it might threaten the foundations of the Danish welfare state, by virtue of harmonisation of tax and social policies on the European level. Moreover, the arguments of opponents to EMU membership have focused on the continuous centralisation of power in Europe, which would make it much harder to pursue a democratic discussion about political issues, which is very important for the Danes.

---

[34] The best example is the special position of the Parliamentary Market Committee, which has a strong impact on Danish international economic affairs. To read more see M. Grzybowski, *Systemy konstytucyjne państw skandynawskich*, Warszawa, 1998, p.78–90.

As far as Danish participation in the European integration is concerned, especially in terms of EMU membership, it is worth mentioning that Denmark has always been keen on deepening cooperation among the Nordic countries. The countries of the region are quite similar, and in that sense their enhanced collaboration is obvious. There are certain features of those countries, namely geographical traits, history, traditions and culture, language, religion, as well as political systems (constitutional monarchies with very strong and influential social-democratic parties) and socio-economic dimensions (basic concepts of justice, welfare programmes with high social allowances, free health care and education, advanced gender equality, cooperative institutions). Analysing reasons for the Scandinavian cooperation one must not forget about the historical background as well as the gradually created interconnections between the countries, which indicate high levels of mutual interdependence, e.g. passport union, agreements on education, research, seasonal workers, trade agreements etc., mostly within the Nordic Union (however, the process started in the inter-war period). In that light, it was natural for Denmark, together with the other Nordic countries, to submit proposals for the creation of an area of enhanced economic cooperation in the region under the Nordic Council, which was introduced in 1969 and was called NORDEK. Regrettably, the Nordic countries failed to fulfil their plans and the whole idea collapsed soon after implementation. As a result, the countries re-established accession negotiations with the European Communities to accomplish their accession to the organisation.[35]

2.3. SWEDEN

Since 1814 Sweden has pursued the policy of neutrality. In 1855, in the November Treaty, Great Britain, France, Prussia and Russia confirmed Sweden's neutral position in European and international affairs. Moreover, the country developed a domestic consensus among the main political parties to pursue a security policy based on 'non-alignment in peacetime leading to neutrality in the event of war'.[36] It was maintained during both world wars and in the post-war period

---

[35] To read more about the creation of NORDEK see L. Miles, [1997], p.156–160; T. Cieślak, [1978], p.437–440.

[36] L. Miles, [1997], p.10.

during the era of the Cold War. The doctrine of neutrality policy largely influenced Swedish attitude towards the process of European integration. European plans for establishing a European Defence Community in the 1950s, as well as continuous endeavours to develop European defence policy, have always caused rather unfriendly responses in Sweden and contributed to the negative Swedish attitude towards the whole process of European integration.

Another reason for abstaining from the European Community was based on the Swedish political system. Sweden is a mature parliamentary democracy with consensus in decision making and a low degree of opposition towards the existing political system. Governments are believed to be open and transparent. European institutions are, by contrast, regarded as exceedingly bureaucratic and obscure. In consequence, strong attachments to national sovereignty and confidence in the success of Swedish democratic standards for the wealth and freedom of all citizens created a feeling of resistance towards the European Community and shaped Swedish European politics for many years. Lee Miles argues that while legal aspects of Swedish democracy are not completely distinct from the democratic model in different countries, 'Swedish politics is different in sprit, which is best exemplified by a high commitment to governing through consensus at all levels of administration.'[37] As a result, in Sweden there is the so-called 'Swedish model' of integrative democracy denoted as 'consensual democracy'. It adheres to a low level of domestic opposition over the main political issues (achieved through frequent consultations among the main political actors), and a high degree of continuation of public policy. Moreover, the model has shaped domestic politicians' behaviour in such a way that the growing role of European integration in creating economic forces has been neglected or underestimated.

Likewise, Sweden is a parliamentary democracy where public power derives from the people. There are two major principles – the principle of open government and the principle of accountability, including free public access to official documents (the principle of publicity) and protection of clerks giving information to the media. Taking these rules into account, both politicians and citizens have resisted any aspect of European integration for many years. They believed that membership in the European Communities would

---

[37] Ibid., p.18.

weaken Swedish constitutional standards, especially those aforementioned. There was a widespread confidence that Swedish democracy was superior to those on the continent, and that it was the organisation which could gain more benefit from Swedish membership rather than Sweden itself.[38]

For many Swedes it is the Swedish parliament, the Riksdag, which is the main democratic institution that symbolises democratic rules and the standards of the country. Hence, society was afraid to lose crucial elements of democracy while joining the European Communities. It is widely known that in the organisation there is a deficit of democracy, and the role of national parliaments in the decision-making process is rather small. Consequently, diminishing the position of the Riksdag on the national political scene has been regarded as lowering democratic standards and losing part of its national sovereignty. Furthermore, there is much wider distribution of information and access to political debate in Sweden than in other European democracies. Accordingly, once a decision is reached, and all political forces have agreed on it (e.g. political parties, pressure groups), the implementation of a decision is considerably easier. In the European Communities it is, however, more difficult to accomplish an agreement (especially in unanimity voting areas), and even though it is done, there may occur some difficulties in its implementation.

Another reason for abstaining from membership in the EEC was a developed notion of local self-government in Sweden. Respect for national identity in order to safeguard powers of national and local authority is highly developed in Sweden. Swedish local self-government is responsible for welfare programmes – education, social and medical care. Moreover, local awareness is very high, much more than in the European Union, and national governments feared that accession to the organisation would diminish it. It was not earlier than the beginning of the 1990s that the principle of subsidiarity was established in the organisation and it has been developing since the Treaty on European Union came into force in November 1993.

One of the main arguments against membership in the European organisation, and involvement in continental matters was the fact that Sweden is quite a small country in population terms. It was said that having joined the European Community, this peripheral and neutral country could be easily outvoted by large European

---

[38] Ibid., p.19.

countries such as Germany, France or the United Kingdom. As a result, it would be forced to accept common decisions which could interfere in its autonomy and change its pursued policy of neutrality. Consequently, another reason from abstaining from the process of European integration was again the Swedish principle of non-alignment and neutrality.

The Swedish doctrine of neutrality consisted of several principles. The most important were connected with first, gaining complete public support based on a high degree of consensus between domestic political parties regarding security policy and neutrality; and second, all decisions in foreign policy needed to be compatible with the doctrine of neutrality.[39] Third, Swedish neutrality was reinforced by a 'principle of total defence', which was connected with preserving large armed forces as well as technological and military industries.[40] Finally, the doctrine of neutrality was combined with internationalism, according to which being a member of the European Community would prevent the country from pursuing an active independent role in international relations (e.g. within the United Nations and the Conference/Organisation of Security and Cooperation in Europe).[41] However, the Swedish policy of neutrality was a concept of an 'active neutrality', according to which Sweden voluntarily decided to remain neutral and continued to reinforce its neutral status. It was the main reason for not joining the European Community until the 1990s, since it was essential for Sweden to clearly define and articulate its neutrality during the confrontation era in Europe. Hence, all foreign decisions had to be compatible with the declared neutrality, so that the actions of successive governments were predictable and credible for foreign partners. However, at the beginning of the 1990s the non-socialist Ingvar Carlsson government announced that joining the European

---

[39] For many years it was impossible for Sweden to join the European Community because Swedish economic sovereignty failed to be compromised with supranational features of the EC Common Commercial Policy. Swedish governments could not allow decisions of a supranational body (as the European Communities were perceived by the Swedish political and economic elites) to prevail against the Swedish doctrine of neutrality.

[40] In the post-war period, budgetary spending for Swedish defence was the highest in Western Europe and the size of the armed forces was disproportional in comparison to the overall population of the country. Sweden is still very biased against European projects of the European Security and Defence Policy within the European Union because it may negatively affect its 'armed neutrality'.

[41] L. Miles, [1997], p.42–43.

Community would not damage the Swedish doctrine of neutrality. On the contrary, EC membership would be quite compatible with it. Consequently, in October 1991 there were some serious changes in Swedish national security policy. Prime Minister Carl Bildt announced a 'revised foreign and security policy with a European identity'. In practice, Swedish security policy was diminished to 'non-participation in military alliances'.[42]

The next reason for being a reluctant partner in the process of European integration is connected with plans to create a 'United States of Europe'. Sweden, together with Great Britain, Denmark and Austria, is against federal concepts of Europe. The arguments have focused on two main reasons. First, Swedish politicians were frightened that their high standard of living would attract a large influx of foreign labour, and then highly qualified Swedish industries could face serious problems. Second, integration with Europe could undermine the social policy and welfare programmes established in Sweden. Moreover, Swedish politicians did not want to replace advanced national institutions with the unknown ones of the European project. Sweden reckons a project for a federal Europe would have positive aspects for those countries 'whose political and economic institutions had been discredited during World War II' – but that was not the case of Sweden.[43]

Integration of the Nordic region seems to be the other reason for reserved Swedish attitude towards the process of European integration. Denmark, Finland, Norway, Iceland and Sweden are homogenous in political and socio-economic terms. However, following the sixteenth century there was a lasting rivalry between Sweden and Denmark for leadership in the region. Maybe this is partly an explanation of why Denmark joined the European Community earlier than Sweden did. Moreover, three other Nordic states, namely Norway, Iceland and Finland, were very afraid of the domination of the major two, since they were newly independent states, concerned about their status in international relations.

Norway, Finland and Iceland gained independence in 1905, 1917 and 1944 respectively, and they were somewhat afraid of any kind of closer integration which would go far beyond intergovernmental

---

[42] S. Åström, 'Continuity or Change? Sweden appraises its security policy', *Current Sweden*, The Swedish Institute, no.434/2001, p.2.

[43] This is the same reasoning as in the United Kingdom after World War II. To read more see L. Miles, [1997], p.54–55.

cooperation. They were rather suspicious about establishing a competitive process of closer integration in Europe and hence, coordination of their relations was based on existing national institutions without creating supranational organs, even though for some, namely Sweden, this collaboration deemed to be 'a second best solution'.

3.   Economic Reasons

Great Britain, Denmark and Sweden have always supported the economic aspects of European integration. The countries agreed on the creation of a free trade zone, adding four free flows and finally the establishment of a common market without internal borders. Nevertheless, successive governments, especially in the United Kingdom, argued that it would be better for the country to be outside the Eurozone. Agreeing on introducing the single currency while its value was low in comparison to the national currencies might have increased foreign imports and decreased national export rates. EMU membership could also contribute to raising unemployment and inflation rates, which could be forced by lowering interest rates caused by the decrease of the number of foreign investors coming to the countries in question. Those elements could cause turmoil in the British, Danish and Swedish economies, erasing all profits from possible participation in the Economic and Monetary Union, namely positive changes in levels of productivity and competitiveness, the higher quality of goods, the elimination of risk of changes in the exchange rates of European currencies, removal of transaction costs, providing transparency of prices across the EU member states, increasing economic growth, currency liquidity, which guarantees higher return on capital because of decreased costs of its keeping on a bank account, and enhance inflow of FDIs.[44]

A serious argument against joining the third stage of the EMU is connected with differences in the business cycles between the United Kingdom, Denmark and Sweden and the other EU member states.

In 1993, in Great Britain, the unemployment rate started to decrease, and this was the case until 2003. On the European

---

[44] A. Moravcsik, [1998]; D. Baker and D. Seawright, [1998]; W. Eltis, *Britain, Europe and EMU*, London, 2003.

continent this rate has diminished since 1998 but it is still higher than in the United Kingdom. The unemployment rate on the British Isles equals 5%, while in the continental EMU members it has consistently increased and equals now around 10%. As one may conclude, unemployment rates in the three countries in question are very satisfactory in comparison to unemployment rates in the EMU members.

Figure 3.1   *Unemployment (%)*

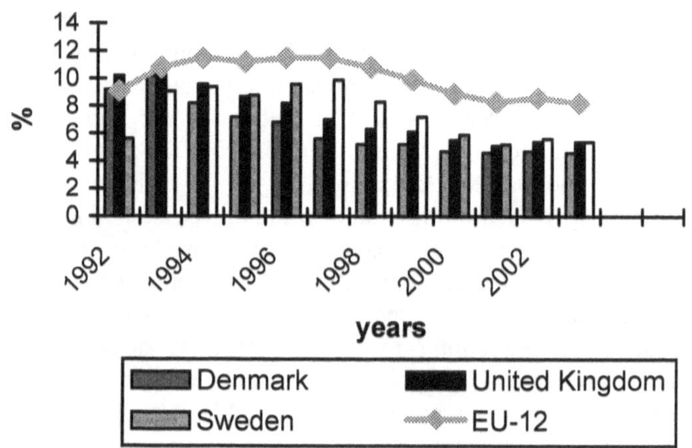

Table 3.1   *Unemployment (%)*

	1992	1993	1994	1995	1996	1997	1998	1999	2000	2001	2002	2003
Denmark	9.2	10.2	8.2	7.2	6.8	5.6	5.2	5.2	4.7	4.6	4.7	4.6
Sweden	5.6	9.1	9.4	8.8	9.6	9.9	8.3	7.2	5.9	5.2	5.6	5.4
UK	10.1	10.5	9.6	8.7	8.2	7.0	6.3	6.1	5.5	5.1	5.4	5.4
EU-12	9.1	10.8	11.5	11.2	11.5	11.5	10.8	9.9	8.9	8.3	8.6	8.3

Source: *European Economy. The EU Economy: 2002. Review: Investing in the Future*, European Commission, Directorate-General for Economic and Financial Affairs, no.73/2002; IMF, OECD.

British economists argue that according to different economic cycles each country needs specific economic solutions, especially in terms of interest rates, which fit well the economic and financial condition of each country. In the Eurozone the short-term interest rate is fixed by the European Central Bank, which cannot take into account all the specific features of the economies of twelve EMU members. The lack of prior cyclical and structural convergence amongst all participating member states may create strains within the Eurozone. Consequently, unsynchronised business cycles and/or structural differences enlarge the effects of asymmetric external shocks (e.g. oil price rises), whilst a unified monetary policy will be unable to meet satisfactorily the needs of all economies, concentrating upon the 'average' member state, as it is likely to do. Thus, incorrectly set interest rates may damage individual economies, increasing their initial misfortunes rather than moderating them. Hence, being outside, in the event of any economic crisis, the United Kingdom can pursue its own independent fiscal and monetary policies, which could help her to overcome the crisis using tools created specifically for her. The European Union Committee of the House of Lords concluded, 'common monetary policy (...), which should fit everyone, may not be good for anybody'.[45]

Danish opponents of the creation of the Economic and Monetary Union also disagree on elimination of a possibility for national institutions to coordinate national economic policy as well as conducting interventions in critical situations. They stress that in the 1980s and 1990s Denmark had substantial economic problems, which were linked to a deterioration of its competitiveness on international markets. They resulted in record deficits in the balance of payments and a flow in overseas debt which in 1986 increased to almost 40% GDP. The only reasonable way to cure the situation was governmental intervention. To improve economic conditions the government decided to reform the fiscal system and put forth a number of indirect and direct tax rises (the so-called 'potato cure'), which included imposing a tax on consumer loans. Moreover, a tax

---

[45] 'Wielka Brytanic: o wspólnej walucie', in *Rzeczpospolita*, 09.12.2000.

reform, aiming at the promotion of personal savings, was introduced. Meanwhile, the indirect tax policy, aimed at promoting competitiveness, was launched. The growth in private consumption and investments was decreased and resulted in a noticeable reduction of imports. With growing exports, a strong improvement in the trade balance occurred. In 1990 the balance of payments showed a surplus for the first time in almost 30 years. However, the package of tax reforms failed to solve domestic problems. Property prices fell, and unemployment rose significantly. The recession was worsened by an international slowdown at the beginning of the 1990s, which diminished export potential in both Great Britain and Sweden. Bearing the above in mind, some Danish economists kept anti-EMU stances. They point out that in case of any turbulence in global economy, Denmark, as an international player, should at least be able to have its own tools to coordinate the economic performance of the country. As in the British case, they also underscore the inappropriateness of the 'one-size-fits-all' policy conducted by the ECB. Furthermore, an argument that the main Danish trading partners, namely Sweden and the United Kingdom, remain outside the Eurozone, is also very popular among opponents of the Danish membership in the final stage of the EMU.[46]

In the Tables 3.2, 3.3 and 3.4, GDP, general government consolidated gross debt as well as budget deficit in the United Kingdom, Denmark and Sweden are shown.

---

[46] In 2002 Swedish Foreign Direct Investments (FDI) in Denmark amounted to 50% of all inward FDI, while the British figure was 22%, the second biggest number. To read more see 'Foreign Investments in Denmark, Royal Danish Ministry of Foreign Affairs Facts', *Invest in Denmark*, June 2002, p.2.

Figure 3.2   *Gross Domestic Product at 1995 market prices (%)*

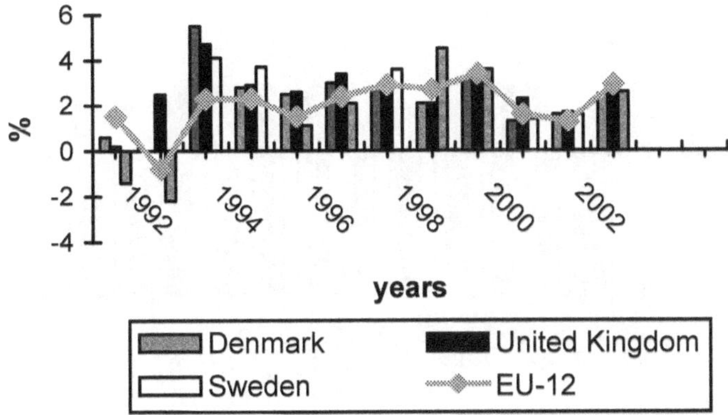

Table 3.2   *Gross Domestic Product at 1995 market prices (%)*

	1992	1993	1994	1995	1996	1997	1998	1999	2000	2001	2002	2003
Denmark	0.6	0.0	5.5	2.8	2.5	3.0	2.8	2.1	3.2	1.3	1.6	2.5
Sweden	-1.4	-2.2	4.1	3.7	1.1	2.1	3.6	4.5	3.6	1.4	1.6	2.6
UK	0.2	2.5	4.7	2.9	2.6	3.4	3.0	2.1	2.9	2.3	1.7	3.0
EU-12	1.5	-0.8	2.3	2.3	1.5	2.4	2.9	2.7	3.4	1.6	1.3	2.9

Source: *European Economy. The EU Economy: 2002. Review: Investing in the Future*, European Commission, Directorate-General for Economic and Financial Affairs, no.73/2002; IMF, OECD.

Figure 3.3 *General Government Consolidated Gross Debt (percentage of GDP at market prices)*

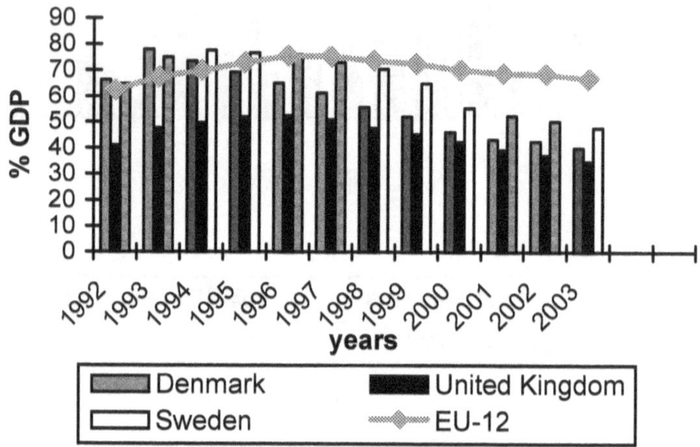

Table 3.3 *General Government Consolidated Gross Debt (percentage of GDP at market prices)*

	1992	1993	1994	1995	1996	1997	1998	1999	2000	2001	2002	2003
Denmark	66.3	78.0	73.5	69.3	65.1	61.2	55.6	52.0	46.1	43.2	42.5	40.0
Sweden	64.8	75.1	77.7	76.6	76.0	73.1	70.5	65.0	55.3	52.3	50.2	47.8
UK	41.0	47.6	49.6	51.8	52.3	50.8	47.6	45.2	42.4	39.3	37.2	34.8
EU-12	62.4	67.5	69.8	72.9	75.4	75.3	73.7	72.6	70.2	68.8	68.4	66.7

Source: *European Economy. The EU Economy: 2002. Review: Investing in the Future*, European Commission, Directorate-General for Economic and Financial Affairs, no.73/2002; IMF, OECD.

Figure 3.4   *Budget Deficit (as percentage of GDP)*

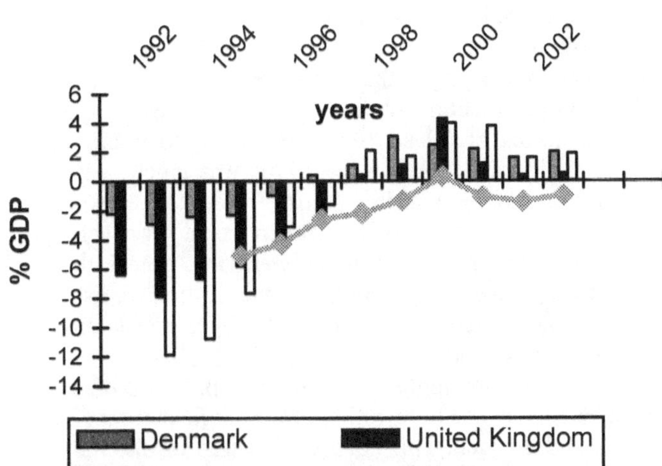

Table 3.4   *Budget Deficit (as percentage of GDP)*

	1992	1993	1994	1995	1996	1997	1998	1999	2000	2001	2002	2003
Denmark	-2.2	-2.9	-2.4	-2.3	-1.0	0.4	1.1	3.1	2.5	2.2	1.6	2.0
Sweden	-	-11.9	-10.8	-7.7	-3.1	-1.6	2.1	1.7	4.0	3.8	1.6	1.9
UK	-6.4	-7.9	-6.7	-5.8	-4.4	-2.2	0.4	1.1	4.3	1.2	0.4	0.5
EU-12	-	-	-	-5.1	-4.3	-2.6	-2.2	-1.3	0.3	-1.1	-1.4	-1.0

Source: *European Economy. The EU Economy: 2002. Review: Investing in the Future*, European Commission, Directorate-General for Economic and Financial Affairs, no.73/2002; IMF, OECD.

The opponents of the EMU membership underline that despite the fixed exchange rate policy, the Danish economic business cycle became significantly desynchronised with that of the main EMU members between 1993 and 1998. Rapid economic growth, in particular in 1993 and 1994, and an impressive reduction of unemployment (from around 10% in 1993 to 5% in 1998), supported by active labour market reforms, made it possible for Denmark to meet the convergence criteria without any problems, which since 1996, Denmark has fulfilled.

The argument of asymmetric shocks is also vivid in Sweden. Swedish economists argue that there are different economic cycles on the European continent and in Sweden, which could pose serious obstacles and lead to higher unemployment rates. The Swedish cyclical downturn in the 1990s was much deeper than in many of the EMU countries. Hence, it could be expected that Sweden would have followed a different route for several years in comparison with France, Spain or Germany, where the cyclical downturn was much less pronounced. And if the Swedish economy were to fall out of step with the rest of Europe, the common interest and exchange rate would have a destabilising effect.

Moreover, labour mobility in the European Union is limited, which also contributes to rejection of the single currency in Britain, Denmark and Sweden. This is an explanation for the failure of the European economies to create jobs, even in periods of economic expansion. Cultural differences, including language differences, substantially reduce labour mobility on the European continent. If labour markets are flexible, there is no need for an active stabilisation policy to deal with asymmetric shocks at all, since shocks (demand-side or supply-side) can be absorbed by changes in wages, rather than changes in employment and output. The available evidence suggests that, while labour market institutions vary across the EU, in general the European labour market is much less flexible than that in the United States. Labour mobility could provide an alternative to wage flexibility as a way of absorbing asymmetric shocks, with workers moving from depressed regions to those where employment is high.[47] Nevertheless, in the European Union it is still a future project.

Likewise, the design of the Economic and Monetary Union implies that the majority of EMU participants must continue to

---

[47] In 1992 the European Commission presented a programme to complete the single market, which abolished many legislative obstacles to the free movement of labour, and so geographical mobility is likely to increase in the future. To read more see N. M. Healey, [2000], p.34–35.

deflate their economies by raising taxes or cutting government spending in order to meet the rigid financial criteria established by the Maastricht Treaty as well as the Growth and Stability Pact. The combination of these measures will result in higher unemployment and slower growth within the Eurozone.

In the last report on global economy, the OECD announced that despite strenuous economic conditions in the world, Britain managed to face them better than the other countries, especially members of the Eurozone. British economists say that if the normal rules of economics were observed, the German government would be cutting taxes and boosting public spending to overturn an economic slowdown.[48] But the Eurozone is not 'normal economics'. Under the rules of the Growth and Stability Pact, Germany is being required to do the exact opposite – raise taxes and cut spending. If that is not enough, it will have to pay a 0.5% of GDP fine, which will worsen the situation. In the meantime, Britain, Denmark and Sweden – outside the Eurozone – can set both monetary and fiscal policy to suit their own needs. This is the main reason for their having such a small number of unemployed in comparison to the rest of Europe, Japan and the United States, for the first time since World War II. Being an EMU member, the countries in question would have to bear the same restrictions now being seen in Germany.[49]

Another reason for abstaining from the third stage of the EMU is an absence of any substantial fiscal redistribution mechanism, which could stabilise the EMU by transferring resources from richer to weaker regions, meaning the less competitive areas may suffer lower incomes and growing mass unemployment, increasing inequality and social turbulence across the single currency area.[50]

---

[48] During the last two years, Ireland has faced very high growth and inflation rates while Germany and Italy were growing slowly. In that case, the European Central Bank should have tightened monetary policy to cool Ireland off and adopted an expansionary monetary policy to stimulate growth in Germany and Italy. To read more see D. Salvatore, 'The Euro, the European Central Bank, and the International Monetary System', *Annals of the American Academy, AAPSS*, January 2002, no.579, s. 157.

[49] J. Bush, 'A tale of two Chancellors', http://www.euobserver.com, 27 November 2002.

[50] This is a common knowledge, but it has been proved to be false since resources will be shifted from one place to another if conditions for that are created and an infrastructure is developed by correct usage of financial aid.

The Maastricht Treaty failed to provide any sort of economic mechanisms, which limit the decline of weak areas within existing 'single currency areas'.

> This process is referred to as 'fiscal transfers' since it refers to government spending (fiscal policy) and it results in money being transferred automatically from areas that are prospering to areas in economic difficulty. It operates through the tax and benefit system, affecting the whole country or a single currency area. No equivalent process would be in operation in the euro area because taxation revenue and public spending would remain locked within the existing nation states. The automatic transfer between regions would not take place and the poor would just get poorer. It would undermine the revenue base from which benefits are funded. If any national currency is overvalued (as is the case of the pound) and its goods are therefore uncompetitive both at home and abroad, then this will cause bankruptcies and higher unemployment. This in turn usually forces a devaluation (or depreciation of the currency) to remove the specific problem. Even being a member of the Eurozone it is quite possible to become a declining region, locked into a vicious cycle of decline.[51]

Likewise, the euro was supposed to be a strong and stabile currency. Nevertheless, its introduction on 1 January 1999 had contradictory results. Until the autumn 2001 the value of the euro was steadily falling against the US dollar and since its introduction it marked a loss of 30%, which contributed in flow of foreign savings out of Europe, and hence the of economic growth was slower in the whole Eurozone. The low value of the euro helped to maintain negative opinions towards the common currency in all the examined countries, but especially in the United Kingdom. The opponents consider the weak euro to have a negative influence over financial operations in the City of London, since the British pound had always remained stronger than the US dollar.[52] Entering the Eurozone 'when the euro has been behaving like a Camembert

---

[51] J. Michie, 'The Economic Consequences of EMU in Britain', in M. Baimbridge, B. Burkitt, P. Whyman, [2000], p.50–51.

[52] Apart from the situation just after World War II when the pound sterling cost less than the US dollar because the latter was more frequently used in trade and financial relations.

currency, melting from one low to the next'[53] would be harmful for the British economy.[54] The Labour Party is particularly afraid of fixing the value of the pound to the euro, because it will be connected with lowering the current value of the pound together with lowering the interest rates. It might cause a disappearance of foreign investors and foreign capital. Moreover, the Prime Minister, Tony Blair, is especially terrified of a possible increase in the inflation rate and cuts in budgetary spending.[55] On the other hand, the pound is overvalued, and the cost of production and imports is much higher than it should be (see below).

The weakness of the common currency was also of great importance for Sweden. As the United States is Sweden's fourth trading partner, joining the EMU would definitely improve the situation of the euro but not the Swedish economy. In that context, the Swedish economy has been gradually changing from a traditional manufacturing and commodity-based economy. Currently, the country appears to have a comparative advantage in the growing hi-tech sectors, such as information technology (IT) and pharmaceuticals.[56] This shift makes the Swedish economy less vulnerable to competition from low-cost producers in Eastern Europe and South East Asia, compared with the main EMU economies. In this respect Sweden has more in common with countries like Great Britain, Denmark and the US than with Germany or France. The opponents of the EMU membership underlined that until mid-2001 the euro was not as stable a currency as many had expected after its introduction in 1999. On the contrary, its value has fluctuated a good deal and was below the lowest margins. In that sense, all expectations of a strong European currency proved to be a misconception. The Swedish krona was in a better position, and joining the Eurozone at that time would be the ultimate economic error.[57]

---

[53] 'This may end the debate in Denmark, but the result will be felt across Europe', in the *Independent*, 20 September 2000.

[54] To read more see J. Bloom, 'British business and the euro', BBC News/Business, 31 March 2000, http://news.bbc.co.uk.

[55] M. White, 'The Path to Euroland', in the *Guardian*, 30 January 2002.

[56] M. Kinnwall, 'Swedish Monetary Policy: On the Way to EMU', in *Sweden and the European Union Evaluated*, edited by L. Miles, London, 2000, p.159.

[57] N. Gottfries, 'Why is Sweden not in EMU?', *Current Sweden*, The Swedish Institute, January 2002, no.435, p.4.

Furthermore, there are also arguments underlining the large amounts of money which would be spent in preparing for the switch to the single currency. However, short-term changeover costs would be vastly outweighed by long-term benefits. The Chamber of British Industry (CBI) has estimated that the 'EMU will reduce business transaction costs by 0.4% of GDP',[58] and this saving could be made every year after joining the EMU. Moreover, it estimated the costs of preparation and transition to be a one-off cost of 'probably no more than 0.5% of GDP'. At the same time, the Bannock Consulting Report shows that the financial gain to the United Kingdom simply from not having to change currencies inside the Eurozone is worth around £4.5 billion each year. By comparing the one-off cost of single currency membership with this ongoing benefit, the Bannock Consulting Report estimates that the 'payback period' for membership in the EMU is approximately two and a half years for the United Kingdom.[59] This means that it is relatively short, and Britain will join the EMU at a certain moment in the foreseeable future. This is also true for two other countries which remain outside the Eurozone.

Each of the examined countries has its own economic reasons for non-participation in the third stage of the EMU. They will be presented and commented below.

3.1. THE UNITED KINGDOM

After World War II, the best known external motives for not participating in the integration process on the European continent involved Britain's special economic relations with the Commonwealth.[60] Great Britain could buy many goods at preferential prices, lower than fixed world prices, from their former

---

[58] 'Bannock Consulting. An estimate of the one-off transition costs to the UK of joining the Euro', Bannock Consulting, July 2001.

[59] It is worth mentioning that this estimation does not take into account any wider potential benefits of membership in the Eurozone, such as increased trade and investment and currency stability. http://www.euro.gov.uk.

[60] The Commonwealth was created in 1867. After World War II it comprised of a quarter of the world's people living in one-sixth of the world's area. Its 49 member states had been included in the British Empire for some time. Today the Commonwealth is a loose association of independent sovereign states, which cooperate with the United Kingdom in different dimensions. To read more see P. Bromhead, *Life in Modern Britain*, Manchester, 1991, p.190–194.

colonies (mainly New Zealand, Australia and Canada).[61] Adding together the additional costs of insurance, loading and transport, these imported goods were still much cheaper than goods bought from the European countries. It is also worth mentioning that British exports to the countries associated in the Commonwealth were six times bigger than to European countries. The economic profits were the most important factor for the British, although in their relationships with the Commonwealth they used political arguments and rhetoric to hide the real advantages they had by pursuing such a policy. Relationships with the Commonwealth could preserve, at least partially, Britain's position of power in international relations. Moreover, in the Westminster Treaty (1931) a Sterling Bloc was created to keep economic and financial relations with the British colonies in pounds, so that the risk of fluctuations in exchange rates between currencies was eliminated.[62] Accession to the EEC might have reduced that advantage significantly.[63]

One may also point out several internal economic causes, among which agriculture, transport regulations and steel production were essential in causing reluctance towards membership of the European Community. First, British economists emphasised that creation of the European Steel and Coal Community would destroy the British steel industry. After World War II the United Kingdom experienced some disturbance in those industrial areas. Having been 'the workshop of the world' for decades, Great Britain now experienced problems with competitiveness of her production on international markets, which were caused by high labour costs and the strengthening value of the British pound resulting from discovering oil in the North Sea. In consequence, British export became unprofitable, since the prices of British goods were higher

---

[61] *Britain in Europe: An Introduction to Sociology*, edited by T. Spybey, London, 1997, p.3.

[62] The Westminster Treaty provided the British dominions and colonies with a possibility to pursue their own foreign policy, but there were British military bases and strong economic relations (*Sterling Bloc*) with the mother country. The only country which was exempted from the Sterling Bloc was Canada. F. Gołembski, [2001], p.24–26.

[63] It is also worth mentioning that there were intensive financial relations between Great Britain and the United States pursued mostly within the Organisation of the European Economic Cooperation (OEEC), later changed to the Organisation of Economic Cooperation and Development (OECD).

than prices of the same goods produced by the continental countries, which thus extended their import on the British Isles. To cure the situation successive British governments introduced social packages for workers to protect them from becoming redundant and in the meantime increased the then very high corporate taxes. Nevertheless, the importance of the British economy in trade relations and international economic relations was gradually diminished. This led to a decrease in the level of trust in British currency in the 1950s.[64]

In negotiating accession to the European Community, the United Kingdom fiercely criticised the plans on which the Common Agriculture Policy (CAP) was to be based. Trading with the former colonies provided Britain with very profitable terms of trade of farm goods, although after World War I she developed her own agricultural sector so as to be independent of external supplies. In 1954 the 'deficiency payment system' was introduced to support British farmers. Its main idea was to offer direct budget subsidies, which led to decreasing prices of British farm goods compared to international prices. In the meantime, the productivity of British farmers was the highest in the world, and the production line was the most modernised.[65] Therefore, approving the rules of the CAP as well as breaking trade agreements with the former British colonies would cause a budget loss of £4.5 billion.[66]

There is also a problem of the relationships between those countries with a tradition of fiscal stability, and those with no such tradition regarding the reduction of inflation rates, together with the reduction of their public deficits and debts. There is fear that such states would not be able to maintain their stances. In particular, concerns were expressed over the so-called 'pension issue'. The population on the European continent is continuously ageing. In the next 25 years the number of EU citizens over 60 will rise by 50%. Since the birth rate is low and life expectancy is still rising, the

---

[64] P. Kennedy, *Mocarstwa Świata. Narodziny – Rozkwit – Upadek*, Warszawa, 1995, p.460–475.

[65] The CAP was designed to maintain artificially created guaranteed prices, which in result were higher than international prices, and protective actions such as interventional purchase and movable equalising fees in case of importing from third countries.

[66] A. Wojtyna, 'Rolnictwo brytyjskie wobec Wspólnej Polityki Rolnej EWG', *Sprawy Międzynarodowe*, 1974, no.2, p.103–109.

number of working people for each retired person will fall from 4 to 2 by 2040. Therefore EU countries will have to face the problem and need to reform their pension systems. 'The OECD has estimated the capitalised (or net present value) cost of current pension arrangements (pension liabilities) to be 98% of GDP in France, 113% in Italy and 139% in Germany, compared with 19% in the United Kingdom.'[67] There was an argument presented by opponents of entering the third stage of the EMU that there was a possibility that demographic pressures in the other EMU member states would threaten stability of the single currency. Moreover, British ability to pay pensions, which was much higher than in the other countries, thanks to the reforms of the pension fund system, would also be endangered. There might also occur pressure for assistance from other EMU members. It must be stressed, though, that Britain would never have to pay pensions due in other countries because, according to the article 104b of the Maastricht Treaty, 'a member state shall not be liable for or assume the commitments of another member state'.[68] However, it cannot be denied that they point to a real public policy dilemma in the countries concerned, even though they are not a problem for the EMU.[69]

Opponents of British membership in the European Economic and Monetary Union maintain an argument on specific rules of the British financial system. In the United Kingdom there are floating credit rates, while on the continent they are stable. Therefore the level of credits and mortgages taken out by British households is higher than in the rest of the EU member states. As a result, the aggregate demand in Britain is more predisposed to changes in the interest rates.[70] The British private financial sector is more sensitive to changes in interest rates since a higher proportion of mortgage debt is denominated in flexible rather than fixed interest rate stock. The aggregate mortgage debt is 60% of GDP in Britain but only

---

[67] L. Talani, 'Who wins and Who Loses in the City of London from the Establishment of European Monetary Union', in *After the Euro. Shaping Institutions for Governance in the Wake of European Monetary Union*, edited by C. Crouch, Oxford University Press, 2000, p.133.

[68] Ibid., p.133.

[69] D. Currie, 'EMU: Threats and Opportunities for Companies and National Economies', in Baimbridge, B. Burkitt, P. Whyman, [2000], p.122.

[70] B. Patterson, 'EMU and the United Kingdom, Task Force on Economic and Monetary Union', European Parliament, April 1998, PE 166.059/rev.3, p.19–20.

40% in Germany, 25% in France and 10% in Italy. The interest rates paid on these lower levels of personal debt are also less flexible on the continent than in the United Kingdom. The variable rate liabilities of the personal sector total 64% of GDP.[71] Consequently, if the ECB varied interest rates in order to stimulate or restrain average EMU economic activity, the United Kingdom would be disproportionately impacted by the corrective measures, causing the economy to diverge further from the EMU average. Thus, a uniform monetary policy would be likely to create fluctuating boom-bust cycles in the British economy rather than a smooth and sustainable rate of economic development.

Likewise, the peculiarity of London as a financial centre was another argument against membership in the Eurozone. It is achieved precisely by its unique international orientation. London is the most international of the leading financial centres, and has the largest share of many global markets. The London Stock Exchange has a greater turnover than all other countries combined. The London foreign exchange market is the largest in the world, with a daily turnover of US$637 billion in April 1998, which is higher than that of New York and Tokyo combined. In February 1997 there were 565 foreign banks in London, two-thirds of which come from non-EU countries, more than in any other city in the world.

British participation in the Eurozone would for sure undermine this leading international role of the City of London by enforcing restrictions on its markets and institutions, and, generally, by submitting the City to tight control of the ECB. Moreover, the EMU could affect the City's international primacy by eliminating the possibility for London to develop as the main offshore market in euro or in euro-denominated assets. This activity, in case of British participation in the EMU, would certainly be developed by one of its major world competitors. Finally, it is necessary to take into consideration the domestic economic consequences of joining a monetary union. These are usually included in the expression of 'loss of sovereignty'; but, in the case of the City of London, it has a clear-cut meaning, namely the loss of the ability to influence domestic monetary and exchange rate policies, which could be

---

[71] W. Eltis, 'British EMU Membership Would Create Instability and Destroy Employment', in M. Baimbridge, B. Burkitt, P. Whyman, [2000], p.140.

interpreted in terms of loss of domestic political power.[72]

Nevertheless, since the success of the City of London has always been linked to its ability to adapt to the changing environment, its markets and institutions are certainly able to catch business opportunities coming from the establishment of a single currency area even remaining outside it. Evidently, the supremacy of the City of London has not been damaged, even though the United Kingdom stays outside the Eurozone. It is characterised by the comparative international efficiency and the fact that much of the business done in the City is independent of whether or not the United Kingdom is part of the single currency area. This could be weakened if banking regulations made in Frankfurt reflected continental rather than British interests. Switzerland offers an example of a country which does not maintain exchange rate stability with the currency of any other country, yet maintains a highly prosperous and competitive financial centre. The City of London could follow this example and thrive even outside the Eurozone.[73]

Another argument against participation in the Eurozone is connected with the structure of production in the United Kingdom. It should be stressed that the British economy has a very different structure of production from continental Europe. The United Kingdom, like the United States, but unlike any other EMU member state, is a significant oil producer. Moreover, the country has a particular competitive advantage in high technology, aeronautical, pharmaceutical, biochemical, scientific instruments and telecommunication sectors, which, together with oil production, are typically priced in US dollars and compete principally with US and Japanese companies. Great Britain has a higher ratio of high-tech production than France, Germany and Italy. In the high-tech industries such as pharmaceuticals, where Britain has some of the world's largest and most efficient companies, success in research and development is more notable than skill in manufacturing. The country has however managed to established a large comparative advantage in the mid-tech industries and excels in original research, with far more Nobel Prizes than any other country except the United States. Thus, the sterling-dollar exchange rate remains far more important to this key

---

[72] L. Talani, [2000], p.130–131.
[73] W. Eltis, [2000], p.144.

element of the British manufacturing sector than the sterling-euro one.

EMU membership might increase exchange rate volatility for these crucial sectors of the British economy. It is often supposed that because 50–60% of British trade is with other EU member states, and only 15% with the United States, sterling's exchange rate with the US dollar matters little in relation to its exchange rates with France and Germany. Such calculations ignore that where the United Kingdom exports high-tech products to Europe, it usually competes on the continent with US companies. Summing up, with a different structure to the European structure of production, Britain often needs a different combination of exchange rates and only the present flexibility of the sterling rate against both the euro and the dollar could offer it.[74]

3.2. DENMARK

The Danish economy is small and open, and very dependent on trade with other countries. However, it does not have a possibility to make an impact on international trading conditions or central economic factors, especially interest rates. The value of both exports and imports constitutes one third of the Danish GDP. About two-thirds of foreign trade is pursued with the other EU member states. Sweden, Great Britain and Germany are the most important Danish trading partners.[75] In fact, strong economic ties and interdependence with the United Kingdom partially caused Danish application for membership in the European Community, submitted at the beginning of the 1960s. Indeed, on account of the great importance of foreign trade for the domestic economy, Denmark was very keen to deal freely in goods and services with other countries.

From the mid-1960s, when oil and natural gas were discovered, Danish industrial exports exceeded agricultural exports. After World War II the country changed rapidly into a fully developed industrial nation, and it currently leads in information and communication high technologies (ICT), computers and telecommunication systems. The transformation into a post-industrial information society is already far advanced, including a

---

[74] Ibid., p.143–144.

[75] Outside the European Union, Denmark trades especially with Norway, the US and Japan. Danmarks Statistiks, 2002, www.dst.dk.

large software export business. Moreover, the public and private service provision has become the largest occupation sector, employing 36% of the Danish working population. However, farming, for which Denmark was famous in the nineteenth century, has not stopped. Furthermore, Denmark established a strong position in international economic relations, especially in cement-making machinery, wind turbines, hearing aids, enzymes for food processing and washing powder production, water purification equipment, draught beer fittings, medical measuring instruments, and medicines such as insulin.[76]

The high rate of economic growth also led to a deterioration of the external current account and put pressure on the labour market followed by wage increases. In 1998, the parliament decided to tighten economic policy significantly (the 'Whitsun Package') in order to reduce domestic demand and ease the pressure on the labour market. During 2000, the inflation rate remained high due to increasing energy prices and the higher value of the US dollar in relation to the euro. Thus, the Danish krone rose 2.8% in October 2000. Nevertheless, since autumn 1999, the inflation rate has decreased significantly, and an increase in private investment and exports appeared.

Like the United Kingdom, Denmark opposes membership in the third phase of the Economic and Monetary Union, pointing out its inclinations in international trade in high-tech goods, traditionally denominated in US dollars. Moreover, the country is afraid of introducing fixed exchange rates because of the negative experience with pegging the Danish krone to the German mark in the past.

Danish Euro-sceptics stress the fact that introducing the euro could bring deeper integration within the monetary and fiscal national policies. Membership in the third stage of the EMU would therefore threaten the foundations of the universal Danish welfare state, causing harmonisation of tax and social policies at the supranational level.

Consequently, opponents of EMU membership attach great importance to the asymmetrical construction of the project. They claim the fact that the monetary and exchange rate policy has been centralised at the supranational level, whereas the general economic policies basically remain national, which could have harmful

---

[76] The Royal Danish Ministry of Foreign Affairs, www.um.dk.

consequences on the European economy. This asymmetry was a main argument in explaining why the Union would either break down or have to be fixed by much deeper political integration. Nationalist or conservative Euro-sceptics emphasised that the European Economic and Monetary Union exists for cooperation among sovereign nation states with particular national interests, national political institutions and stable loyalties between them and citizens. However, in the light of past experiences and the different national traditions in Europe, it would be difficult to achieve a sufficient political solidarity among all the EU member states required to ensure a successful ending of the project. On the contrary, the asymmetrical construction of the EMU would give rise to a persistent tension between the supranational monetary body and the national institutions of the participating countries. According to Karsten Skjalm:

> ...the tension would be likely to reach the boiling point, and this could result in the breakdown of EMU. For this reason it was better for Denmark to remain on the outside, or at least wait and see how the project would evolve.[77]

The political tensions could lead to much deeper political integration in terms of a higher degree of 'harmonisation' of the most important economic areas. The main fears are expressed against 'centralisation' in such aspects as taxes, labour market policies, pensions and social policies, which are key elements of the Danish welfare programmes. The opponents of the EMU membership emphasise that this could not only worsen the democratic deficit in the EU, but also threaten the foundations of the Danish welfare state. The counter-argument of pro-Europeans focuses on the lack of consistency in such reasoning. They point out that the Maastricht Treaty and secondary legislation clearly stipulated the rights and obligations of the member states and the EU institutions which would participate in the Eurozone. Moreover, they underline that the experience gained from more than 40 years of European integration generally shows that the EU member states have tended to bear their obligations as long as these are clearly formulated. Finally, the construction of the EMU is not as asymmetrical as it looks at the first glance. During the whole

---

[77] K. Skjalm, [2000], p.34.

process of European integration, economic policies of the member states have been unified. In most areas of economic policy, the European Communities first, and now the European Union, has been making use of 'soft' coordination instruments such as broad economic guidelines, best practices, benchmarking, surveillance, information exchange, code of conducts and peer group pressure. The EU institutions try to accommodate the special needs of each EU member state and respect their prerogatives, but at the same time such a policy ensures a certain coordination of the economic policies of EU members, which is also evident because of the high level of economic interdependence in the organisation.[78]

3.3. SWEDEN

Sweden has relatively high degree of natural resources, namely large amounts of forestry, iron ore and water reserves, which have contributed to and secured the affluence of the country.[79] For centuries it had developed and expanded its industry, trade and economic relations with the other Scandinavian and Nordic countries, and in consequence it was able to become a strong international player reliant on export of raw materials (iron, grain, metal ores, timber), combined with highly converted engineering products, textiles and paper pulp. Nevertheless, such an economic structure caused dependency on international markets, although it contributed to the considerable wealth of the country. The latter aspect also enabled Sweden to pursue economic and commerce relations independently from European countries, although Europe has been the main Swedish trading partner. This factor should be analysed together with the aforementioned non-alignment in international conflicts in the first half of the twentieth century. According to this, economic cooperation was pursued with both hostile sides during the Cold War, which prevented the Swedish economy from serious damage in industrial and manufacturing sectors. Furthermore, it helped to develop new areas of involvement.

After World War II, Sweden became an economy dependent on international trade and industrial relations with other countries. Swedish exports were extensive and eclipsed the number of

---

[78] Ibid., p.37–40.
[79] S. Hadenius, [1999], p.8.

imported goods. The importance of agriculture gradually diminished, whilst industrial production reached its highest point in the 1960s. At that time Sweden became 'a matured industrial society with (...) high standards of living, advanced welfare policies and a harmonious labour market'.[80] High rates of growth in all export-oriented industrial sectors laid down the economic foundations for industrial modernisation, and participated in increasing employment in public service as well as securing the costly welfare state. Moreover, Sweden introduced the export of capital and services, creating branches of Swedish companies abroad. As a result an intensive economic expansion appeared. The country has exported high quality technical and mechanical items and electro-technical goods.[81] However, leading politicians were concerned about Sweden's status as a small country heavily dependent on European markets and trade. Therefore they postulated the establishment of a free trade zone, internationalisation of the global economy, and full access to European markets for Swedish exports.

Sweden's main reason for remaining outside the Economic and Monetary Union was connected with a need to peg national exchange rates to the euro. When the international Bretton Woods system of fixed exchange rates collapsed in the early 1970s, Sweden maintained a fixed rate for the krona. The Swedish officials thought that it would have a controlling effect on wage levels. Labour and management in Sweden were likely to understand that substantial pay increases would cause reduced profits and a loss of market shares for industries in the competitive sector. Nevertheless, 'Sweden was caught in an inflation-devaluation cycle, in which periods of high demand and high inflation were followed by crises and devaluations. The Swedish krona was devalued in 1976, 1977, 1981 and 1982',[82] in accordance with successive governments' decisions. At the end of the 1980s, there was an economic boom in Sweden, but it led to financial speculation. Wages and prices rose faster than elsewhere. Within a few years, a deep economic crisis appeared. The Swedish Central Bank (*Riksbank*) struggled to maintain a fixed rate in relation to the

---

[80] L. Miles, [1997], p.7.

[81] T. Cieslak, [1978], p.411.

[82] N. Gottfries, [2002], p.1.

ECU until 1992, when it let the Swedish krona float in the currency market. When this happened, new guidelines for Swedish monetary policy were required. In consequence, the Riksbank was endowed with considerably more rights and tools to pursue an independent role in monetary policy affairs.[83] Opponents of EMU membership highlighted that by virtue of the economic turbulences Sweden experienced at the beginning of the 1990s, it had to impose floating exchange rates. In joining the EMU, Sweden would have to impose fixed exchange rates again, which could cause more problems for the Swedish economy. This was fiercely discussed, since the costs of pursuing an independent monetary policy could be too high. Moreover, unilateral exchange rate pegs were vulnerable and costly. All in all, the bad experience of a unilaterally fixed exchange rate was one reason why Sweden refused to join the 'broad band ERM', having become a EU member in 1995.[84]

Another aspect of Swedish reluctance towards the process of European integration is connected, as in Denmark, with the development of the Swedish model of the welfare state. Since the 1930s, the Social Democratic Party (*Socialdemokratiska Arbetare-partiet*, SAP), has been the main actor on the political scene in Sweden, which has had major implications for Swedish European policy.[85] Stig Hadenius argues that:

> ...the party commitment to develop a social welfare state was in clash with supranational integration movements as they were perceived to undermine the sovereignty of social democratic economic policy.[86]

Moreover, arguments against full membership in the EEC originated from the social democratic perspectives and the ideology of the party. Not only until the 1980s and the 1990s did the European debate become more pluralist, thanks to the non-socialist parties, which held power in Sweden in 1976–1982 and 1991–1994.

---

[83] Ibid., p.1.

[84] M. Karlsson, 'Swedish Interest Groups and the EU', in L. Miles, [2000], p.85–87.

[85] From 1932–1996, the SAP governed in Sweden for 55 out of 64 years. To read more see S. Hadenius, [1999], p.44–49.

[86] Ibid., p.73–80 and 116–118.

4.   Socio-cultural Reasons

There are several socio-cultural factors on which British, Danish and Swedish societies base their negative attitude towards the European Economic and Monetary Union and the common currency.

Great Britain has not been defeated in any war for centuries, on account of being an island. In the absence of invasion or defeat, Britain 'felt no need to exorcise history'. The 'Dunkirk Spirit' and the struggle of the 'Battle of Britain' shaped later public attitudes. They strengthened the feeling of nationhood and reinforced sovereignty, which continued as main assumptions in English politics.[87] Therefore, British society was convinced of the influential position of the home country both in Europe and in the world. The British did not trust European nations because they regarded the continent as the main source of conflicts and disturbances in international relations in the past decades.[88] Furthermore, citizens of the United Kingdom 'identified more with the white settler population of Australia, Canada, New Zealand, and South Africa than with the peoples of France, Germany, the Low Countries, and Italy'.[89] British inhabitants were convinced of the necessity for special relations with the US as the main source of peace on the continent and they did not like ideas of closer European cooperation in that context. This cautious and critical approach is still maintained nowadays, and hence the British nation is the least supportive of the European Union. There is a kind of a psychological barrier, according to which British consider any European proposal as more dangerous than profitable.

Bearing the above in mind, one may easily understand why the United Kingdom prefers to keep the European cooperation at the governmental level, being rather unwilling to create common policies, especially if they are not directly connected with economy and finances. Andrew Moravcsik in his book, *The Choice for Europe. Social Purpose and State Power from Messina to Maastricht*, argues that politicians were in favour of introducing the free flow of goods, services, workers and capital as well as creating a common market because such steps might have raised British

---

[87] K. Dyson, K. Featherstone, [1999], p.558.

[88] J. Kendle, *Federal Britain. A History*, London, 1997, p.155.

[89] S. George, *Politics and Policy in the European Union*, Oxford, 1996, p.133.

competitiveness as well as restructuring and modernising the British economy. From the political point of view, membership in the EEC could have confirmed the British international position both in Europe and in the world.[90] On the other hand, developing the European security and defence policy as well as plans to introduce the common currency in the 1990s were perceived as attacks on the British nation. British politicians warn that handing over new areas of life to Brussels may result in depriving British citizens of the ability to make decisions which could have a direct impact on their life. Consequently, the British government regards joining the Eurozone as contributing to losing national sovereignty and political independence.

Denmark and Sweden are the biggest players in the Nordic region, and for many years back in history they pursued a natural rivalry for leadership in the region. There were also permanent tensions between them, as the major countries, and the minor ones in the Nordic region. In the nineteenth century, Sweden, united with Norway, developed relations with the United Kingdom, while Denmark and Iceland were linked with Germany.[91] Partly, therefore, Danes have always had a rather ambivalent attitude towards cooperation among the European countries. Following its defeat by Germany in 1864, the country has felt a certain distrust towards binding international cooperation. Being a small nation with only 5.2 million inhabitants, Denmark is naturally worried about the possibility of its disappearing in the greater Europe.

Opponents to the EMU membership in Denmark and Sweden enumerate social reasons for staying outside the project. First, they underline developments of the Danish and Swedish welfare state policies after World War II.[92] As social-democratic-led economies

---

[90] It was necessary because the United States did not need any mediator in its relationship with Europe and preferred the United Kingdom to be a member of a new European organisation. The countries of the Commonwealth did not respect British leadership in the organisation either (e.g. the Suez crisis of 1956; the introduction of apartheid in the Republic of South Africa in 1961).

[91] L. Miles, [1997], p.142.

[92] A *welfare state* is a state in which organised power is deliberately used (through politics and the administration) in an effort to modify the play of market forces in three directions: a) by guaranteeing individuals and their families a minimum income irrespective of the market value of their property or work; b) by narrowing the extent of insecurity by enabling individuals and their families to meet certain 'social contingencies' (e.g. sickness, old age, unemployment), which lead to family

with built-in welfare structures and a heavy emphasis on full employment, both countries provide their citizens with large numbers of different social allowances and entitlements. Therefore, the question of the economic influence of EMU membership on the welfare model is fiercely debated in those Scandinavian countries. Moreover, it is worth stressing that welfare and the process of European integration have been intensely examined ever since the 1950s. During the negotiations on Danish membership in the European Communities in 1961–63, welfare provisions provided by the country underwent dramatic attacks in the light of a future membership. Therefore, entering the third stage of the EMU caused social discussion on that matter. It is emphasised that there was a low degree of social concerns at the European level.

Since the end of the nineteenth century, Swedish politics and regulations have contributed to forming a leading social democratic and corporate country. Sweden can be characterised by its own model of the welfare state, comprising a social democratic, corporate and consensus policy, representing a 'middle way' between capitalism and communism.[93] Moreover, Swedish citizens are endowed with social rights (e.g. unemployment allowances, pensions for the retired) and can use social services (e.g. free health care, care of children and older people), which was known as 'People's Home' (*Folkhemmet*). 'It was a combination of the Keynesian approach to solving unemployment and welfare policy as containing the main points of the Saltsjöbaden Agreement between employers' and employees' organisations.'[94] This agreement shaped and governed industrial relations in Sweden for the next 50 years, maintaining unprecedented labour peace in the country.

---

crises; c) by ensuring that all citizens without distinction of status or class are offered the best standards available in relation to a certain agreed range of social services. To read more see A. Briggs, 'The Welfare State in Historical Perspective', in R. E. Goodin, B. Headey, R. Muffels, H-J. Dirven, *The Real World of Welfare Capitalism*, Cambridge, 1999.

[93] L. Miles, [1997], p.7.

[94] The Saltsjöbaden Agreement (*the Basic Agreement*) was signed in 1938 between the Swedish Employers' Confederation (*Svenska Arbetsgivareföreningen, SAF*) and the Swedish Trade Unions Confederation (*Landsorganisationen, LO*). It introduced a system of collective bargaining between business and labour (centralised but without the interference of government), as well as contributing to the development of the so-called '*Swedish Model*'. To read more see S. Hadenius, [1999], p.49–55.

It contributed in development of corporate and consensual approaches to decision-making and facilitated the expansion of the welfare state, which were to become the other main Swedish characteristic of the post-war era.[95]

The compromise also embodied the consent of Swedish business to welfare reforms, while on the other hand, the trade unions restricted themselves from pushing for nationalisation of industrial companies. The main goals of the 'Swedish model', namely a consolidated wage policy, welfare policy, full employment with low inflation and high economic growth, were possible to achieve thanks to pursuing the active labour market policy.[96]

Moreover, Swedish and Danish opponents towards EMU underline that its creation has failed to take the environmental and energy supply aspects into consideration. The European Union also disregards the social and regional problems, especially maintaining high levels of employment on the European continent, which could threaten the basis of the Danish and Swedish welfare states.

Sweden and Denmark are still afraid that membership of the Economic and Monetary Union would diminish those standards, as they were more strict than in the organisation. This was connected to the special regional policy towards the rural populations in the arctic and sub-arctic northern regions of Sweden. Furthermore, the agricultural policy needed special conditions. Sparsely inhabited rural territory as well as a short growing season and the arctic conditions of the Norrland region, including special treatment of the Sami people, were always mentioned while speaking about membership of the European Community.[97]

Another social reason for staying outside the Economic and Monetary Union is the relatively low degree of the so-called 'green taxes' in other EU member states. In the 1990s, as part of the tax reform, the Danish and the Swedish governments have moved a larger part of the income base from direct to indirect taxes, including the green taxes, which aim at reducing the consumption of scarce resources and materials causing environmental pollution. In Denmark, in the so-called 'Whitsun package', approved by the parliament in 1998, a substantial increase in the number of green

---

[95] L. Miles, [1997], p.9.

[96] Ibid., p.31.

[97] S. Hadenius, [1999], p.127–129.

taxes was included. There are only a few countries on the European continent where such taxes exist. With the Danes' high awareness of environmental issues, a need to remove this solution after joining the EMU entry would be unacceptable.

The next reason for non-participating in the third stage of the EMU was a threat that the Union could pose to the Danish and the Swedish systems of collective wage bargaining. Nevertheless, a report entitled 'Jobs and the single currency', prepared by economists from the Danish Confederation Trade Unions (*Landsorganisationen I Danmark,* LO) and the Economic Council of the Labour Movement (*Arbejderbevaegelsens Erhvervsrad*) was published on 9 September 1999. It recommended that Denmark should join the third stage of the EMU since in the long-term it would lead to a European harmonisation and coordination of collective bargaining systems. According to the report, the Stability and Growth Pact had no effect on the size of the public sector, as well as the size of the public expenditure or revenue which was not part of the EMU criteria. Nevertheless, the report indicated that the EMU might result in a sharp fall in wages and incomes, because the countries with the lowest incomes would pull the average level down. 'It would be the richest countries which would adjust downwards.'[98] Moreover, the EMU might have an effect on the whole Danish collective bargaining system, since its implementation could force labour movements in the EU member states to coordinate both their collective bargaining demands and the bargaining rounds themselves. It must also be expected that, at the European level, framework agreements might arise between the social partners, the details of which would subsequently be filled in at national level. The summary of the analysis states the following:

> The focus on the framework for collective agreements which we are already seeing in neighbouring countries will no doubt be intensified after the establishment of EMU where the differences in wages and prices between the countries will inevitably be high-lighted. Therefore, there may be increased co-operation on the coordination of collective agreement demands and bargaining.[99]

---

[98] *LO report recommends that Denmark should join EMU,* European Industrial Relations Observatory on-line, www.eiro.eurofund.ie.
[99] Ibid.

For Swedes, a very important social reason for not participating in the process of European integration was also a characteristic feature of Sweden's economic environment: the lack of expensive monopolies established by private enterprises, since the state was present in many fields of national economy.[100] Nonetheless, a special regime for producing, importing and selling alcohol, namely the allowance of operating for commercial monopolies, was also needed. They were, however, 'based on important health and social policy considerations'.[101]

---

[100] Olaf Petersson argues that the 'Swedish model' incorporates a specific type of policy, namely capitalism, parliamentary democracy and welfare policy, which operates on the principles of consensus through state administration and interests group. On the other hand, it is a specific type of public policy, in which welfare provisions are comprehensive, universal and institutionalised (*Beveridge model*). To read more see O. Petersson, *Swedish Government and Politics*, Stockholm, 1994, p.50–58.

[101] L. Miles, [1997], p.226.

IV: Attitudes towards Membership in the Economic and Monetary Union

The issue of British, Danish and Swedish membership in the third stage of the European Economic and Monetary Union is a very controversial one, on which everyone has their own opinion. Accordingly, politicians, economists, representatives of business and industry as well as ordinary citizens present certain views on creating the EMU within the European Union. While politicians and economists are mostly in favour of this undertaking, society usually strongly opposes joining the Eurozone. The reasons for such a situation are often explained with the limited knowledge of the whole European project, its complexity, and lack of clear benefits and gains. Moreover, after observing the last five years of existence of the euro in international finance, trade and economic relations, one may conclude that the three countries abstaining from membership in the Eurozone perform better in micro- and macroeconomic terms than the EMU members. Therefore, the negative stances towards the third stage of the European Economic and Monetary Union are preserved.

The chapter is divided into three parts, presenting certain political, business and societal attitudes in each country in question. In the first part, political arguments for and against membership in the third stage of the EMU are presented. In the following parts the methodology is the same: first business and industrial organisations and associations are examined, and in the last part the results of the public opinion polls in Great Britain, Denmark and Sweden are observed.

1. Political Attitudes

In the three countries, namely Great Britain, Denmark and Sweden, which are the subject of this survey, most politicians and political parties are in favour of membership in the third stage of the Economic and Monetary Union. However, each country in question is characterised by specific features and factors, distinct from the ones observed in other countries.

1.1. THE UNITED KINGDOM

In spite her opting-out clause in the third stage of the EMU, Britain has started to conduct a policy which could bring her closer to the European continent. First, the Bank of England became independent. Moreover, the Labour government published detailed plans for the possible later accession to the Eurozone.[1] During the electoral campaign, Labour politicians had called for working closer with the continental countries of the European Union. Even though the Labour Prime Minister, Tony Blair, never said he would immediately accept the euro as legal tender in the United Kingdom, he sent signals to consider such a solution. Furthermore, during its presidency of the European Union in the first part of 1998, Great Britain chaired preparations for the EMU. The Conservative government's 'wait and see' policy was replaced by a 'prepare and wait' policy.[2]

Moreover, the Blair government announced that introducing the euro could be acceptable for the United Kingdom. In October 1997 the Chancellor of the Exchequer, Gordon Brown, introduced a 'National Changeover Plan', consisting of five economic tests to prove whether economic conditions in the United Kingdom were favourable for starting preparations for the third phase of the Economic and Monetary Union. The tests are examined further.

At the same time, the policy of the Conservative Party was to keep all options open, but in its manifesto published in late 1997, it stated that:

> ...it would be unlikely to maintain sufficient convergence of economic conditions across Europe for a single currency to proceed safely on the target date of 1 January 1999 (...) and without such convergence a British Conservative Government will not be part of it.[3]

---

[1] Power in Britain shifted to the Labour Party in 1997.

[2] H. Larsen, [1999], p.473.

[3] B. Patterson, 'EMU and the United Kingdom', Task Force on Economic and Monetary Union, European Parliament, April 1998, PE 166.059/rev.3, p.15–16.

A new leader of the Party, William Hague, who replaced John Major, indicated that the United Kingdom should not join the EMU in the possible scope of ten years. Consequently, the Tory Party remains hostile to EMU entry, although in 2002 the succeeding Conservative leader, Iain Duncan Smith, insisted to call a referendum on the single currency, promising at the same time that he would never take Britain into the Eurozone.

However, in February 1999 the Prime Minister, Tony Blair, started an official euro campaign, although he said that nothing would be done until the British economy was in better condition. Furthermore, social approval for introducing the common currency was needed in order to gain positive results in a referendum on this question. According to the Prime Minister, only when the majority of British citizens were in favour of the euro could preparations to replace pound sterling be started. Unfortunately, it could take 2–3 years.[4]

As mentioned above, the Chancellor, Gordon Brown, said that Britain would introduce the common currency in the country only if results of the 'National Changeover Plan' were positive. The aforementioned tests were to answer such questions:

- Are business cycles and economic structures compatible, so that we and others could live comfortably with euro interest rates on a permanent basis?

- If problems emerge is there sufficient flexibility to deal with them?

- Would joining the EMU create better conditions for firms making long-term decisions to invest in Britain?

- What impact would entry into the EMU have on the competitive position of the UK's financial services industry, particularly the City's wholesale markets?

- In summary, will joining the EMU promote higher growth, stability and a lasting increase in jobs?[5]

---

[4] K. Kołodziejczyk, [2000], 136–137.

[5] 'UK Membership of the Single Currency. An Assessment of Five Economic Tests', HM Treasury, October 1997, p.5.

These additional criteria that the Blair government has attached to EMU membership serve the interests of the government well. Nevertheless, they are severely criticised by both British and European economists, since the questions overlap to a certain extent. For example, it is difficult to meet the first four criteria without also fulfilling the fifth one. Moreover, they are rather vague and open to interpretation, which would enable the government to declare that they are satisfied, in that way opening for a referendum, if public opinion changes in favour of the euro.[6]

When the Treasury reviewed the five criteria in October 1997, numbers 1, 2 and 5 were not met, while number 3 was uncertain. Only number 4 was fulfilled. In 1998, answers to questions concerning economic cycles, flexibility and inflow of foreign investments were negative because of the higher interest rates in the United Kingdom compared with those on the continent (7% in comparison to 3%) and a different economic cycle on the British Isles. Nevertheless, the capital and labour markets are judged to be prepared for the euro.[7]

The first test compares the business cycles in the United Kingdom and in the Eurozone, which became increasingly synchronous during the late 1990s. The GDP growth rates in Britain and on the European continent are moving closer to each other, in 2001 amounting to 1.9% and 1.4%, respectively, and 1.4% and 0.9% in 2002. Several factors have contributed to the observed greater convergence, especially as macroeconomic policies have had similar goals in recent years. British monetary policy has pursued a successful course of price stabilisation, and accordingly the Bank of England has kept the key interest rate above the level observed in the Eurozone. On the other hand, the fiscal policy has become more compatible with the Stability and Growth Pact.

One of the most important factors behind cyclical convergence is the increasing European integration of the British economy: 54% of exports and 47% of imports are traded with the Eurozone, and

---

[6] 'Have debate – Need timetable', edited by J. Birger Christensen, *Focus EMU*, Danske Bank Research, February 2002, p.8.

[7] 'The debate will not die', in *The Economist*, 15 June 2000; J. Glover, 'The five tests', in the *Guardian*, 29 September 2000; K. Niklewicz, '*Rząd Wielkiej Brytanii sprawdza, czy kraj jest gotowy na przyjęcie euro*', in *Gazeta Wyborcza*, 16 August 2001; 'Continental drift', in *The Economist*, 18 April 2002.

hence, joining the EMU would bring a permanent exchange rate among the main British trading partners from Europe, which would contribute to even more similarity with the EMU member states.

The same test also examines the level of flexibility of the labour market in the United Kingdom and the Eurozone. Entry to the third stage of the EMU would increase benefits from euro financial markets for the City of London. Nevertheless, the question of a 'one-size-fits-all' policy (in regards to the ECB monetary policy) still brings a lot of controversy in the debate on joining the EMU in Great Britain. Opponents argue that a European-wide monetary policy, which takes into account the inflation performance of the whole Eurozone, cannot consider specific British issues. However, on entering the Eurozone the United Kingdom would be the second largest economy within it, behind Germany but more or less equal to France, and would therefore be an important player for the European Central Bank. Proponents of accession to the third stage of the EMU emphasise that there already are 'one-size-fits-all' interest rates in the United Kingdom. They point out that no interest rate would ever be ideal for all parts of Britain, whether set by the Bank of England or elsewhere. Currently the monetary policy conducted by the Bank of England does not always fit the economic demands of different areas of the British Isles, either. Different industries and regions within national boundaries require different interest rates. For instance, manufacturing exporters in northern England have complained that rates have been set in the interests of the South Eastern part of the country. Moreover, currently, the key central bank rates do not differ significantly, with 4% for the Bank of England and 3.25% for the ECB.[8]

The second test deals with flexibility, namely it tries to answer the question whether the British economy will be able to resist asymmetric shocks after giving up her monetary and exchange rate policy as policy tools. The United Kingdom has the most liberalised product market in the European Union, and the labour

---

[8] Nevertheless, in 1999 the level of the interest rates in the United Kingdom was circa 6%, while in the Eurozone they were lower (ca. 4%). Differences in the interest rate level reflected the availability of capital. High interest rates attracted capital and pushed the interest rates down, while low interest increased demand for capital, which was not diminished by investments in the British economy but with transfers abroad. www.euro.gov.uk.

market provides flexible employment conditions together with low firing and hiring costs. The British unemployment rate (5.4% in 2001) is much lower than the rate in the Eurozone (8.6%). Nonetheless, most of the EMU members have not yet conducted structural changes in their labour markets, even though one of the expected results of introducing the single currency was to encourage such reforms; but it ought not to be a reason for staying out of the EMU. It is also underlined that greater economic cooperation with the Eurozone would increase macroeconomic stability and reduce possible risks of the existence of asymmetric shocks in Great Britain. If shocks occurred, the more flexible product and labour markets would enable Britain to absorb them relatively smoothly.

The third test refers to foreign direct investment (FDI). The United Kingdom has been a very attractive investment area for foreign companies during the past years. It has the first place among the EU member states, having received about 30% of all inward investment coming to the European Union since the early 1990s. Nevertheless, some foreign investors have pointed out the overvalued and volatile exchange rate of pound sterling, which causes serious problems for exports to the European continent. Hence, elimination of the exchange rate risk would lead to a better calculation basis for trade and investment in the British Isles. Then the country could become an even more attractive location for FDI. Since the introduction of the single currency, the British share of foreign investment in Europe has significantly fallen. In 1998 the country drew 28% of new European investment, in 2000, 26%, and in 2001 it was down to just 19%. Moreover, some Japanese car companies have threatened to withdraw their factories from the United Kingdom if the country does not join; but on the other hand, inward investment from Japan is only about 5% of the total volume of FDI.[9]

The fourth test deals with the competitive position of the British financial markets. In that sense the City of London, which is the most important financial centre in Europe, attracts the most attention. The competitive strength of the City has rested on a number of factors: a

---

[9] G. Bishop, D. Hiller, 'News analysis: Has Britain passed the Treasury's tests for joining the euro?', in the *Independent*, 3 May 2002.

large pool of financial expertise, a wide range of ancillary support services, light regulation of security trading, a favourable tax regime for expatriates moving to London, language and location in a major political and cultural centre. Moreover, high volumes of trade allow London to offer competitive terms for trading; London's position has made it easier to attract first-rate financial experts; the availability of expertise makes London attractive both for trading and locating an operation. However, Paris and Frankfurt are making strenuous efforts to catch up. They are modernising their trading systems, and France is changing fiscal laws to attract overseas experts to locate in Paris.[10] At the launch of the single currency one of the most pressing questions was whether the City would be disadvantaged by the British non-participation in the Eurozone. This could happen by virtue of the following: European exchanges and markets could merge; new debt and currency instruments could be the preferred medium of trade and hedging activity. In fact, the financial services sector still produces about 10% of the country's GDP, and the City of London remains very competitive even without participation in the Eurozone.[11]

The fifth test examines both employment and growth levels after accessing the EMU. British economists are concerned that growth in the Eurozone is beset by structural inflexibilities, in particular in the labour markets. In that sense, British GDP levels could be lowered upon EMU membership. However, all members of the Economic and Monetary Union keep autonomy over a wide range of economic and financial policies and, accordingly, if monetary and exchange rate policies are centralised, structural policies become more important inside the Eurozone. Furthermore, the British point out that fiscal policy will be too inflexible after joining the third stage of the EMU, since the Stability and Growth Pact would impose certain limits on budget deficits, whose violation is submitted to the sanctions of this document. Nevertheless, the requirement of a balanced budget provides room for automatic stabilisers in a downswing. Given the relatively

---

[10] D. Currie, 'The pros and cons', HM Treasury, July 1997, p.17.

[11] J. H. Bryson, 'Special Report: Prospects for EMU Expansion', Wachovia Securities, Economic Group International, March 2002, p.2–3. To read more about the economic situation of the City of London see T. Edmonds, 'The Euro-Zone: Year One', House of Commons Library, , Economic Policy and Statistics Section, March 2000, Research Paper 00/34, p.23–26; L. Talani, [2000], p.113–137.

sound position of British public finances, the country is unlikely to suffer from the rules of the Pact. On the contrary, joining the EMU would eliminate the exchange rate risk, improve planning capabilities for companies and contribute to a more stable macroeconomic environment. Therefore, it may be concluded that participation in the EMU would indeed have a beneficial long-term effect on investment, growth and employment on the British Isles.[12]

HM Treasury has promised to provide its assessment of five tests on 7 June 2003, which is crucial for an announcement of a referendum. It will only happen if the five self-imposed tests are fulfilled. Furthermore, the results of the European Convention and the future institutional structure of the European Union, presented in mid-2003, played a politically important role in the process of taking the British decision on the EMU, because the Brits are not only 'Euro-sceptics' but also 'EU-sceptics'. As is now clear, arguments for accepting the European Convention prevailed over those accepting the EMU membership, but the coming referendum, even if dedicated directly to the new EU treaty, would partly give an answer to the question on British membership in the Eurozone. However, the Prime Minister, Tony Blair, is trying to convince voters that the time for EMU membership has come.[13] Nevertheless, the United Kingdom has already widened the scope of the five tests. The Chancellor of Exchequer, Gordon Brown, added an additional two elements, namely assessment of the Growth and Stability Pact on the British economy, as well as checking the impact of the single currency on shop prices.[14]

On 9 June 2003 the Chancellor, Gordon Brown, informed the House of Commons about fulfilment of the 'National Changeover Plan'. He stressed that the intention of the Blair government was to join the Eurozone, but at the same time he underlined that the United Kingdom was still not well prepared to introduce the common currency in the country. According to Brown, only one test, namely that of retaining competitiveness in the British financial markets, has been met. However, certain economic

---

[12] W. Becker, A. Järvbäck, 'EMU Watch. The United Kingdom, Sweden and Denmark on the Way to EMU', Deutsche Bank Research, August 2002, no.95, p.6–8.

[13] Ibid., p.9.

[14] 'Gordon Brown widens scope of 5 euro tests', http://www.euobserver.com, 9 September 2002.

reforms have already been announced to ensure the others be met in the foreseeable future. The Chancellor also said that a draft referendum bill and a plan for euro preparations would be presented in the coming autumn; however, he emphasised a need to adjust the Stability and Growth Pact as well as the need to reform the European Central Bank before the United Kingdom would join the Eurozone.[15]

As it was mentioned above, the issue of the British membership in the third stage of the EMU was shifted aside because of the debate on the European Constitutional Treaty, which was to be ratified via referendum in spring 2006.[16] Moreover, fiercely debated questions such as intervention in Iraq, contributed to cooling down discussions on the euro. Currently, politicians concentrate more on the state of international relations and a future treaty for the European Union than possible membership in the EMU.

1.2. DENMARK

As in the United Kingdom, in Denmark politicians, economists, representatives of businesses, as well as public opinion, are divided on the issue of EMU membership. While Danish politicians and economists are mostly in favour of this European undertaking, Danish society strongly opposes joining the Eurozone, feeling especially threatened about losing its sovereignty. There is an opinion in Denmark that 'integration is like nuclear power – it is OK as far as it goes, as long as it is not too close to one's own back yard'.[17]

Until the mid-1980s, Danish European policy was strongly influenced by internal turmoil within the Social Democratic Party (SDP), on the question of an economic and monetary cooperation in the organisation. Adopting the Single European Act in 1987 was a culminating moment in domestic political disagreements, and contributed towards a more active Danish European policy. This attitude developed mostly into seeking improvements of the environmental and social policies pursued on the supranational level, but it focused on the creation of greater openness in the

---

[15] 'Brown: It is our intention to join the euro', http://www.euobserver.com, 9 September 2003, 'Brown rules out euro decision for another year', http://www.euobserver.com, 10 June 2003.

[16] Since France and the Netherlands rejected the Treaty in referenda in the summer of 2005, the debate is frozen in Britain.

[17] Quotation in 'LO report recommends that Denmark should join EMU', *op. cit.*

European Communities as well. In that sense, Danish politicians came to an agreement that the country should participate in most vital European projects, namely increasing economic cooperation and shaping political integration. It was an indirect consequence of the fall of the Iron Curtain and ending the Cold War. After World War II Denmark found itself next to the German Democratic Republic, and in consequence, an immediate security threat to its territory was continuously present until the beginning of the 1990s. Membership in the North Atlantic Treaty Organisation secured Denmark in political and military terms, and therefore accession to the European Community was seen only as a guarantee of economic security for this small country. Nevertheless, changes in the geopolitical situation in Europe enabled members of the EEC to develop their cooperation.

All in all, dilemmas of the European policy of the Social Democratic Party (conflicting views on integration between Nordic and European partners, on ways to reconcile the requirements of international economy and domestic employment, as well as closer integration and national welfare strategies) have always had a disruptive impact on political programmes and strategies of the party. Primarily, the SDP was very sceptical, if not hostile, to the idea of a European economic and monetary union, but its opposition weakened considerably at the beginning of the 1990s, since the project was viewed as a natural extension of the single European market. However, certain steps towards launching a union contributed to a negation of its existence. The SDP is against EMU membership, viewing it as economically unsound, and considering it to cover too large a geographical area. Moreover, the convergence criteria are believed to focus too much on economic aspects, without taking social issues into account.

The opposition parties (the SDP, the Greens and the Progress Party) agree that the Economic and Monetary Union would stimulate more economic growth, but they stress that it would take place without adequate consideration for environmental and energy supply aspects, as well as the social and regional problems. They also criticise extension of the qualified majority voting and shifting national power to the European level. Furthermore, the Progress Party is very much in favour of a highly independent Danish economy, and does not want to be too closely linked to the other EU member states and their 'unstable and less solid economies'. In that sense, creation of the single European market is a sufficient achievement for Denmark.[18]

On the other hand, the Liberal Party is in favour of Danish participation in the third stage of the EMU. The Party believes that full Danish membership will contribute to increased influence on European monetary policy, and will give the country a substantial say in coordination of the employment issue at the European level. In that context, the Party is against the four Danish exemptions from the Maastricht Treaty, and calls for their immediate removal. Moreover, the Liberals highlight that the EMU entry would bring the EU member states closer together, which in turn would create a more favourable environment for the organisation, and Denmark as part of it.

The Conservative People's Party also supports joining the Economic and Monetary Union. It fears that maintaining the Danish opt-out clause will lead to weakening Danish industrial competitiveness, and thus result in a higher unemployment level, brought about by increased exchange rate risks, higher interest rates, more costs and possible currency speculation.

According to the Prime Minister, Anders Fogh Rasmussen, the single currency has enhanced the dynamics of the internal market and served as an advantage to Europe in international competition. Furthermore, it has already led to a consolidation in the European industries, thanks to which Europe could become more attractive for foreign investments.

Even though there were contradicting political views on EMU membership the country organised a referendum on joining the Eurozone.

At the end of 1998 Denmark pursued its monetary policy towards maintaining a fixed exchange rate against the euro. The Danish government, in consultation with the European Central Bank, has remained in the Exchange Rate Mechanism 2 (ERM2) since introduction of the euro in January 1999, which has continued to contribute to economic stability and to certainty in policies. Likewise, there were strong economic fundamentals in Danish policy – export growth, a return to external current account surplus, a relatively well functioning labour market, a budget surplus, and a flexible fiscal policy, which suggested that Denmark could adopt

---

[18] M. Andersson, 'EMU and Denmark', Task Force on Economic and Monetary Union, European Parliament, April 1998, PE 166.168/rev.2, p.12.

the single currency. In his New Year address in January 1999, the SDP Prime Minister, Poul Nyrup Rasmussen declared, 'I believe that we should join the EMU. I believe that it is the best solution for Denmark, and the future of the welfare state'. In his speech, the Prime Minister argued that Denmark should approve introduction of the euro on its territory in order to avoid serious changes of its position on the international markets. Such a move would also protect the Danish welfare system. Secondly, he stressed that if Danes rejected EMU membership, Danish jobs would be at stake due to the lack of Danish influence on European labour policies. Moreover, the number of FDIs would diminish. Lastly, the Prime Minister emphasised the importance of possibly spreading Danish values in the European Union. He points out that 'it is about setting limits to the market forces, as we have done it in Denmark, as we are about to do in Europe – and that we can extend to the world.'[19]

It was important that even the Confederation of Danish Industry supported that view. At the same time, Hans Ejvind Hansen, the chairman of the Copenhagen Stock Exchange, suggested that membership in the Eurozone would have a positive impact on foreign demand for Danish securities, although it could also expose Danish financial instruments to increased competition, particularly in the government bond market. According to the Foreign Affairs Minister, Niels Helveg Petersen, introduction of the common currency would enhance the dynamics of the single European market and benefit trade partners, as well as protecting Europe against international financial crises and speculation. A third strong global currency beside the US dollar and the yen would contribute to stabilising the world economy, which would be profitable to all economies and allow smaller states, like Denmark, to have a substantial say in international monetary policy. It could also be a shield towards the pressures of international financial relations. Moreover, the members of the Danish government emphasised that introduction of the euro would be important for the future of the Danish welfare state model.[20]

Proponents of organising the referendum on EMU membership

---

[19] H. Collet, 'On the Outside Looking In: Pragmatic Danes in Quick Reversal', Yale University, November 1999, p.17–19.

[20] V. Miller, 'The Danish Referendum on Economic and Monetary Union', House of Commons Library, International Affairs and Defence Section, September 2000, Research Paper 00/78, p.8–9.

pointed out that in 1999 and 2000 Denmark met the economic convergence criteria to enter the Union, and its economy moved along the cycle with the EU members of the Eurozone. Accordingly, Denmark could accept interest rates set by the ECB easily, but the government was cautious about early entry because the Danish electorate was very sceptical on the issue. On 9 March 2000 the Prime Minister suggested that the referendum on Danish membership in the third stage of the EMU should be held on 28 September 2000.[21]

The pro-euro group was supported by the ruling Social Democrats and Social Liberals, the opposition Liberals, the Conservatives and the Centre Democrats, most of the business community, a majority of trade unions and employers' federations, as well as by most of the media. On 15 November 1999 an official pro-euro campaign, which aimed to be impartial and inform citizens of both advantages and disadvantages of a membership in the Economic and Monetary Union, commenced. On the other hand, the opposition to joining the Eurozone came mainly from the far left, the far right and the centre right Christian People's Party. Pia Kjaersgaard, leader of the right-wing Danish People's Party (DPP), launched the main anti-euro campaign with the slogan 'Keep the krone – vote Danish'.

The speech in May 2000 by the German foreign minister, Joschka Fischer, on a federal Europe, was not welcomed in Denmark, as leading to German dominance in the European Union. According to some analysts, Danes were also against the diplomatic sanctions imposed by the other EU member states on Austria for including the populist Austrian People's Party in the governing coalition. The action of the organisation was regarded as unnecessary aggression against another small EU member state, leading to a possible loss of national sovereignty by Denmark itself.[22] As a consequence, opinion polls showed diminishing support for the euro. Moreover, opponents of the EMU membership concluded that since the Danish krone was already in the ERM2 and stayed within margins of ±2.25%, Denmark could just easily maintain the status quo and remain outside. The popular arguments

---

[21] The Bill 'Concerning Denmark's Participation in the Single Currency', was introduced in Parliament on 2 May 2000 and was adopted on 6 September 2000 by 81 votes in favour to 29 against, and with 69 abstentions.
[22] V. Miller, [2000], p.16.

focused on loss of sovereignty, a move towards creating a federal Europe, and increased immigration from less prosperous EU member states, as well as the weakness and volatility of a single currency, compared with the strength of the Danish krone. Euro-sceptics argued that participation in the Eurozone would pose strains on the welfare state and could lead to supranational tax harmonisation, undermining pension and unemployment benefits in Denmark. There were also murmurs about threats to the Danish monarchy. The Euro-sceptics also asked whether the Danish government had calculated the costs of changing all the computer software, machinery, price lists and slot machines into euros. Furthermore, the leading Danish professors of economy showed in their papers that there were few purely economic gains to be had from joining the third stage of the EMU, and they repeated they would vote for the membership mostly for political and not for economic reasons.[23]

Danish public scepticism about entering the European Economic and Monetary Union originated not only from a feeling of reluctance to give up the Danish krone for the single currency, but from the belief that this was the start of a process leading to the eventual loss of Danish sovereignty and creation of a federal 'United States of Europe'. One of the main fears was the possible weakening of the generous Danish welfare system. For many, the economic arguments for joining were simply not convincing, and they saw no significant negative economic consequences from remaining *outside* the Eurozone and staying in the ERM2. There seemed to be an unwillingness to trust either the government or the opposition. Instead, there was a growing frustration that domestic politicians failed to admit that the EMU was as much a political project as an economic one.[24]

On 28 September 2000 the Danish government held a referendum on joining the third phase of the Economic and

---

[23] British euro-opponents set up a trust called 'The Danish Referendum Campaign', to help their Danish allies in the 'No' campaign. The British appeal aimed to raise £50,000 to pay for advertisements in the Danish press before the referendum. The British Conservative MEP, Daniel Hannan, participated in the annual congress of the Danish People's Party in September 2000, although not all Danish anti-euro campaigners welcomed the United Kingdom, warning that it might push voters to the pro-euro camp. To read more see V. Miller, [2000], p.18.

[24] Ibid., p.18–20.

Monetary Union. Nevertheless, 53.2% of the population voted 'no' to merging the Danish krone with the euro; 46.9% supported such a change. The turnout was over 85%.[25] Professor Hans Jorgen Nielsen suggested that Denmark rejects the common currency mostly because the referendum took place when the value of the euro was the lowest in its short history.[26] Nevertheless, harmful economic effects were limited. The outcome had little impact on the Danish currency, and the value of the krone as well as that of the euro were maintained. The Danish Central Bank raised the basic interest rate by 0.5%. However, being outside the EMU, the country would fail to participate in a more favourable political and socio-economic environment for the organisation as a whole, and for Denmark as a member. Abstaining from the Eurozone and maintaining opt-outs could lead to a further weakening of Danish industrial competitiveness, and thus result in higher unemployment levels, caused by increased exchange rate risks, higher interest rates, more costs and possible currency speculation.

Politically, the negative outcome of the referendum left Danish European policy in a state of disarray. Commenting on the results of the plebiscite, the Danish Prime Minister emphasised that, in spite of the vote, Denmark would continue to play a full part in the future development of the European Union. The Danish Finance Minister admitted that the vote reflected a general discontent with the EU developments. He turned to recent speeches on European integration, EU corruption scandals and the impact of globalisation on the whole process. He also suggested that the government did not present correct arguments to the voters, and that the plebiscite became a protest vote against the traditional ruling parties.

The Danish euro referendum was followed with great interest in Britain and Sweden since the outcome was likely to have an important impact on the outlook for an early referendum on EMU membership in these countries. In part, the Danes were also voting for the Britons and Swedes.[27] The British government insisted that the Danish vote would not affect the plebiscite in the United Kingdom. The Prime Minister, Tony Blair, said before the Danish result that a 'no' vote would not influence the timetable for a

---

[25] Ibid., p.7.

[26] *Gazeta Wyborcza*, 29 September 2000, 30 September – 1 October 2000.

[27] K. Skjalm, [2000], p.1.

referendum in Britain planned after the general elections in the following year. The Swedish Prime Minister, Göran Persson, admitted that the Danish result would influence domestic debate in Sweden, but when a referendum was held in Sweden, the decision on whether or not to join the Eurozone would be based on Swedish issues and concerns alone.

Economists concluded that the economic consequences of a 'no' vote outside Denmark would be limited by the fact that the country represented a relatively small part of the EU economy. The reaction in the other EU member states was generally one of disappointment but resignation. The political analysts emphasised that the negative Danish vote made it more difficult for the supporters of the euro in Britain and Sweden. Anti-euro groups in these countries were reinforced by the Danish result, and although their ability to change anything in Eurozone countries would be limited, they would no doubt try to extend their influence to the countries outside the EMU. Moreover, the result of the Danish referendum undermined international confidence in the single currency, and complicated the negotiations on a new EU treaty, which was completed in Nice in December 2000. In the long run, it might also influence Swedish and British citizens to vote *against* the euro in their prospective referenda on joining the third phase of the EMU. While fears of the collapse of the single currency and a 'domino effect' in other potential members of the Eurozone might be exaggerated, there was a real fear that public trust in the single currency might be diminished as a result of the Danish vote.

1.3. SWEDEN

While submitting an application for full membership in the European Communities in June 1991, the Bildt government declared its acceptance of the entire contents of the Treaty on European Union, including membership in the European Economic and Monetary Union. However, just after accession, the following government of Ingvar Carlsson presented a very cautious stance towards possibly entering the EMU. He pointed out that Sweden would have to examine its fulfilment of convergence criteria as well as consequences of membership for the Swedish economy. In June 1995 the government presented a convergence programme, in which it stated that Sweden met convergence criteria, together with employment and environmental objectives, and was prepared to become a full EMU member. The programme consisted of budgetary goals focused on stabilisation of central government debt in relation to GDP by 1996, and the deficit measures as the consolidated general government financial balance to be eliminated by 1998. The programme was underpinned by a consolidation plan, including measures reinforcing public finances by SEK118 billion by 1998. Needless to say, Sweden failed to enter the Eurozone on 1 January 1999, explaining its position with serious political and economic reasoning.[28]

In 1995, during the preparations for the EU Intergovernmental Conference in 1996, the Social Democratic government decided to keep a cautious stance on EMU entry. On the one hand, there were rising pressures from business organisations to participate in the Eurozone. Nevertheless, there was also an internal pressure from the SAP to hold another referendum on the project. However, taking into account the previous plebiscite on EU membership in 1994, it could cause serious problems. Therefore in January 1996 the Prime Minister, Göran Persson, announced that a decision on EMU membership would be delayed 'as a result of any future downturn in the country's or the European economy'. He decided to remain static until 1998, when a decision would be concluded by consensus.[29] The Social Democratic government adopted a 'wait and see' attitude, partly because it itself consisted of both opponents and proponents of the EMU. Its members expressed doubts about moving towards a federal Europe, where important decisions on tax and social welfare policy might be centralised. Moreover, the contrasting views of economic experts made it difficult to support the theory that membership in the Eurozone would certainly lead to significant economic benefits for Sweden. Politically speaking, the Swedes, who had only recently joined the European Union, were comparatively sceptical and distrustful, as they saw how a growing number of decisions were being shifted to the European level. Public opinion was hardly ready for another step towards federalism. In consequence, a decision on the EMU membership was to be made by Swedish citizens via referendum.

It is worth mentioning that at the beginning there was also the lack of political support for the EMU. In 1996, 4 out of 7 parties in

---

[28] The Swedish Government, http://www.regeringen.se.

[29] L. Miles, [1997], p.291.

the Riksdag (the Left Party, Greens, Christian Democrats and the Centre Party, with all together 83 seats out of 349) declared against Swedish EMU membership. The situation has not changed recently. The Centre Party (*Centern*), although it supports Swedish presence in the European Union, is against joining the Eurozone. The same is true for the Christian Democratic Party (*Kristdemok-raterna*), which highlights that it is simply to soon to join another big undertaking after recent EU entry. The Left Party (*Vänsterpartiet*) and the Greens (*Miljöpartiet*) maintain critical stances towards the EMU. On the other hand, the Moderate Party (*Moderaterna*) and the Liberal Party (*Folkpartiet*) were strongly in favour. The latter argues that rejection of EMU membership might pose obstacles to development of trade and export policies. The former underlines that Swedish membership of the Eurozone would be a vital step towards the better performance of the single European market with a common currency and free competition between enterprises, as well as in terms of taxes and public services. 'It would bring Europe the economic dynamism and prosperity it strongly requires.'[30] However, both parties agree with the government that a referendum on accession to the EMU should be conducted before any decision is made.[31]

In 1996 the governmental report on the Economic and Monetary Union, entitled 'EMU – A Swedish Perspective', prepared by a group of economists and political scientists under the leadership of Lars Calmfords (the *Calmfords Commission*), was presented. The report summarised various economic and political aspects of the European project. Political arguments were mostly in favour of membership in this European undertaking, while economic ones suggested that Sweden should remain outside the Eurozone.

The most important political reason for membership was increasing Sweden's influence on European affairs. The Commission focused on the so-called 'integration argument'. It reported that economic integration was only a step towards and prerequisite for political integration. In this light, the EMU was an important step on the way to fulfilling the goal, and therefore it was smart enough to stay outside. Nevertheless, the report also

---

[30] A. Widfeldt, 'The Swedish Party System and European Integration', in L. Miles, [2000], p.74.
[31] Ibid., p.74–75.

indicated that Sweden's position in the European Union could be weakened if the country remained outside the Eurozone.

> By choosing not to participate in the Community's most important project to date, Sweden would be removing itself from the inner core of the EU, Swedes would be regarded as 'unwilling Europeans', and the country would lose influence in other areas.[32]

The authors agreed that economic benefits of the EMU were to be found mainly at the microeconomic level in the form of reduced transaction costs, elimination of the uncertainty caused by fluctuations in exchange rates, simpler price comparisons and enhanced competition in the European single market. Moreover, the Commission saw the euro as bringing more credibility to the Swedish economy, and the trust of foreign investors in Swedish industries and economic factors. Nevertheless, the lack of the possibility of national governments to adapt monetary policy according to their current economic situation was deemed to be the main negative point of the idea. They simply had to accept the common interest rates and the exchange rates applied throughout the European Union, which could be a problem in the event of asymmetric shocks.

The Commission concluded that the economic gains from joining the third stage of the EMU would be 'small but certain'. On the stabilisation issue, loss of monetary policy independence would not ordinarily create any great problems. The report underlined that:

> ...choosing to remain outside the euro zone was like choosing an insurance policy where the annual price in the form of, for instance, higher transaction costs, could be viewed as an insurance premium that Sweden has to pay if it wishes to take independent monetary policy action whenever its economy behaves in a radically different way from the rest of Europe.[33]

The Commission, instead of recommending joining the Economic and Monetary Union, favoured the alternative scenario, which focused on continuation of the floating exchange rate, greater independence for the Riksbank and low inflation as the principal

---

[32] The Swedish Government, http://www.regeringen.se.

[33] N. Gottfries, [2002], p.3.

targets of Swedish monetary policy. Moreover, the report advised the pursuit of comprehensively restructuring government finances, which would cause such credibility that Sweden would eventually acquire interest and inflation rates roughly the same as those in the Eurozone. The Commission advised that Sweden should not join the third stage of the EMU in the first wave in 1999, but instead should adopt a 'wait and see' policy, which was already true for the Social Democratic government. The political costs of remaining outside the Eurozone and the comparable economic goals of economic efficiency would increase from membership in the EMU if the most important Swedish trade partners joined.[34]

In its summary and conclusions, the Commission stated that in the short run the political arguments *against* the Economic and Monetary Union would outweigh those in favour. It explained that participating in the European project when the level of unemployment is very high could be risky. Any change in Swedish productivity, output and employment rate would be higher if Sweden adopted the common currency than if it kept the krona. Any negative shock could cause a rise in unemployment to an even higher level. Macroeconomic turbulence that could not be counteracted by monetary and exchange rate policies could lead to further increases in unemployment. Therefore, Sweden should join the Eurozone when the situation on the labour market significantly improved. Second, the Commission underlined a Swedish fiscal position, for which participation in monetary union would pose great risks. Third, EMU entry would need long and broad public debate, so that any future decision would be democratic and legitimate. Finally, Sweden would not be the only country to stay outside the Eurozone. The case of the United Kingdom, Sweden's main trading partner, as well as Denmark, was indicated. Nevertheless, the Commission highlighted that if the unemployment rate diminished and the fiscal situation stabilised, Sweden should join the EMU. Entry at a later date should therefore be the aim, thought it ought not to occur until the

---

[34] When it became obvious that both the United Kingdom and Denmark would remain outside the Eurozone, Sweden hardened its attitude even more. Moreover, the relatively favourable economic development in the United Kingdom also affected Persson's government view on EMU membership. It appeared that it was not just Sweden, as an 'EMU outsider', who could 'manage best on her own' without the single currency.

economic and political conditions for participation were more favourable.[35]

In 1997 the Social Democratic government, supported by the Swedish parliament, approved a strategy of not participating in the EMU from its very beginning. The reasons were twofold. First, the labour market situation needed to be improved, including lowering the rate of unemployment, liberalising the wage negotiation system and job security laws. Second, Swedish membership in the Eurozone would need a great public support, which in that time was impossible to achieve. Moreover, the Riksdag decided that the final decision on participation in the EMU could be taken only in a referendum after the next general elections. However, taking into account the practical preparations for the changeover to the euro, a government bill of 1997 stated that Sweden was to maintain the highest level of freedom of decision with regard to the EMU membership 'by continuing the work on practical preparations to enable a positive future transfer to the euro to be implemented successfully'. The Riksbank and the Swedish financial sector have been working together with the government on preparations for the potential EMU membership. Nevertheless, the final phase of practical preparations for the changeover in the financial, corporate and public sectors can only begin when the political decision on participation in the Eurozone has been made.[36]

In November 2002 the Prime Minister, Göran Persson, announced that the referendum on the Swedish membership in the third stage of the EMU would be held on 14 September 2003. On 12 March 2003 the Swedish parliament approved the date of the referendum on EMU membership. However, Swedish officials ruled out an early move to join the Eurozone, even if voters gave backing to the single currency in the referendum. Gunnar Lund, the minister responsible for EMU issues, wanted to give Sweden enough time to prepare for the currency changeover in the event of a successful plebiscite. In that case, Sweden would not join the Eurozone until 1 January 2006, but would tie the krona to the single currency in the ERM2 from 1 January 2005. Nevertheless, the banking system in particular needed time to adjust.[37]

---

[35] N. Gottfries, [2002], p.2; M. Kinnwall, [2000], p.154–155.

[36] W. Becker, A. Järvbäck, [2002], p.13.

[37] 'Sweden in no hurry to introduce euro', www.euobserver.com, 29 January 2003.

Accordingly, the Swedish Minister of Trade, Leif Pagrotsky, said that Sweden needed to keep control of its own monetary policy because of its negative experiences of the high inflation of the late 1970s and 1990s. On each occasion, Sweden lost competitiveness and interest rates rose sharply. If Swedish companies reached inflationary wage arrangements in future, the ECB would not put up interest rates to deal with it.

> Bigger countries, like Britain can pool their monetary policy with others of equal size. But small countries have to give up their monetary policy. If we say 'yes' to the euro, we are saying 'yes for ever', because there is no going back once we have joined. What I am saying is 'no, not now'.[38]

He added that the proposal for new voting rules in the ECB meant that Sweden would not be a full member of the Economic and Monetary Union, even if it decided to join the Eurozone.

> Those who want to join the EMU in order to have a seat at the table where decisions are made can forget about that now. There will be no seat for us there. The Swedish people will not be full participants. We are not going to have any fully worthwhile vote when decisions are taken.[39]

The group *supporting* introduction of the single currency in Sweden consisted of the Social Democratic Party, supported by the Moderates, the Christian Democrats and the Liberals, who represent three out of the four non-socialist parties within the Riksdag. Moreover, the Association for Receipt of 'yes' Campaign was established by the Sweden in Europe Foundation, the Social Democrats for Europe and the Federation of Swedish Farmers.

The two remaining centre-left parties, the Green Party and the Left Party, along with the Centre Party, have firmly opposed adoption of the euro. They were supported by the Partnership against EMU, whose well-known members came from the Social Democratic Party, Christian Democrats and Centre Party, including

---

[38] C. Brown-Humes, 'Swedish minister out of step over joining euro', *The Financial Times*, 26 February 2003.

[39] 'Swedish minister of trade: Forget about EMU influence', www.euobserver.com, 23 January 2003.

several Swedish cabinet ministers, i.e. the Deputy Prime Minister, Margareta Winberg, and the Industry Minister, Leif Pagrotsky. As it is seen, political support for the euro was divided not only along party lines, but also internally within each political party.

The Swedish government, having conducted talks with the party leaders in December 2002, agreed to allocate SEK140 million to spread information on the EMU and the euro to the public. The campaign organisations received SEK90 million of this sum; the political parties in the Riksdag, SEK30 million; adult education initiatives, SEK15 million; and the Riksdag's EU Information Centre, SEK5 million. All together, the 'no' campaign received SEK48 million while the 'yes' campaign SEK42 million.

From the end of 2002, Swedish opinion polls showed that the majority of the electorate opposed introducing the euro in Sweden, although a large number of voters remained undecided. The 'no' camp led in opinion polls long before the plebiscite, while the supporters for the euro averaged around 38%. Opinion polls prepared between May and July 2003 by Gallup indicated support for the single currency at around 33%, while the opposition held approximately 48–49%. About 18–20% of voters remained undecided. Polls by the Danske Bank showed a higher degree of support for the 'yes' campaign, although opposition to the euro was continuously higher than 50%.

A few days before the referendum, on 10 September the Swedish Foreign Minister and pro-euro campaigner, Anna Lindh, was attacked in Stockholm and died the next day; but the Swedish police did not link the murder to the Mrs Lindh's political beliefs. Nevertheless, both the 'yes' and 'no' camps suspended their campaigns following the murder. The leaders of the parliamentary parties announced in a joint statement on 11 September that the euro referendum would take place on the previously decided date.

On 14 September 2003, the Swedes voted in a referendum on joining the third stage of the Economic and Monetary Union. They answered the following question: 'Is it your opinion that Sweden should introduce the euro as its currency?'.[40] 56.2% of the population voted 'no' to merging the Swedish krona with the euro,

---

[40] 'Anser du att Sverige ska införa euron som valuta?', G. Jonnson, 'Uppgörelse klar om EMU-fråga', in *Dagens Nyheter*, 17 December 12.2003; L. Hennel, 'Rakt ja eller nej till euron', in *Svenska Dagbladet*, 18 December 2002.

while 41.8% supported such a change; 2.1% submitted blank votes. The turnout was over 81.2%.[41]

> The 'no' vote meant that Sweden would have less influence in Europe, although the result did not have any immediate economic consequences. The observers underlined that the outcome of the plebiscite 'was not necessarily important for the Swedish economy or useful for Europe, but good for the Swedish people's opportunity to live on at some kind of peace with itself after an unrelenting and sometimes brutal debate with a shocking, tragic end'.[42]

In Great Britain and Denmark, most comments emphasised that the result of the Swedish referendum would have implications for future referenda on the euro in both countries, erasing the possibility of merging both the Danish krone and the pound sterling with the single currency. The analysts underlined the fact that many Swedes decided to reject the euro because they considered Sweden was doing better outside the EMU, with stronger growth, lower unemployment rates and stable public finances. In their opinion, the welfare state was secured by an independent monetary policy. Furthermore, the rejection of the single currency was not a surprise, since the campaign had been conducted when economies of the leading EMU members, especially Germany, were in recession.

The European Commission expressed its disappointment about the result of the Swedish referendum on membership in the third stage of the EMU. It emphasised the role and position of the single currency in international trade and financial relations, and it showed the strong belief that the euro would continuously bring advantages to the economy of the Eurozone. Nevertheless, the Commission called upon the Swedish government to keep the euro project alive in Sweden.[43]

It must be emphasised that even though the Swedish 'no' to EMU membership seemed not to be negative for Swedish credibility and influence in the European Union, Sweden signed the

---

[41] E. Potton, V. Miller, C. Taylor, 'The Swedish Referendum on the Euro', House of Commons Library, Economic Policy and Statistics Section, International Affairs and Defence Section, September 2003, Research Paper 03/68, p.7–9.

[42] Cited in E. Potton, V. Miller, C. Taylor, [2003], p.27.

[43] 'Commission Statement on the Swedish Referendum', Brussels, 15 September 2003, IP/03/1242.

EC Treaty and should fulfil the obligations imposed by it. Therefore the 'no' opened debate in Sweden about the future role of the country within the European Union.

2.   Business Attitudes

Representatives of British, Danish and Swedish industry and business have their own opinion on the issue of membership of their countries of origin in the Economic and Monetary Union. In most cases industrial organisations are in favour of the common currency, while labour associations present negative stances on joining the Eurozone.

2.1.   THE UNITED KINGDOM

Business opinion in the United Kingdom has been divided on EMU membership for some years. The Confederation of British Industry (CBI), which represents the larger and more established British companies, together with the National Farmers' Union, is in favour of participation. On the other hand, the Institute of Directors, which represents smaller firms, is against by a significant margin (almost 70% in 2001). The main demand of industry and commerce is to prepare an adequate 'time frame' for membership in the Eurozone. It is connected with the necessary preparations for a possible membership, but without a certain date, while companies are not willing to commit themselves to the necessary expenditure unless EMU membership is agreed. Furthermore, in a recent statement, Alan Greenspan, Chairman of the US Federal Reserve, said that London was thriving and 'has stayed on top despite the emergence of the euro'.[44]

In 2001 three-quarters of British companies would have supported a government decision to introduce the single currency in the British Isles, but on condition that there would be no harmonisation of taxes and no influence of European laws over British social policy. The firm agreement was represented by 21% of British companies, while 36% consider deciding on the euro to be too early a decision.[45] In 2002 in an ICM poll of chief British

---

[44] 'Greenspan says British better off outside the euro', http://www.euobserver.com, 26 September 2002.

[45] 'Firmy o euro', in *Rzeczpospolita*, 17–18 March 2001.

executives, 56% of them said that introduction of the euro in the British Isles would harm the British economy, and 78% believed that Britain could prosper even outside the Eurozone.[46] On the other hand, 56% surveyed by the Engineering Employers' Federation believes that abstaining from the Eurozone would not harm British manufacture, and only 29% of British companies would want to adopt the single currency, while 16% did not want to join ever.[47] In the most recent survey by the British Chamber of Commerce, two-thirds of British businesses said 'no' to the single currency within the next two years, 49% said that the 'wait and see' policy adopted by the government was an appropriate one, and 13% would never vote in favour of the euro.[48]

The British Trade Union Congress (TUC) has strongly supported EMU membership, arguing that 'a prolonged absence from the euro will be harmful to British jobs'.[49] However, in a new poll, conducted in March 2003, 67% of members of the Britain's General Union (GMB) did not want to join the Eurozone. Moreover, the then general secretary of the Transport and General Workers' Union, Bill Morris, said, 'If Britain enters the euro at the wrong time and the wrong rate it will create major problems for the stability of the British economy and her ability to invest in quality public services, and it will lead to higher prices.'[50]

2.2. DENMARK

Many of the employers' organisations, including the Danish Employers' Confederation (*Dansk Arbejdsgiverforening*) are in favour of Danish membership in the final stage of the EMU. The Confederation of Danish Industry (*Dansk Industri*) has even taken the initiative of establishing a new movement, 'Denmark in Europe' (*Denmark i Europa*), to support joining the EMU and spread knowledge about the project amongst Danish companies. On

---

[46] *British Businesses prefer to stay outside the euro*, http://www.euobserver.com, 16 September 2002.

[47] P. Thornton, 'Delayed euro entry "will not harm industry"', in the *Independent*, 28 October 2002.

[48] 'UK Businesses say "no" to euro for now', http://www.euobserver.com, 9 January 2003.

[49] B. Patterson, [1998], p.18–19; K. Dyson, K. Featherstone, [1999], p.562–563.

[50] 'British trade union turning against euro', http://www.euobserver.com, 17 March 2003.

the other hand, the Danish Confederation of Trade Unions (*Landsorganisationen i Danmark, LO*), which has around 1.5 million members and numerous affiliated unions, has remained loyal to the opinion of the Danish people expressed in the referendum on the Maastricht Treaty, including the Edinburgh opt-outs. However, LO has recently worked on reaching a new position on the EMU with about 58% of their members supporting Danish participation in the project. The chairman of LO, Hans Jensen, in his open letter argued that Denmark had two main reasons to join. First, the costs for smaller countries in terms of non-membership are much higher. Denmark would get lower interest rates, reduced transaction costs, as well as more stable and transparent prices. Second, Denmark has lost political influence in several areas, especially in the area of labour politics.[51]

2.3. SWEDEN

Swedish industrial organisations wanted to establish and practise private ownership and development of competitive business in Sweden. In consequence, they were mostly in favour of gaining EMU membership. In their view, Swedish participation in the European single market could enhance and accommodate Sweden's competitiveness in external relations.[52] The Federation of Swedish Farmers, the Swedish Confederation of Professional Associations (*Tjänstemännens Centralorganisation, TCO*) and the Swedish Industry (*Svenska Industriförbundet, SI*) emphasised the efficiency gains deriving from participation in the Eurozone in the form of reduced transaction costs, the elimination of currency uncertainty in Europe, and more effective competition. They also pointed out macroeconomic advantages from greater financial integration in the monetary union, which could enhance competition in financial markets and lead to a greater supply of financial services. Another argument in favour of the EMU membership was that it would offer secure guarantees of low interest rates and low inflation. Lower interest rates would make it easier to counteract unemployment.

---

[51] H. Collet, [1999], p.19.

[52] However, it is openly claimed that EU regulations constrain competition within the sectors of transport, agriculture and public activities. Moreover, at the beginning, Swedish industry feared that the European integration process would constrain the competitiveness of European industry by increasing regulation and bureaucracy.

The single currency would also have a restraining effect on wage formation. In the opinion of the Swedish Employers' Confederation, (*Svenska Arbetsgivareföreningen, SAF*) the Economic and Monetary Union was mainly a political project, and by remaining outside Sweden would drastically reduce its chances of exercising influence in the European Union as a whole. In February 1995 the SAF announced that Sweden should become a member of the third stage of the EMU in 1999. In its view the Union is a natural consequence of socio-economic integration in Europe, and Sweden should join in order to maintain economic efficiency. Participation in the Eurozone could improve Swedish conditions for growth and industrialisation, thanks to lower transaction costs and interest rates. It mainly called for coordination effects focused on competitive conditions to avoid serious disturbances on the single European market.[53] In 1998 the opinion polls showed that no less than 89% of Sweden's largest companies, and a 4 to 1 majority amongst the small and medium-sized enterprises, were in favour of Swedish membership in the EMU.

Yet, the Swedish Trade Unions Confederation (*Landsorganisationen, LO*) stated that the majority of its affiliated unions were *against* Swedish entry to the Eurozone. The organisation underlined that the EMU membership would impose considerable demands on wage formation, and for this reason wage formation needed reshaping prior to entry. Swedish wages are still higher than on the European continent, which may threaten growing unemployment after a few years in the Eurozone. Solving this problem will mean problems for the Prime Minister, Göran Persson, and his own supporters in the trade unions. According to Scop polls, 57% trade union members say 'no' to EMU membership. Swedish business circles no longer see EMU membership as an unquestioned advantage.[54] The LO simply promoted socio-economic interests of their members. A large part of the Swedish economy is based on collective agreements to cover working and employment conditions and therefore the LO called for keeping them unchanged after accession to the third stage of the

---

[53] M. Karlsson, [2000], p.81–83.

[54] 'Persson to set euro referendum date in December', www.euobserver.com, 22 November 2002.

EMU.[55] On the other hand, the TCO is also afraid of dismantling its traditional economic and labour market policy, which secured the Swedish model of welfare state. On the other hand, the SACO considers joining the EMU as desirable in terms of long-term economic development, as the project brings stable economic conditions, including low inflation and a stronger exchange rate. Furthermore, SACO emphasises the political need to influence formation of the EMU conditions from inside from the very beginning. In February 1999 TCO, SAF and SACO published a joint common report, in which they stated that the EMU would substantially influence Sweden, even if the country stayed outside the Eurozone, and they would do anything needed to prepare Sweden for the future membership.[56]

3.   Societal Attitudes

As was shown above, most politicians and representatives of both industrial and labour organisations are in favour of British, Danish and Swedish membership in the third stage of the EMU. Nevertheless, the main opposition is found in the public opinion of the countries in question. In the United Kingdom the percentage of those who support British engagement in the Eurozone is only half that of those who want the country to be a part of the EMU. In Sweden, before the referendum on replacing the Swedish krona with the euro, the number of euro proponents in the population fell significantly. The best situation is in Denmark where the numbers of proponents and opponents of the euro are more or less the same, with a slight majority of those who are against the single currency. The issue of positive public attitude is crucial because all the countries examined decided to call a referendum before introducing the euro on their territory.

3.1. THE UNITED KINGDOM

The British are on the whole against the common currency. On average, about 60% of the respondents of different opinion polls and surveys are against the common currency. This outcome was

---

[55] A. Widfeldt, [2000], p.73–74.
[56] M. Karlsson, [2000], p.84–85.

reinforced by the negative result of the Danish and Swedish referendum on entering the third stage of the Economic and Monetary Union. After the Danish plebiscite on 28 September 2000, the support for the euro in Britain fell to 22%.[57] Meanwhile, the British Foreign Secretary, Robin Cook, said that 'it would be very unwise for us to close off the option of membership of the euro',[58] and the Prime Minister, Tony Blair, emphasised that the result of the Danish referendum would not change his plans to organise a referendum on agreeing to the common currency in Britain at the beginning of the next term of parliament, namely in the middle of 2001.

Today one can say that such declarations were exaggerated, and up till now there have been no plans to pursue a referendum on the euro in Britain. The economists have said that the most reasonable date for a plebiscite would have been spring 2004, after the referendum in Sweden in September 2003. Nevertheless, Robert M. Worcester, Professor of the London School of Economics, reckoned that the Prime Minister would not take up a decision on a referendum earlier than after the next general election in 2005. According to his survey, there were 10% of committed supporters of the euro, while 36% of committed adversaries.[59] It is obvious that Tony Blair would like to win the referendum, because it will also be judged as an approval for his policies given by the public opinion. Nevertheless, he must be very cautious, as the greater part of British society is against the euro, just as it was at the beginning of its operation in 1999.[60] However, opinion polls show that a large majority of the population (79%) believes that participation in the EMU is unavoidable in the long run, which could be regarded as a supportive attitude.[61]

---

[57] J. Glover, 'Where Does the Danish Euro Vote Leave Britain?', in the *Guardian*, 29 September 2000.

[58] S. Castle, P. Waugh, 'Danish Vote Prompts Calls for "Two-Speed Europe"', in the *Independent*, 30 September 2000.

[59] R. M. Worcester, 'Dlaczego rządowi Blaira nie opłaca się przystąpić do euro', in *Gazeta Wyborcza*, 2 July 2001.

[60] S. McGuire, 'To Join or Not to Join?', in *Euroland. Year One*, Newsweek Special Report, 29 November 1999.

[61] J. Birger Christensen, [2002], p.9.

Figure 4.1   *Support of UK citizens for the euro*

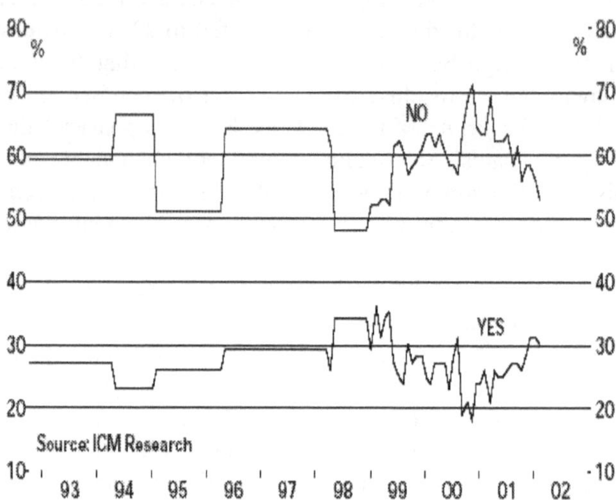

In the opinion polls conducted in July 2002, 55% of the British population would vote against the introduction of the euro, while only 31% would vote in favour. However, the majority against the EMU has become smaller than in the preceding years, when more than 60% of the population rejected EMU entry.[62] In May 2003 only 19% of British citizens surveyed by the ICM Institute would vote for the euro, while 45% were against and 14% strongly against; 9% were in favour but they could change their opinion, and 13% were undecided.[63]

3.2. DENMARK

While the government and political elites approved of the Economic and Monetary Union, opinion polls indicated that a substantial majority of the Danish population was rather negative towards further European integration. The major part of the Danish population supports cooperation in a whole range of

---

[62] W. Becker, A. Järvbäck, [2002], p.3.

[63] 'Silny opór Brytyjczyków przed przystąpieniem do strefy euro', PAP, 20 May 2003.

concrete areas on the EU level, rather it was against closer EC integration. In 1999 public support and opinion polls showed that some 55% of Danes were in favour of staying out of the third stage of the EMU, with 31% in favour, and 14% with no opinion on the subject,[64] even though the Danish government warmly welcomed the introduction of the euro as a very important step in preparing Europe and the European economies for the 21st century.

Figure 4.2   *Danish support for the euro*

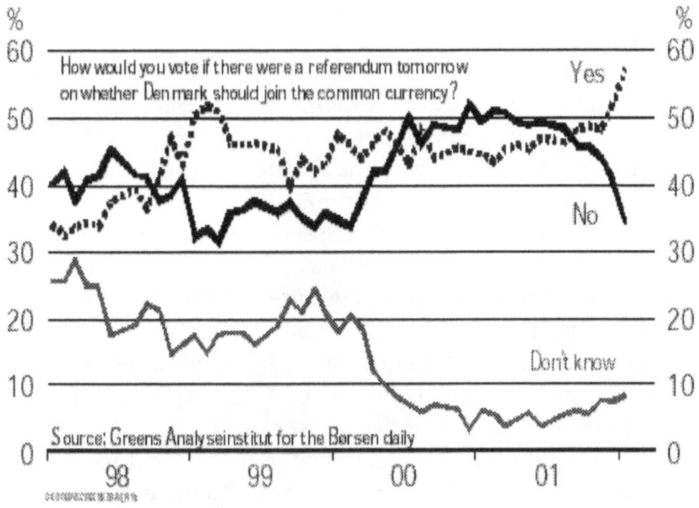

Source: Greens Analyseinstitut.

It is worth stressing that recent support for the EMU membership has gradually risen, especially following introduction of the euro as legal tender in the Eurozone. Since the referendum on EMU membership in September 2000, the support for the single currency has risen from 44% to 56% in August 2001, while the 'no' side decreased from 49% to 34%.[65] The smooth adoption of the euro into circulation in January 2002 has significantly changed public

---

[64] M. Andersson, [1998], p.14.

[65] J. Birger Christensen, [2002], p.6–7.

opinion in Denmark. In June 2002, a majority of nearly 59% was in favour of adopting the euro, and only 34% against, while in January 2003, 58% supported joining the Eurozone, 33% were against, and 9% were undecided.[66]

3.3. SWEDEN

In 1995 opinion polls showed that only 20–30% of the Swedish society supported possible EMU entry.[67] Public opinion on the Economic and Monetary Union has changed in recent years, which probably shows the substantial uncertainty that most people feel about the EMU membership. Today, those in favour of Swedish participation slightly outnumber those against. Changes in public opinion depend mostly on economic improvements in both Sweden and the Eurozone, which both reinforce or weaken the economic arguments for or against. But more important is the political attitude that Swedes adopt towards the European Union and its everlasting goal of 'an ever closer union'.[68]

Prospects for a referendum depended largely on the citizens' attitude toward the single currency. The government called a plebiscite only because it was quite sure that the 'yes' camp would prevail, what in fact was a misjudged opinion. At the beginning, popular feeling toward joining the EMU has been boosted in Sweden, as in Denmark and the United Kingdom, by the successful introduction of euro-denominated notes and coins in the twelve countries that use the single currency. For the first time in nearly three years, more Swedes were in favour of joining the EMU than opposed it.[69] Nevertheless, in December 2002 public support for the euro fell back again. In a SIFO survey, 42% were against adopting the euro in Sweden, while 36% would vote 'yes' in the referendum of 2003.[70]

---

[66] W. Becker, A. Järvbäck, [2002], p.15.

[67] L. Miles, *Sweden and the European Union Evaluated*, 2000, p.7.

[68] N. Gottfries, [2002], p.4–5.

[69] J. H. Bryson, [2002], p.2.

[70] '300,000 non-Swedes to vote on EMU issue', www.euobserver.com, 19 December 2002.

Figure 4.3   *Public support for the EMU in Sweden*

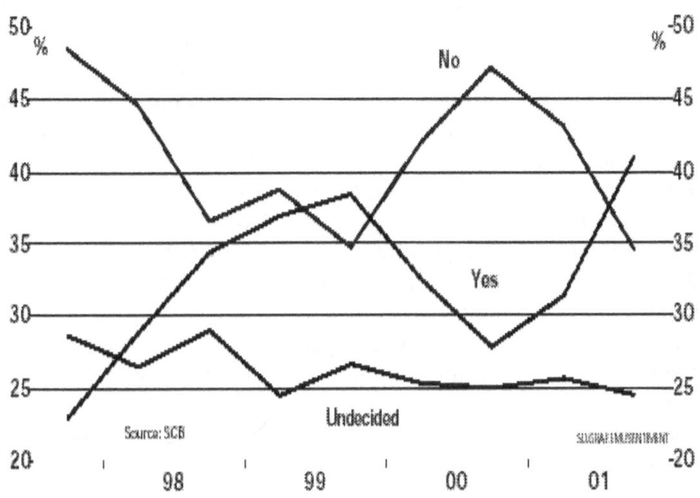

Source: The Swedish Central Bank, http://www.riksbank.se

The final and most difficult obstacle to Sweden joining the Eurozone is public opinion.[71] According to the polls before the referendum, a relative majority of the Swedish people – still not over the 50% level – would have voted for membership in the Eurozone.

Well-known economists founded an organisation called: *Medborgere mot EMU* ('Citizens against EMU'). In their letter, published in *Dagens Nyheter* on 2 July 2002, they wrote that they supported extensive cooperation among nations, but they opposed changing the European Union into a federal state. According to them, introducing the single currency was a big step towards a federal state because the European nations were deprived of their ability to conduct an independent monetary and currency policy. Consequently, the instability of Swedish economy would increase with EMU membership. The state government would have to have a higher budget surplus in order to be secured during shocks, which might harm its economy. It may lead to further overtaxation of the

---

[71] J. Birger Christensen, [2002], p.3.

Swedish people with 'a new heavy and everlasting EMU tax'.[72] The economists emphasised that Sweden's positive balance of trade with the rest of the world expanded faster than with the EU members, which was due to faster growth in the outer world than the European Union. As a result, Sweden was not becoming more dependent on the euro area, but rather the opposite was true. The other issue concerned the exchange rate regime. Since the world changed to floating exchange rates, fluctuations between the great currencies, namely the US dollar, now the euro and the Yen, have been significant. This was not connected with changes in the underlying competitive powers but with the enormous amounts of international capital flow. Fixing the Swedish krona to the euro would force the country to follow the euro both up and down, which could expose the large part of the Swedish industry dependent on the US dollar, mainly the timber industry, to heavy pressure.[73]

In July 2002, a new anti-euro group, 'Europe yes - euro no', which includes some well-known figures such as Karl-Gustav Löfgren, Professor and Dean at Umeå University and a member of the Nobel Prize Committee, Stefan de Vylder, Professor at the Stockholm School of Economics, Kerstin Jacobsson, Associate Professor in Sociology at Stockholm University, Nils Lundgren, Professor of Political Economy, and Sören Wibe, Social Democrat MP, presented a three-point memorandum against EMU membership. The group argues that the existing floating exchange rate has served Sweden well, since recent Swedish economic development had been more positive than those of the EMU countries. They underline that Sweden's economic growth was higher and unemployment rate lower than in the Eurozone. The group adds that EMU participation would be connected with significant loss of Swedish autonomy: 'Decisions on Sweden's economic policy would be taken by the ECB in Frankfurt without insight and by persons who cannot be called to account.' According to them, the Maastricht Treaty does not want to see any democratic control over interests and exchange rates. Moreover, it says that the

---

[72] Such a fear is rather unrealistic since no country will put new taxes on its citizens in the environment of liberalised capital flows, as this would result in a fall of budget revenues in the short run.

[73] 'Keep Sweden out as long as Britain stays out', www.euobserver.com, 3 July 2003.

government of each member state is unable to influence the central bank governors.[74] Furthermore, the economic policy would be decided by the economic development in the bigger countries: 'If Sweden's economic conditions do not follow theirs, we will suffer from economic imbalances and lower growth. The EMU will divide – not unite the peoples and countries of Europe.'[75]

---

[74] J. Redwood, 'Sterling Democracy or European Bureaucracy?', in M. Baimbridge, B. Burkitt, P. Whyman, [2000], p.211.

[75] 'Swedish euro camps gear up for crucial referendum', www.euobserver.com, 13 March 2003.

V: Consequences of being out of the Economic and Monetary Union

Being outside the area of the common currency adopted by the majority of the EU member states puts the United Kingdom, Denmark and Sweden in a quite new situation. The consequences of 'being out' are always discussed bearing their positive and negative aspects in mind. The positive ones are seen in terms of the economic and financial gains, despite non-participation in the Eurozone, that may accrue to the three countries in question. On the other hand, negative ones concentrate on those benefits Britain, Denmark and Sweden could have if they were full members of the third stage of the EMU.

Economists say that for a medium-sized country like Great Britain it is not advisable to keep a separate currency. The United Kingdom is too involved in international trade and therefore it is not able to neglect her interest rates, as for example the US can. Nowadays Britain seems to be caught between two large currency blocs, and only by joining the Eurozone can the country protect herself against the danger of exchange rate fluctuations. Such a possibility endangers investments and deters medium-sized companies from expanding abroad. Furthermore, currency fluctuations redirect management attention towards exchange rate risks instead of preparations for higher productivity, lower costs and improved quality. It is impossible to avoid such perils, especially for firms which plan to invest or to produce goods and services to be sold in different European countries in uncertain quantities and at uncertain prices over many years. They simply cannot maintain such threats for a long period of time.

Many international observers had long anticipated that Denmark was much closer to deciding on participation in the Eurozone than Great Britain and Sweden. The country is already a shadow member of the EMU, as it meets all the convergence criteria. Moreover, in contrast to Sweden and Great Britain,

Denmark has participated in the ERM2 since 1999. Given the stable development of the Danish krone to the euro, Denmark easily meets the exchange rate criterion. Nevertheless, trade and foreign direct investment would benefit from the elimination of the exchange rate risk in relation to the euro. The business cycle in Denmark is closely in line with those of the rest of the European continent. Regarding monetary policy, Denmark behaves as if it were already part of the Eurozone, however, with none of the advantages of the single currency. The Danish Central Bank must more or less follow the monetary policy of the ECB. The remaining small exchange rate risk is associated with somewhat higher interest rates in Denmark than in the EMU. The euro is highly important for the Danish economy, since 43% of its exports are to EMU countries and 50% of its imports are from the euro area.[1]

Sweden is a special case insofar as the country is legally committed by the EC Treaty to adopt the euro. Unlike the United Kingdom and Denmark, which also remain outside the Eurozone, Sweden does not have an opt-out clause in this sphere and thus it is obliged to join the project once the convergence criteria are met. This implies a political commitment to fulfil those criteria and the conditions for secondary legislation. The Swedish government, however, has hesitated to do so, even though meeting the conditions for EMU membership would not cause any serious problems. It declared that it would adopt a final position on the union 'in the light of further developments and in accordance with the provisions of the Treaty'.[2] Sweden has preferred to miss the convergence criteria by not participating in the ERM2, which can be called the 'Swedish way' of achieving an opt-out clause, and it is certainly not in line with the spirit of the Maastricht Treaty.[3]

1.   Economic Consequences

The economic benefits which Britain, Denmark and Sweden lose

---

[1] W. Becker, A. Järvbäck, [2002], p.15.

[2] However, in order to become a full member of the EMU, Sweden changed its constitution, especially the legislation of the Riksbank so that it could be less dependent on the policies of Swedish governments. M. Kinnwall, [2000], p.146–147.

[3] W. Becker, A. Järvbäck, [2002], p.11.

while not participating in the EMU, focus on increasing productivity levels and the competitiveness of their economies on international markets. Consequently, the quality of British, Danish and Swedish goods would become higher if the countries were part of the Eurozone. The fluctuations in the exchange rates between European currencies would be eliminated which could lead to a decrease in the exchange risk. There would be no transaction costs if one single currency were adopted in the three countries, which remain outside the third stage of the EMU. Moreover, it would provide more transparency in prices across the EU area, increase the economic growth and currency liquidity, as well as guaranteeing higher returns on capital and enhancing inflow of FDI on the British Isles and the two Scandinavian countries.[4]

The most obvious economic advantage connected with the disappearance of the currency borders is the elimination of transaction costs. This removal of the cost and risk involved in exchanging currencies while visiting or trading with different countries in the Eurozone, for the economy as a whole, would have, however, a relatively small symbolic cost. Nevertheless, it serves as a small customs union. A somewhat larger cost has arisen from the handling charges companies make to hedge against undesirable fluctuations in exchange rates. This cost is not particularly large in relation to GDP either – perhaps a few tenths of a percentage point. Furthermore, a single currency promotes competition within the European Union and benefits the consumers, who experience lower prices and thereby save more.[5]

Needless to say, when everyone uses the same unit of currency, it is easier to compare prices between countries. It can be an advantage for the national economy as a whole, since competition facilitates lower inflation. Some differences in prices are unavoidable, arising from transport and information costs, but not all of them can be connected with these costs. Despite the fact that there is the single European market, with free trade for goods and services throughout the entire EU territory, there are still large differences in prices between different countries within the union. The average price difference is 16%, which means that it is approximately 40% larger

---

[4] A. Moravcsik, [1998]; D. Baker and D. Seawright, [1998]; W. Eltis, [2001].

[5] This is a false statement to some extent, since after introducing the single currency in the Eurozone, prices went up significantly, for example in Germany by almost 20% in comparison with original prices.

than between various states and regions in the US. The price of an ordinary Volvo, for instance, can differ by 15–20% between countries in Europe. Some of those disparities are created by divergences in cultures and languages, but new studies indicate that the actual psychological barrier involved in differing units of currency may be responsible to a certain extent.[6]

The largest negative effects of having different currencies probably have to do with trade and resource allocation, combined with fluctuating exchange rates. In addition, the allocation of resources in society is distorted by an exchange rate that is not fully motivated, which has particular significance for trade. Many economists have long attempted to estimate this gain by looking at the extent to which fixed and relatively floating exchange rates affect trade. Surprisingly they have found a very small difference. However, a single currency is not the same as a fixed exchange rate. In studies by professor Torsten Persson, it was estimated that the benefits of a monetary union would bring 30% higher trade figures in comparison to those for Sweden outside the Eurozone.

Moving to a single currency offers three main benefits for business. First, the lower costs of managing cash. For companies operating across national boundaries in Europe, elimination of the costs of changing money from one national currency to another within the Eurozone might be quite significant, especially for small and medium-sized companies. Second, with the euro, less currency risk appears. The manufacturing sector, with long-lived factories, would benefit most from the elimination of exchange risk. Companies with long-lived assets are most subject to exchange rate uncertainty, which is not the case for financial businesses and the trading sector. Therefore, abstaining from the Eurozone is especially negative for companies operating in the United Kingdom, Denmark and Sweden. The exchange rate between different countries contributes to the inflow of speculative capital and artificial increases in levels of interest rates in a country, and can cause periodic irrational fluctuations. As a result, appreciation

---

[6] The US economist, Charles Engel, has calculated in extensive studies of price differences between the US and Canada that a currency border creates price differences corresponding to a geographical distance of almost 8,000 km, even though the countries on either side of the currency border (as in the case of Canada and the US) are entirely open to one another and share the same language and culture.

of a national currency appears but the relevant macroeconomic indicators do not sustain it.[7] Moreover, a single currency contributes to effectiveness in productivity, and an increase in the level of economic growth, especially in the employment rate. 'If Britain stays out, the dangers of falling further behind the rest of core Europe will steadily increase'.[8]

Furthermore, the single currency will sharpen competition throughout Europe and it could influence the markets in three important ways: by cheaper transaction costs; exchange rate certainty; and more transparent price differences. With the euro, firms could have a clear choice, namely presenting prices in the common currency and differentiating their products in terms of quality, innovation, and price.[9] Moreover, these three effects will lead to major changes in the business environment throughout Europe, making it more competitive and effective. Likewise, for businesses, transparency of process and the elimination of exchange rate uncertainty within the Eurozone will make it easier to level costs across suppliers. With the single currency firms will be able to make direct comparisons between suppliers' costs in different countries. An efficient customer-oriented company will have opportunities for functioning across a much larger customer base. But an inefficient company will find itself under pressure from the more intensive competition. It will result in making European industries more rational, and therefore customers will benefit through price reductions and better quality.[10] The introduction of the single currency also provides the opportunity for firms to realign their products in two ways – their geographic market, and product positioning. Acceleration in the globalisation of trademarks has been recently observed. The euro may present an opportunity for smaller and medium-sized firms to follow this lead. Furthermore, it should also be a motivator for firms to review the

---

[7] At the turn of 1999 there was an unexpected increase in the value of the pound, and its strength crippled many export and import competing companies and was one of the reasons why BMW sold Rover. To read more see R. Layard, W. Buiter, D. Currie, C. Huhne, W. Hutton, P. Kenen, R. Mundell, A. Turner, *'The Case for the Euro'*, London, 2000, p.4.

[8] Ibid., p.5.

[9] D. Simon, 'EMU and the Opportunities for British Business', in M. Baimbridge, B. Burkitt, P. Whyman, [2000], p.171.

[10] D. Currie, [1997], p.14.

organisation of their distribution system, eliminating the extra management time devoted to managing new currencies.[11]

British, Danish and Swedish politicians and economists argue that positive aspects of the membership in the Economic and Monetary Union are connected with an increase in productivity in comparison to being outside the Eurozone. The countries examined need to belong to a large market, one that is comparable to that existing in the United States. In consequence, companies will be able to sell their products more widely and will profit from the economies of scale, which are observed in the American market. On the other hand, the variety of products and suppliers which exist in the single market influence their quality and increase price competitiveness. A survey by KPMG Consulting showed that 86% of companies that have different prices across Europe thought the price range would narrow as a result of the euro; 64% expected convergence *downwards*.[12]

The same arguments were presented in the report published by the Danish Ministry of Economic Affairs and the Danish Central Bank in March 1998. It enumerated the main consequences for Denmark of being outside the Eurozone. With the fact that around 50% of Danish foreign trade in goods would be with the future Eurozone, the expected strength of the single currency and the economic size of the Eurozone would contribute to changing Danish external economic relation by eliminating barriers to free trade, such as exchange rate uncertainties and transaction costs between euro countries, as well as increasing transparency of prices on European markets. All those factors would enhance competition between enterprises, including the financial sector, and create lower prices, benefiting consumers. In consequence, the euro would influence the strategies of Danish enterprises with regard to sales, marketing, price, and product differentiation, as well as the geographical location of investments. They would need to adjust to changes concerning invoicing and pricing in the single currency, supply and sales material directed towards the euro area, and sales via the internet. Nevertheless, the report emphasised that the costs of adapting should not be overemphasised. The consequences for import and export

---

[11] Ibid., p.175.

[12] *Europe's Response to EMU*, 4th Annual Report, KPMG Consulting, January 2000.

enterprises would be significantly larger than for national companies. Finally, the authors of the report suggested that amplified competition on the single European market would dampen prices and increase prosperity also for Danish consumers.

Likewise, the report summarised the economic consequences for Denmark of non-participation in the third stage of the EMU. The country would formally keep their existing powers in the field of monetary and exchange rate policy. It would participate in the ERM2 but not in the Stability and Growth Pact, and therefore it would not be subjected to the fines it introduced. Furthermore, while abstaining from the Eurozone, Danish economic policy would be more ambitious than the economic policy of the EMU members in order to secure room for manoeuvre in fiscal policy and the credibility of the fixed exchange rate policy. In the case of interest rates, a slightly higher Danish real interest rate could be expected. It would influence the costs of domestic financing for Danish companies and consumers, even though financial markets seemed to expect only a small interest rate differences. Consequently, Danish influence on economic affairs might be diminished, even though Denmark participates fully in all areas of economic cooperation in the European Union other than the Economic and Monetary Union.

Last but not least, the report indicated the legislative consequences of non-participation in the third stage of the EMU. They included certain changes in Danish legislation connected with the introduction of the single currency, further adjustments according to developments in other countries outside the Eurozone, as well as allowing Danish enterprises to keep and present accounts in foreign currencies, including the euro (only as a supplement to presentation in Danish krone). Moreover, Danish legislation would be continuously adjusted to improvements in international financial relations. Finally, the report also looked at the consequences for industry, the financial sector and for consumers.[13]

Another negative aspect of non-participation in the Eurozone is linked with inflow of FDI in three countries in question. Many foreign investors use Britain as a base for their operations in Europe. Between 1958 and 1973, the period when the United Kingdom was outside the European Community, Britain's share of investment into Europe declined from around 40% to 15%. Since

---

[13] The Danish Ministry of Economic Affairs, http://www.oem.dk.

joining the organisation, her share of projects has risen to 26%. At the turn of 2000, foreign investors provided more than 40% of British investments. Nevertheless, Britain's share of new foreign investment projects has been falling after introducing the common currency on the continental Europe. A report by Ernst and Young showed that in the first half of 2001, Britain attracted 21% of new European investment projects. In 1998 the country attracted 28% of such projects, and 26% in 2000.

Denmark is regarded as an attractive country for business establishment, partly because it offers a well-educated and highly motivated workforce as well as stable economic and political conditions. The total wage costs are lower than in most neighbouring countries and, in an international context, corporate taxes of 32% are very attractive. Denmark has the potential to become one of the leading nations in the new economy due to its high technological development and openness towards foreign investment. The country is also a natural (and actual) bridge between continental Europe and the Nordic countries, while the dissolution of the Soviet Union in 1991 has opened up entirely new opportunities in the Baltic region.[14]

As a result of globalisation, Danish companies are increasingly active abroad, just as many foreign companies establish themselves in Denmark. The country is in eighth position in the world as a recipient of FDI. Thanks to non-discrimination features of the Danish regulations and policies on foreign direct investments, in the period 1993–2001 inward inflow has tripled. In 1999, net investments by Danish companies abroad amounted to DKK65 billion, while foreign companies invested DKK40 billion in Denmark. In the period 1995–1999, the relating figures were DKK120 billion and DKK100 billion respectively. In 2001, investments were mostly focused on the financial and business services sectors and the other EU member states accounted for almost 70% of total investments.[15] It is worth mentioning that most of the inward FDI come to Denmark from the United Kingdom and Sweden, so remaining outside the Eurozone has not affected the country in a significant way.

---

[14] *Factsheet Denmark. Economy*, The Royal Danish Ministry of Foreign Affairs, August 2001, p.2–3.

[15] *Foreign Direct Investments in Denmark, Royal Danish Ministry of Foreign Affairs Facts*, Invest in Denmark, June 2002, p.1.

Until the mid-1980s the Swedish approach to direct investment from abroad was quite restrictive and governed by a complex system of laws and regulations. During the latter part of the decade, doubts were raised about the effectiveness and desirability of controlling FDI. Such considerations, as well as Sweden's present membership of the European Union, low corporate taxes and trade agreements with neighbouring former communist countries, have developed fast and have greatly improved the investment climate to attract foreign investors to the country. Combined with the well-educated labour force, the outstanding telecommunications network and a stable political environment, Sweden has become a very competitive choice for foreign enterprises.[16] According to the OECD statistics, Sweden had the world's second highest rate of inflow of FDI as a percentage of GDP in 1999.

Since 1993, Swedish investment growth has been significantly higher than the EMU average. There is also no tendency for Swedish investments to decrease in relation to the Eurozone. Admittedly, Swedish investments have slowed down in recent years, but in 1995, just after accession to the European Union, full participation in all policies of the organisation was regarded as an opportunity to diminish the negative economic experience of recession, which occurred at the beginning of the 1990s. Fears of a capital drain, namely rising outwards investments and relocation of production facilities abroad, were overthrown. Furthermore, Swedish participation in the European single market enabled it to fully benefit from inward FDI, which led to improved international competitiveness, higher levels of employment and assured generous welfare programmes. FDI were seen to bridge the domestic economy with existence on European and international markets.[17]

Moreover, the value of the Swedish krona, interest rates and inflation are influenced to a lesser extent than previously by the Swedish government because of the liberalised capital flow and deregulated currency restrictions. This situation has opened Sweden up

---

[16] US Foreign Commercial Service http://www.export.com and US Department of State http://www.state.gov.

[17] M. Kinnwall, 'How well has Sweden managed outside the EMU?', the article published in Swedish as *Hur klarar sig Sverige utanför EMU?*, Journal of the Swedish Economic Association, 3/2002, article published in English in Svenska Nätverket för Europaforskning I Ekonomi, Stockholm, 2002, p.5–6. http://www.snee.org/filer/papers/153.pdf.

to global financial markets. The highest rates of capital inflow come from France, Germany, the United Kingdom and Benelux countries. The main investors come from the other Nordic countries, the United States and Switzerland. Sweden invests its money in the United Kingdom, Germany, France, the Netherlands, Denmark and Finland. During the first three years after the establishment of the European single market existing, almost 30 branches of the Swedish banks were situated abroad.[18]

Inflow of FDI to the United Kingdom, Denmark and Sweden is presented in Figure 5.1.

Figure 5.1   *Inflow of FDI (in %)*

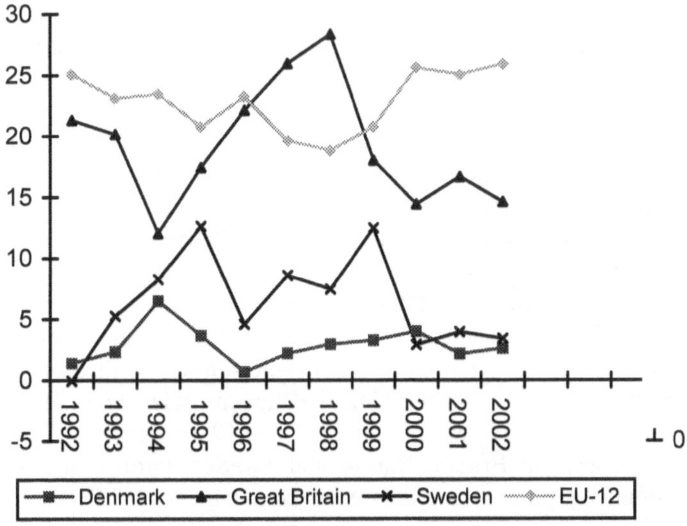

---

[18] R. Matera, [2001], p.199.

Likewise, foreign trade is also very important to the British national wealth. International trade has been the foundation of Britain's prosperity for the last two hundred years. Trade is equivalent to 27% of Britain's GDP, compared to 21% in the OECD as a whole. Britain trades more with Europe than anywhere else. In 1973, when she joined the European Community, only 35% of goods and services exports went to continental Europe. By 2000, 57% of goods and services exports went to the EU member states while 54% of this export went to the Eurozone. By comparison, only 16% of total trade is with the US.[19] Separate national currencies are said to act as a barrier to trade. Creation of the euro means that British firms exporting to the Eurozone face additional transaction costs compared to their continental competitors. In January 2002, Britain's trade deficit with the Eurozone countries rose to its highest level for almost 3 years, reaching £759 million, the highest level since April 1999. Since 1 January 1999, when the euro was introduced, Britain's trade with the European Union has diminished from 23.4% of GDP in 1998 to 22% in 2001.[20]

The situation of Sweden's economy was very good in the post-war period. By the 1970s half of all Scandinavian exports originated from Sweden, and one-third of all imports was destined for the Swedish market. Sweden's foreign trade was twice as much as Denmark's during the period of 1950–1970. The Swedish trade policy after the Second World War concentrated on European markets, especially on those of the European Communities, although its significant part headed for the Nordic partners. Moreover, Sweden continued to develop trade with overseas partners, especially with the United Kingdom, with which export figures circulated between 20% in 1960 and 12% by 1970.

Tendencies in British, Danish and Swedish intra- and extra-Community export and import are shown in tables 5.2–5.7.

---

[19] www.euro.gov.uk.

[20] Over the same period, Germany's trade with the European Union has leapt from 27.2% of GDP in 1998 to 32.2% in 2001; France's trade has risen from 28.0% to 32.2% and Italy's from 23.0% to 24.2%. www.hm-treasury.gov.uk.

Figure 5.2   *Export of goods and services at 1995 prices (national currency; annual percentage change)*

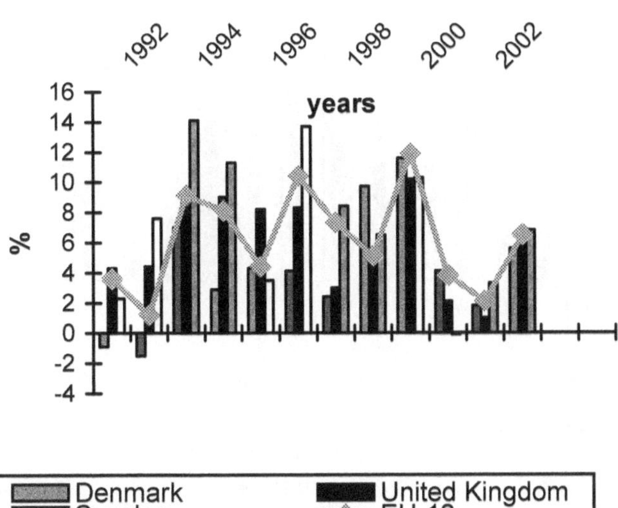

Table 5.2   *Export of goods and services at 1995 prices (national currency; annual percentage change)*

	1992	1993	1994	1995	1996	1997	1998	1999	2000	2001	2002	2003
Denmark	-0.9	-1.5	7.0	2.9	4.3	4.1	2.4	9.7	11.6	4.1	1.8	5.6
Sweden	2.3	7.6	14.1	11.3	3.5	13.7	8.4	6.5	10.3	-0.1	3.3	6.8
UK	4.3	4.4	9.2	9.0	8.2	8.3	3.0	5.4	10.2	2.1	1.0	5.8
EU-12	3.6	1.2	9.1	8.1	4.4	10.4	7.3	5.1	11.9	3.8	2.1	6.5

Source: *European Economy. The EU Economy: 2002, Review: Investing in the Future*, European Commission, Directorate-General for Economic and Financial Affairs, no.73/2002; IMF, OECD.

Figure 5.3   *Import of goods and services at 1995 prices (national currency; annual percentage change)*

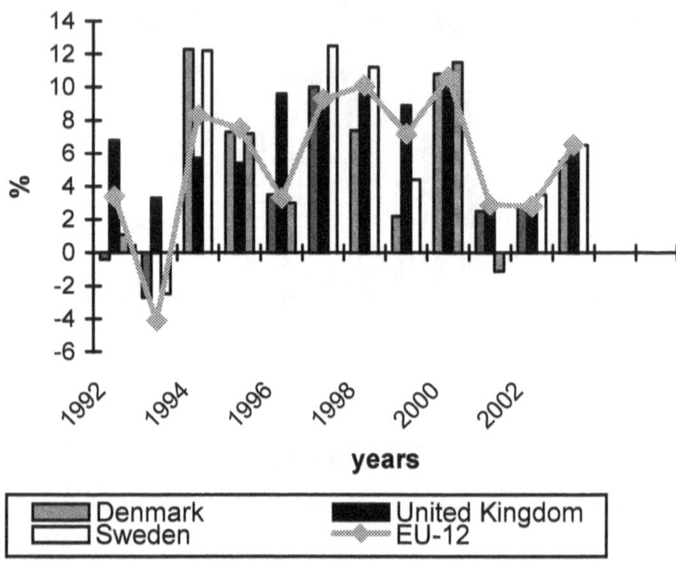

Table 5.3   *Import of goods and services at 1995 prices (national currency; annual percentage change)*

	1992	1993	1994	1995	1996	1997	1998	1999	2000	2001	2002	2003
Denmark	-0.4	-2.7	12.3	7.3	3.5	10.0	7.4	2.2	10.8	2.5	2.8	5.5
Sweden	1.1	-2.5	12.2	7.2	3.0	12.5	11.2	4.4	11.5	-1.1	3.5	6.5
UK	6.8	3.3	5.7	5.4	9.6	9.7	9.6	8.9	10.7	2.9	2.7	6.1
EU-12	3.4	-4.1	8.3	7.9	3.3	9.3	10.1	7.2	10.6	2.9	2.8	6.5

Source: *European Economy. The EU Economy: 2002, Review: Investing in the Future*, European Commission, Directorate-General for Economic and Financial Affairs, no.73/2002; IMF, OECD.

Figure 5.4   *Intra-EU import of goods (as percentage of GDP)*

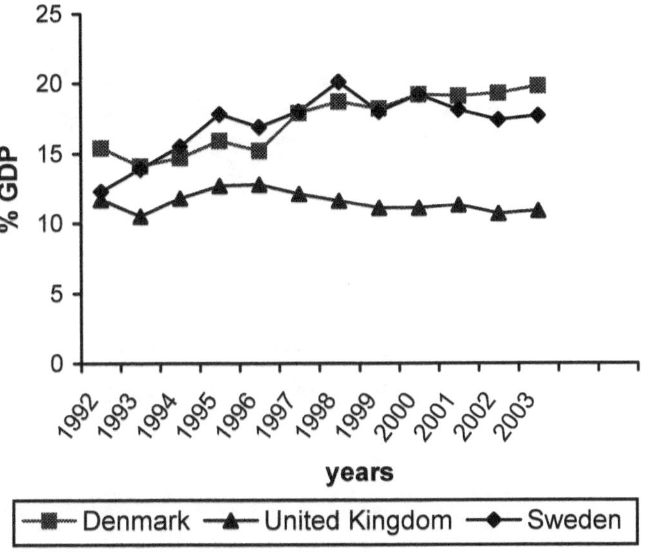

Table 5.4   *Intra-EU import of goods (as percentage of GDP)*

	1992	1993	1994	1995	1996	1997	1998	1999	2000	2001	2002	2003
Denmark	15.4	14.1	14.7	15.9	15.2	17.9	18.7	18.2	19.2	19.1	19.3	19.8
Sweden	12.3	13.9	15.5	17.8	16.9	18.0	20.1	18.0	19.2	18.1	17.4	17.7
UK	11.7	10.5	11.8	12.7	12.8	12.1	11.6	11.1	11.1	11.3	10.7	10.9

Source: *European Economy. The EU Economy: 2002, Review: Investing in the Future*, European Commission, Directorate-General for Economic and Financial Affairs, no.73/2002; IMF, OECD.

Figure 5.5   *Extra-EU import of goods (as percentage of GDP)*

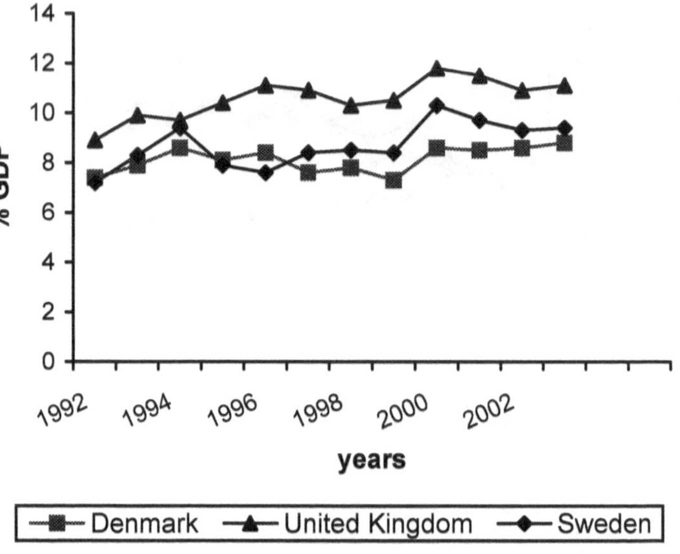

Table 5.5   *Extra-EU import of goods (as percentage of GDP)*

	1992	1993	1994	1995	1996	1997	1998	1999	2000	2001	2002	2003
Denmark	7.4	7.9	8.6	8.1	8.4	7.6	7.8	7.3	8.6	8.5	8.6	8.8
Sweden	7.2	8.3	9.4	7.9	7.6	8.4	8.5	8.4	10.3	9.7	9.3	9.4
UK	8.9	9.9	9.7	10.4	11.1	10.9	10.3	10.5	11.8	11.5	10.9	11.1

Source: *European Economy. The EU Economy: 2002, Review: Investing in the Future*, European Commission, Directorate-General for Economic and Financial Affairs, no.73/2002; IMF, OECD.

Figure 5.6   *Intra-EU export of goods (as percentage of GDP)*

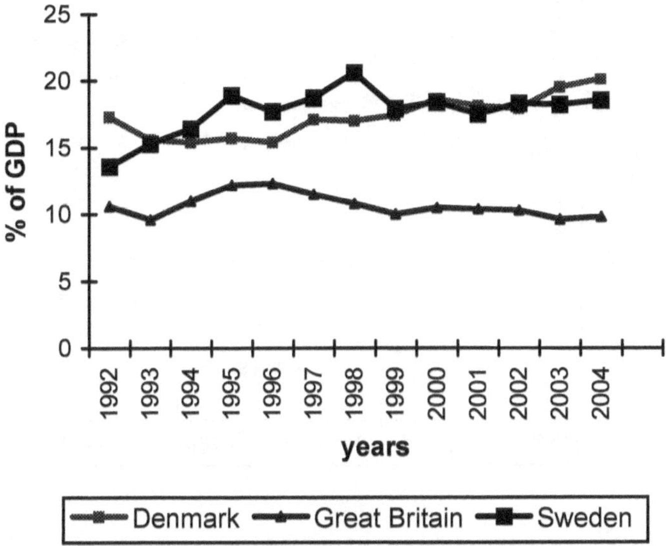

Table 5.6   *Intra-EU export of goods (as percentage of GDP)*

	1992	1993	1994	1995	1996	1997	1998	1999	2000	2001	2002	2003
Denmark	17.3	15.6	15.4	15.7	15.4	17.1	17.0	17.4	18.6	18.1	17.9	17.7
Sweden	13.6	15.3	16.4	18.9	17.7	18.7	20.6	17.9	18.4	17.5	17.0	17.1
UK	10.6	9.6	11.0	12.2	12.3	11.5	10.8	10.0	10.5	10.4	9.9	10.1

Source: *European Economy. The EU Economy: 2002, Review: Investing in the Future*, European Commission, Directorate-General for Economic and Financial Affairs, no.73/2002; IMF, OECD.

Figure 5.7   *Extra-EU export of goods (as percentage of GDP)*

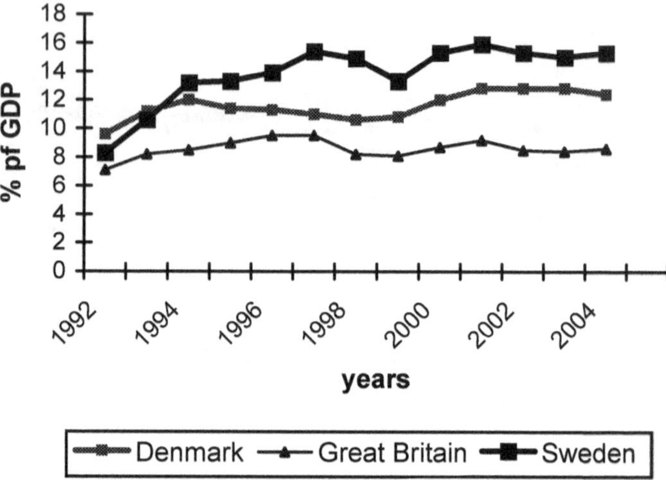

Table 5.7   *Extra-EU export of goods (as percentage of GDP)*

	1992	1993	1994	1995	1996	1997	1998	1999	2000	2001	2002	2003
Denmark	9.6	11.2	12.0	11.4	11.3	11.0	10.6	10.8	12.0	12.4	13.0	13.7
Sweden	8.3	10.6	13.2	13.3	13.9	15.4	14.9	13.3	15.3	14.4	14.1	14.6
UK	7.1	8.2	8.5	9.0	9.5	9.5	8.2	8.1	8.7	8.4	8.3	8.5

Source: *European Economy. The EU Economy: 2002, Review: Investing in the Future*, European Commission, Directorate-General for Economic and Financial Affairs, no.73/2002; IMF, OECD.

However, opponents of the Swedish participation in the EMU feared that, connected to a high interest rate, widespread exchange rate uncertainty would make Sweden less attractive for investments, which in turn caused lower growth. Moreover, it could also affect economic growth by restricting foreign trade through expensive currency hedging. The exchange rate of the Swedish krona against the single currency has reflected the relative economic conditions in Sweden and the Eurozone, with the exception of the years 2000–2001, which were characterised by inflation in CIT sector, the stock market and for the krona. Admittedly, a stable exchange rate in relation to the euro might be important for Sweden, since the EMU region is the largest trading partner for Sweden so far. However, in this perspective it is again not certain that volatility in the Swedish exchange rate has been excessive.[21]

The uncertainty of exchange rates stops the market from being unified and deters investing. The common currency contributes to a lack of currency fluctuations. Keeping national currencies will increase business risk for any company, which exports or which competes with imports.

British industry faced the problem of a strong pound at the turn of 1999 and in 2000. The United Kingdom is an important part of international trade relations, and therefore changes in the level of exchange rate of the British pound pose a threat to the overall condition of the British economy. It is now even more strengthened because of the existence of two large currency blocs – the US dollar one and the euro one. All British companies must face the problem of trading in those two currencies, which is connected with the risk of exchange rates. From 1996–2000 the value of the pound rose by 25% against the euro, which had serious consequences for the British economy at that time.[22] The high value of the pound contributes to the low profitability of British exports and, on the other hand, causes a higher inflow of continental imported goods to the British Isles.

---

[21] M. Kinnwall, [2002], p.4–5.

[22] R. Layard et al, [2000], p.10–11.

Figure 5.8   *GBP/EUR exchange rates*

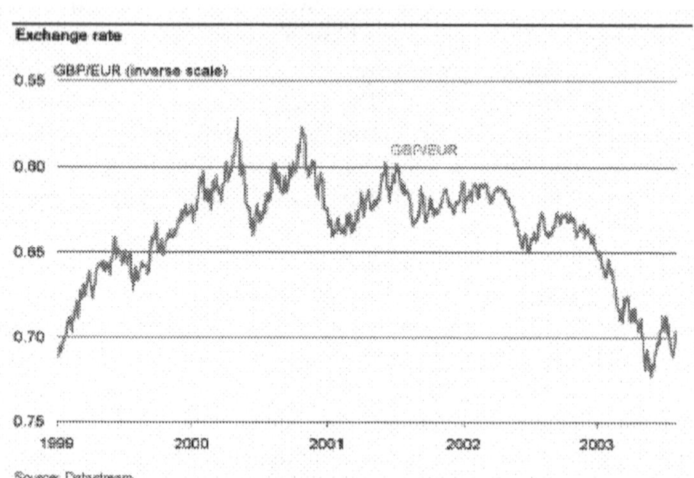

Source: Datastream.

It will be very important for the United Kingdom to enter the Eurozone at a competitive exchange rate. Otherwise, joining at too high an exchange rate would lead to lower competitiveness of British exports, a higher unemployment rate and lower economic growth. Most companies, and many economists, believe that the pound is overvalued at the moment by between 10% and 30% and it is trading at a rate not much higher than when the United Kingdom left the EMS in 1992. Nevertheless, lowering the value of the pound on international currency markets could be a difficult operation. British politicians hope that a long-awaited weakening of the US dollar, which would strengthen the euro, could have the side effect of reducing the pound's value against the single European currency.[23] A recent analysis from HSBC suggests that the pound could join the third stage of the EMU at a rate of €1.54, only 6% below the present rate, partly because Britain's trade performance has not been weak against that of the Eurozone. However, the latest economic survey

---

[23] *Q&A: Understanding the five tests on the euro*, BBC Online, www.bbc.co.uk, 16 May 2002.

from the OECD gives estimates ranging from €1.04 to €1.54, though with most falling between €1.20 and €1.50.[24]

The level of Danish interest rates is closely linked to developments of international interest rates. From the beginning of the 1960s to the 1990s, higher Danish interest rates were maintained in order to ensure a sufficient inflow of capital to finance the deficit on the balance of payments and the current account. The liberalisation of capital movements in the 1980s, however, changed the situation substantially. The Danish interest level has increasingly reflected the credibility of the Danish krone exchange rate. In general, the Danish interest rate is fixed with a margin for the expected change in the exchange rate against the euro.[25]

Figure 5.9   *DKK/EUR exchange rates*

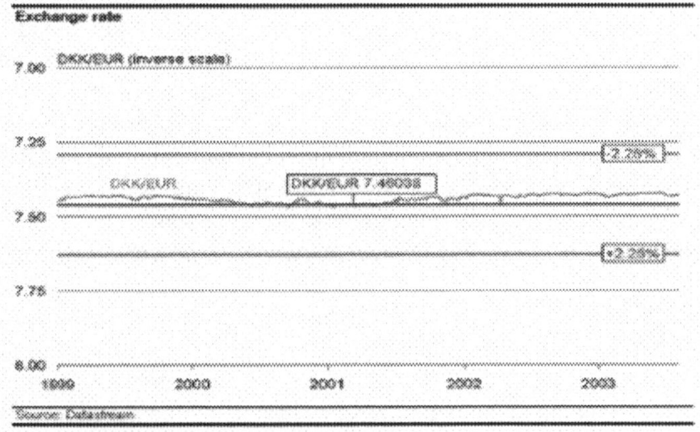

Source: Datastream.

The countries which are not participating in the Eurozone are interested in 'borrowing into' the credibility of the EMU in order to avoid paying higher interest rates. The problem for the countries outside, like Denmark, is that the common currency forces a higher

---

[24] M. Wolf, 'The price of entry to the euro', in the *Independent*, 5 May 2002.

[25] Expectations for changes in exchange rates are determined by historical changes in exchange rates as well as by inflation trends, budgetary developments and changes on the balance of payments.

interest rate because of the theoretical possibility of an interest rate cut. In remaining outside the Eurozone, Denmark would have to pay more, mostly in terms of a stricter financial policy, than the EMU member states, without gaining the advantages of lower interest rates and a safer currency. Furthermore, the companies have started to feel the side effects of the relatively higher interest rates. First, Danish investors pay for being outside the Eurozone because the main attention is on euro-stocks. Second, the higher interest rate influences the stock market, which is then priced lower than would have been the case while being an EMU member. Meanwhile, the higher interest rates make it more expensive to get loans, which influences the success of enterprises.[26]

Swedish market rates have also converged towards the EMU level in recent years. In the early years of floating exchange rate, the interest rate gap with the main EMU countries was volatile and occasionally very large. The 10-year nominal rate spread was around 4 percentage points for more than one year, reaching its highest value of 4.53 percentage points in April 1995. It was interpreted as a huge risk premium, linked to a distrust of Swedish economic policy in general and Swedish government finances in particular. However, the interest rate gap diminished after launching the Social Democratic government's fiscal reform programme in mid-1995. Since early 1998, the gap has been less than 0.5 percentage points, with a few exceptions. During the latter half of 2000, Swedish bond yields were actually lower than their German counterparts. Since 1997, Sweden has exceeded Germany in terms of GDP growth by an average 1.3 percentage points/year, while the real interest rate difference has been 1 percentage point.

Moreover, relative to the whole Eurozone, Sweden's advantage in productivity has been significantly larger. Thus the statement that a higher Swedish real interest rate could reflect a higher economic growth, rather than a credibility premium for remaining outside the Eurozone, cannot be overruled. Summing up, there was some truth in Euro-enthusiasts' view that prevailing Swedish interest rates would be significantly higher than those in the EMU. Obviously, these differences would have been significantly less if Sweden had quickly introduced the policy of a fixed exchange rate, especially in relation to short-term rates. However, the interest rate

---

[26] H. Collet, [1999], p.14–16.

costs for remaining outside the EMU have fallen sharply in recent years as a result of Sweden's own efforts, and not through borrowed credibility from foreign central banks.[27]

By mid-2002 Sweden had higher short-term interest rates than in the euro area and the United States. Nevertheless, given the current inflation rates and the prospect of growth, interest rates would need to rise further. According to the OECD projections, an increase of around 1 percentage point over the year 2003 would be required. Nevertheless, if fiscal easing continued a sharper rise would be necessary to keep inflation within the target range of 2%. It must be taken into account that in September 2003 the referendum on approving the single currency took place in Sweden. Therefore the public debate focused on comparing the role and effectiveness of a stabilisation policy inside and outside the Eurozone. For Sweden as a full member, it would be more difficult to fight asymmetric shocks through an active stabilisation policy in the absence of an independent monetary policy. On the other hand, the greater effective exchange rate stability result from EMU membership would significantly reduce one potential source of such shocks.[28] However, being radically out of synch with the rest of Europe, there is an alternative to using an independent exchange rate and monetary policy as shock absorbers. One can also introduce building up buffer funds to pay for a reduced payroll tax in crisis situations, which is known as an internal devaluation.[29]

The Swedish have had good experience of floating exchange rates. The reform of the Central Bank has brought its greater independence as well as establishing low inflation as the principal goal of the national monetary policy. For a number of years, interest rates in Sweden were significantly higher than in Germany, which indicated a lack of faith in Swedish monetary and fiscal policies; but nowadays they are at roughly the same level as in the Eurozone.

Contrary to what many predicted five years ago, the new monetary policy regime in Sweden with a floating currency rate, an independent Central Bank and an explicit inflation target has led to low inflation and low rates of interest. Meanwhile, however, the value of the krona

---

[27] M. Kinnwall, [2002], p.2–4.

[28] 'Economic Survey of Sweden, 2002', *OECD Observer*, July 2002, p.4.

[29] *Stability and stabilisation policy in the EMU*, (SOU 2001:62), http://finans.regeringen.se/propositionermm/sou/index.htm.

fluctuated a good deal in the 1990s, and like the euro, the Swedish currency has become weaker than many expected.[30]

The value of the dollar rose from SEK/USD 8.05 in December 1998 to SEK/USD 10.56 in December 2001. The euro initially fell from SEK/EUR 9.48 in December 1998 to SEK/EUR 8.24 in May 2000, before recovering to SEK/EUR 9.44 in December 2001. 'This confirms a known fact that when exchange rates float, currency values vary a good deal, but they also properly accommodate the economic conditions.'[31]

Figure 5.10 *SEK/EUR exchange rates*

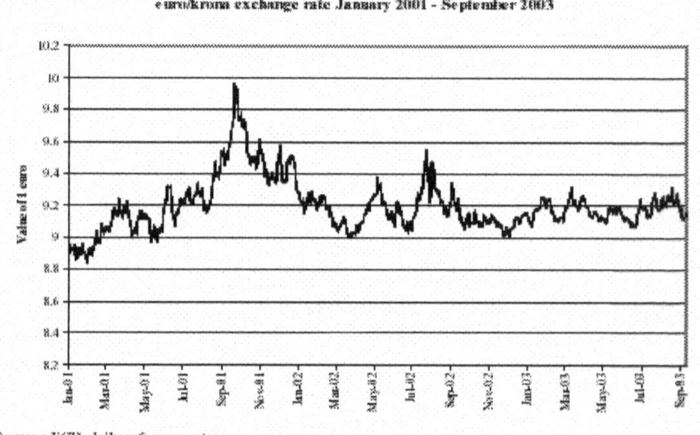

Source : ECB, daily reference rates

Source: European Central Bank.

Staying outside the Eurozone has also a strong impact on small and medium-sized enterprises. There are approximately 3.7 million such firms in the United Kingdom and they account for 99.8% of the British businesses, providing 55% of business employment (12 million people) and generating 51% of business turnover in the country, which is over 40% of the GDP. A great number of small and medium-sized enterprises (53%) have direct or indirect trading

---

[30] N. Gottfries, [2002], p.4.

[31] Ibid., p.5.

connections with the European Union. Joining the Eurozone would bring benefits to such enterprises, for whom it would be simpler to sell products on the continent, especially when linked with the greater national prosperity and economic stability that Britain would have as a member of the EMU. Moreover, participation in the Eurozone would not introduce any additional regulatory burdens. On the contrary, it would make it easier to do business with the continental countries.[32]

The common currency influences the capital market, increasing currency liquidity and return on capital, but the United Kingdom could not benefit from introducing the euro in terms of more liquid markets (e.g. the government bond markets) and more instruments (e.g. creation of a large corporate bond market). Moreover, the euro diminishes the costs of gaining and keeping capital on bank accounts as global financial markets integrate and become more liquid as well. Likewise, membership in the EMU could obviously bring some additional advantages, mostly connected with elimination of the exchange rate risk. The inflow of capital could bring the highest-return investment opportunities in the Eurozone. The pressure on management to perform would increase, stimulating productivity growth. Such an effect would not be achieved without a currency union, since the long-term exchange risk is very difficult to hedge, especially for returns on equity. Thus, only the power of the market could allocate the capital well.

> A company with potential revenue streams could design its business system and invest capital on a maximum efficiency basis and therefore achieve large productivity improvement. There would be no need to maintain branches of production in different countries to gain the best performance and the highest return on capital.[33]

Furthermore, there are at least two negative elements caused by non-participation in the EMU: first, less British influence on shaping EU financial market legislation; second, offering the financial expertise of the City for the euro financial markets. Consequently, inclusion of the large British financial market would contribute in increasing the global position of the Eurozone in international financial relations.

---

[32] www.euro.gov.uk.
[33] R. Layard et al, [2000], p.14–17.

In the light of the introduction of new sectors of hi-tech production, information and communication technologies, as well as pharmaceuticals, Britain, Denmark and Sweden have responded well with the international challenge of the new economy. Nevertheless, new sectors are also more risky. Banks have become more conservative in their credit policies, and they would probably be less willing to allocate capital in emerging new industrial sectors. It is claimed that the three countries in question would be able to keep their 'comparative advantage' in this field, even though the Economic and Monetary Union gradually contributes to the formation of a more efficient capital market in main European economies. However, there are factors which can hamper British, Danish and Swedish growth relative to the EMU member countries. For example, Sweden has the highest tax burden on labour income within the European Union. Low marginal taxes on mobile human and physical capital will be an essential 'growth-enhancing' factor in an appearing high-tech economy, and the EMU membership would probably be required to harmonise Swedish regulations with the EU standards. However, Swedish membership in the Eurozone could reduce differences in the business environment, and it will lead to a long-term interest rate development that is more comparable with the positive business climate.

Positive consequences from non-participation in the Eurozone contribute to the ability of the British, Danish and Swedish authorities to conduct a proper economic policy for the country.

One of the most important positive aspects of staying outside the EMU was connected with turbulences in the EMU economy and the fact that its member states were not moving in step. Paradoxically, and in contrast to common belief, different growth trends might be *strengthened* by a common monetary policy, so that the monetary union creates divergence instead of convergence. There are already signs that tensions have arisen in the EMU due to different growth conditions, where a common monetary policy does not include a common inflation rate. Inflation has been much higher in leading countries, such as the Netherlands, Portugal and Ireland where economic growth is high. At the same time, Germany has also had the lowest inflation. Given the common nominal key rate, the fast growing/high inflation countries thus enjoy a lower short-term real interest rate.

Figure 5.11 *Inflation (%)*

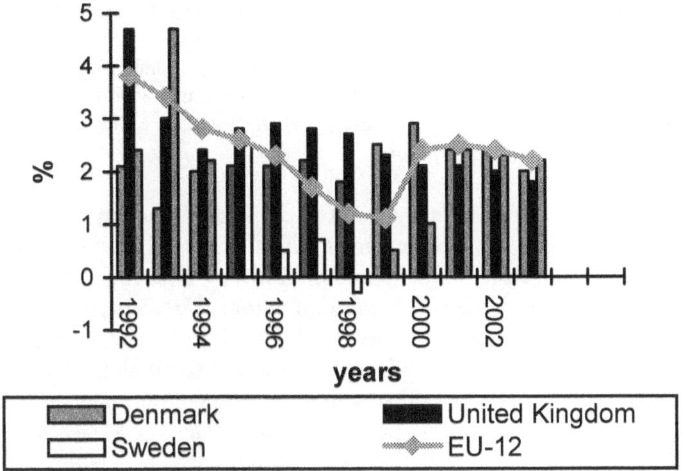

Table 5.11 *Inflation (%)*

	1992	1993	1994	1995	1996	1997	1998	1999	2000	2001	2002	2003
Denmark	2.1	1.3	2.0	2.1	2.1	2.2	1.8	2.5	2.9	2.4	2.4	2.0
Sweden	2.4	4.7	2.2	2.5	0.5	0.7	-0.3	0.5	1.0	2.4	2.3	2.2
UK	4.7	3.0	2.4	2.8	2.9	2.8	2.7	2.3	2.1	2.1	2.0	1.8
EU-12	3.8	3.4	2.8	2.6	2.3	1.7	1.2	1.1	2.4	2.5	2.4	2.2

Source: *European Economy. The EU Economy: 2002, Review: Investing in the Future*, European Commission, Directorate-General for Economic and Financial Affairs, no.73/2002; IMF, OECD.

The low inflation countries are similarly affected by a higher short-term real interest rate, which further reduces economic activity. The inflation pattern in the EMU is a good illustration of how monetary policy institutions cannot short-circuit underlying trends in real foreign exchange rates. With a common currency, change takes place only through different inflation paths. With floating exchange rates, adjustments can take place as a combination of inflation differences and movements in nominal exchange rates.

> Diverging growth trends between, e.g. Sweden and the Eurozone, together with an underlying pressure for the Swedish krona to appreciate in real terms, indicate that a common monetary policy would poorly suit Sweden. Experiences from the 1980s are a painful reminder of what can happen when monetary policy is too expansive for too long a period.[34]

However, loss of monetary policy could be compensated by alternative adjustment mechanisms such as increased nominal wage flexibility and transnational labour mobility. Consequently, fiscal policy becomes an issue of crucial importance. There is an element of uncertainty concerning how well fiscal policy can replace monetary policy as a stabilisation policy instrument. Another question concerns the extent to which monetary union may lead to centralisation of EU fiscal policy as well. This is a politically sensitive issue, since a major part of the British, Danish and Swedish populations are sceptical of the idea of further steps towards a federal Europe. Steps towards a European fiscal policy might also be considered as a threat to the Swedish and Danish models of welfare state, with their high taxes and developed social welfare programmes. Monetary policy may be perceived as a technical problem, but matters such as taxes, transfers and central government activities are far too sensitive for national parliaments to let them go. The question of coordinating fiscal policy will, however, be a subject of broad discussion in the EU over the next few decades.[35]

All in all, outside the EMU, the United Kingdom, Denmark and Sweden have the freedom to set interest rates according to their domestic economic conditions. The loss of monetary policy as an independent tool for dealing with economic cycles would not matter if two conditions were satisfied. First, if economic cycles in the different EMU member states were more or less the same, and second, if the effects of a given monetary policy were the same in each of the EMU countries. In fact, in the British case neither condition applies. Accordingly to British Euro-sceptics, if a bigger

---

[34] Ibid., p.9–10.

[35] N. Gottfries, [2002], p.5.

group of countries joined the EMU there would be greater risks of asymmetric shocks. 'Nevertheless, with growing integration among European economies, the significance of differential shocks may well diminish. Moreover, differences in financial structures are largely a product of different economic policies and history, and with time these will decline.'[36]

Figure 5.12 *Nominal short-term interest rates (%)*

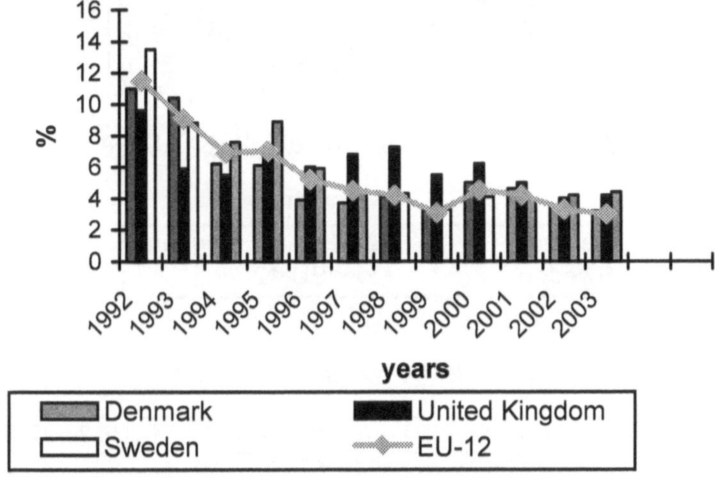

Table 5.12 *Nominal short-term interest rates (%)*

	1992	1993	1994	1995	1996	1997	1998	1999	2000	2001	2002	2003
Denmark	11.0	10.4	6.2	6.1	3.9	3.7	4.1	3.3	5.0	4.6	3.5	3.2
Sweden	13.5	8.8	7.6	8.9	5.9	4.5	4.3	3.3	4.1	4.0	4.2	4.4
UK	9.6	5.9	5.5	6.7	6.0	6.8	7.3	5.5	6.2	5.0	4.0	4.2
EU-12	11.5	9.1	6.9	7.0	5.2	4.5	4.2	3.1	4.5	4.2	3.3	3.0

Source: *European Economy. The EU Economy: 2002, Review: Investing in the Future*, European Commission, Directorate-General for Economic and Financial Affairs, no.73/2002; IMF, OECD.

---

[36] D. Currie, [1997], p.9–10.

Figure 5.13 *Nominal long-term interest rates (%)*

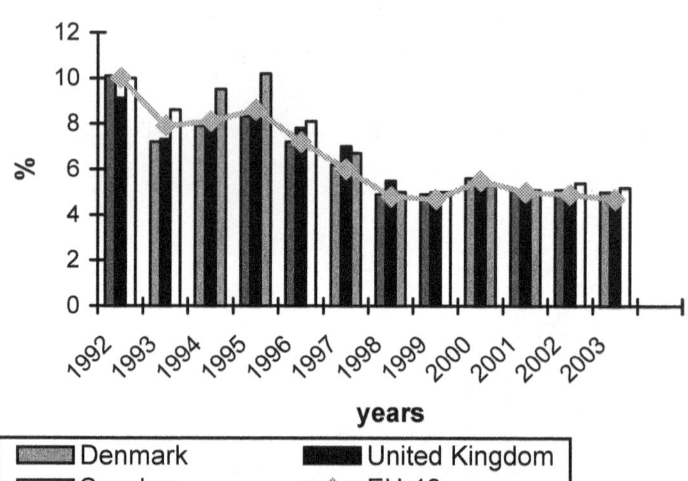

Table 5.13 *Nominal long-term interest rates (%)*

	1992	1993	1994	1995	1996	1997	1998	1999	2000	2001	2002	2003
Denmark	10.1	7.2	7.9	8.3	7.2	6.2	4.9	4.9	5.6	5.1	5.1	5.0
Sweden	10.0	8.6	9.5	10.2	8.1	6.7	5.0	5.0	5.4	5.1	5.4	5.2
UK	9.1	7.3	8.1	8.2	7.8	7.0	5.5	5.0	5.3	4.9	4.9	4.7
EU-12	10.0	7.9	8.1	8.6	7.2	6.0	4.8	4.7	5.5	5.0	4.9	4.7

Source: *European Economy. The EU Economy: 2002, Review: Investing in the Future*, European Commission, Directorate-General for Economic and Financial Affairs, no.73/2002; IMF, OECD.

For Britain, there are certain unique positive effects of non-participation in the Eurozone. First, the British mortgage market, which is different from markets in the Eurozone, is not seriously affected by existence of the single currency. In short, mortgage rates in the United Kingdom, taken by two-thirds of British households, are variable and based on money market rates. British politicians and economists are afraid that having joined the EMU, homeowners would become dependent on money market rates created by the ECB. But it is worth emphasising that money market rates in the Eurozone have always been lower than in the United Kingdom; so, in consequence, British mortgage rates would have been lower as well. The researchers from the Deutsche Bank Research Unit predict that:

> ...if the United Kingdom decides to join EMU, British homeowners would have the additional advantage of direct access to long-term mortgage loans with fixed rates without running an exchange rate risk.[37]

Second, the offshore markets, if the United Kingdom were inside the euro area, would necessarily be set outside the City of London and possibly in one of its international rival finance centres. This is very strong case against British membership in the Eurozone. Alternatively, it could allow London to become the centre for euro-euro deposit trading, as it would become a natural location for excess liquidity to escaping the tedious ECB regime. Moreover, 'its position as an international money market centre, namely its dominant place in the already established Eurocurrency and Eurocommercial paper markets, would not undergo any threat.'[38]

Third, another positive argument relating to membership in the Eurozone is that if the United Kingdom, France, Germany and the other EU member states had the same currency, each of them would no longer have a balance of payments deficit with the others. As Jonathan Michie concludes:

> In fact, however, the deficit would still be there. More money would still be going out of Britain than was coming in. What would change is that this deficit would no longer be recorded, and it would no longer be seen as the duty of the government to do anything about it. So to that extent, the underlying problem would actually be made worse. This real imbalance in economic activity would have to be balanced instead by falling relative income and wealth in Britain, which would continue until the country could no longer afford the imports that were causing the problem. People

---

[37] W. Becker, A. Järvbäck, [2002], p.7; D.

[38] L. Talani, [2000], p.112–113.

would be made poorer; jobs would be lost. However, as the economy becomes impoverished, less is bought from domestic firms as well, so some of these will be forced out of business.[39]

In the case of Denmark, positive elements of non-participation in the third stage of the EMU were included in another report by the Danish Economic Council on the effect of the Economic and Monetary Union on Denmark, which was published in April 2000. It concluded that there were various gains in saved transaction costs, a probable reduction in the interest rates towards Germany, ending of exchange rate fluctuations against the currencies of the EMU member states, and probably beneficial effects from increased competition in some sectors. However, these gains were not expected to be very significant for the long-term development of the Danish economy.

The report underlined that in relation to stabilisation policy, empirical analyses showed that Denmark differed from the main EMU members with respect to changes in GDP and other economic conditions. Future Danish membership in the Eurozone might in itself change these differences, but the change could be in either direction. Hence, differences between the Danish business cycle and that of the other EMU countries were hardly possible, but maintaining an independent Danish monetary policy would be useful.

According to the report, the restrictions concerning fiscal policy in the Maastricht Treaty did not limit Danish stabilisation options. However, because of demographic changes, these restrictions would be likely to cause problems in the future for several members of the Eurozone, and partly because of this, future pressure on changes in the fiscal policy rules of the European and Monetary Union could be expected. The report emphasised that it was advantageous in economic terms to join the Economic and Monetary Union (the efficiency gains and their relation to the costs of definite exclusion of an independent monetary and exchange rate policy). The value of an independent monetary policy depends on the extent to which a monetary policy based on the whole Eurozone would be suitable for Denmark, and if it were not suitable, on the readiness of Danish politicians to use other stabilisation mechanisms. However, the authors of the report pointed out that

---

[39] J. Michie, [2000], p.51.

Denmark had been able to maintain a fixed exchange rate against the German mark for several years, which showed that an independent monetary policy was not necessarily needed to be able to react to differences in the business cycle.

In short, the report concluded that purely economic costs and benefits for Denmark of the EMU membership were small and uncertain. If Denmark decided to stay *outside* the Eurozone, one possibility was to continue the fixed exchange rate policy within the ERM2, but in an expanded fluctuation band. The fixed exchange rate policy had gained credibility, and it was well included into economic policy and expectations formation. The main advantage of participation in the ERM2 was lower sensitivity of the currency to speculative attacks, and in consequence the need to raise the interest rates temporarily to defend the value of the currency would be smaller. On the other hand, a monetary policy based on inflation targets was less transparent than a fixed exchange rate policy. It also allowed greater exchange rate changes.

> However, if the inflation target was the same in two areas, and economic policy was credible, the exchange rates would also move in parallel in the long run. Short-term fluctuations in the exchange rate would be unlikely to have any importance for foreign trade.[40]

Last but not least, in the case of Sweden, there are some fundamental distinguishing factors between Sweden and the Eurozone, among which demographic composition is the most important. Demographic conditions in most European countries will be much less favourable in the future, compared to recent decades. Most especially, the rate of growth of the working population will decline significantly, which applies to Sweden as well. Nevertheless, even if it happens, the Swedish labour force will grow significantly faster that the EMU average in the coming decades. This means that Sweden will have a higher average growth rate than the Eurozone, which could have implications for the Swedish position on the EMU issue. Sweden has already exceeded the EMU in terms of economic growth in recent years, and the demographic factors show that this pattern will persist.[41]

---

[40] K. Skjalm, [2000], p.42–45.

[41] M. Kinnwall, [2002], p.8.

2.   Political Consequences

Participating in the third phase of the EMU and agreeing on an introduction of the euro would have considerable political consequences for the three countries in question. It will embrace strengthening national bargaining positions of the countries within the European Union as well as in international economic and financial relations, which would consequently lead to reinforcing their political situation on both fields.

Entering the Eurozone will increase the influence of the United Kingdom, Denmark and Sweden in Europe and in the world. Joining the EMU will not mean passing laws, which will directly affect and limit the countries. Such powers already exist, no matter whether the countries join the Eurozone or not. However, being inside would enable them to have a greater influence on how these powers are used. Furthermore, being members of the European Central Bank would give Britain, Denmark and Sweden an influence on the European business cycle, which is now regarded as the main obstacle in the way for the EMU by national politicians and economists. Nevertheless, in the Eurozone, the countries will obtain more influence outside the European continent as well.

Successive Danish governments have been trying to strengthen the country's involvement in international relations. Proponents of the Danish participation in the third stage of the EMU underline changes in Denmark's position in the European Union if the country decides to stay outside the Eurozone. It will primarily lead to less power to influence decisions and regulations taken within the organisation, which could result in being isolated from the rest of the world. On the other hand, membership in the Eurozone could give Denmark and other small states the chance to find solutions to common problems, and therefore the country should not observe the new developments from a distant position but as part of the economic cooperation.[42]

Jesper Gronenberg, a member of the Social-Liberal Committee for Foreign Affairs, said in his speech:

No matter whether we join the euro zone or not, we shall be

---

[42] 'It's about Denmark's future in the European Union', by Jesper Gronenberg, member of the Social-Liberal Committee for Foreign Affairs, *Newsletter*, [2000], p.3–4.

obliged to pursue the same kind of economic policy as the rest of the EMU member states. If we do not join, (...) it is and always will be an illusion, which has been advanced by those opposed to joining the euro zone, that we can lead an independent economic policy. It is thus the formal sovereignty by remaining outside. But in case we remain outside the EMU it means that Denmark will not be able to speak with the same kind of importance in the European Union, and this will also apply to the areas that do not concern the single currency (...). Denmark will become marginalised, and the other EU member states will see us as bad partners that want to benefit from the advantages of the co-operation without committing to a greater European responsibility. It will be in the marginalisation that the real loss of sovereignty is found, and that is far more serious than the fact that we shall be prevented from devaluating in the future.[43]

Likewise, the Economic and Monetary Union has already been progressing and encompasses as many as twelve countries. This is a greater number than many had thought would be the case five years ago. It is due partly to the fact that convergence regarding inflation, interest rates and budget deficits proceeded faster than many had expected, and that the convergence criteria were interpreted liberally. As the EMU grows in size, the political costs for Britain, Denmark and Sweden of remaining outside grow as well. It will unavoidably further reduce their political influence and marginalise them in Europe.[44]

It was said that with a 'no' vote to participation in the Economic and Monetary Union in the referendum, Sweden's role in the European Union of the future might have to be questioned. Unlike Denmark and the United Kingdom, Sweden does not have an opt-out clause, allowing the country to withdraw from the third phase of the EMU. The lack of decision in this area has not had any impact on the government's policies so far, but there might be a debate on whether Sweden can continue to be a EU member without respecting the basic agreements it signed. However it is impossible that Sweden would be required to leave the organisation. Therefore, the result of a 'no' vote for Sweden was to stay out of the Eurozone, like Denmark, and the question will need

---

[43] Ibid., p.7–8.

[44] L. E. O. Svensson, [2002], p.2.

to be raised again after a number of years. Until then, economic fundamentals such as inflation gaps and borrowing requirements would formulate interest rate and exchange rate trends, just as is the case today.[45]

However, the common currency is seen to move closer to a political union. The commitment of a number of key EU member governments to further political integration suggests that over time the EMU could indeed favour federalism. Therefore, for Great Britain, Denmark and Sweden, which are hostile to any ideas of closer cooperation in Europe, not to mention federal solutions, joining the EMU would partly mean agreeing on creation of the United States of Europe.[46]

3.   Social Consequences

There are also significant social consequences following the decision on restraining from the third stage of the EMU for the United Kingdom, Denmark and Sweden.

Up to 3.5 million British jobs depend on exports to the European Union, nearly 2 million of which are in manufacturing and almost half a million in banking, finance and insurance. Inward investors, who usually come to Britain to have better entrance on the single European market, employ around 25% of the total number of manufacturing workers. It is an issue strictly connected with currency volatility. The overall unemployment rate in the United Kingdom is low (around 5% for the last 26 years), but jobs have been lost in sectors exposed to the volatility of the pound caused by staying outside the Eurozone. Since the launch of the euro, currency volatility was a factor in an estimated 115,000 manufacturing job losses, which originated from significant reductions in the ability to compete in export markets by British companies due to the strength of sterling. The exchange rate also matters to tourism. In April 2000, David Quarmby, chair of the British Tourist Authority, said that volatility of the pound outside the euro meant that Britain's tourism industry had missed out on £2 billion of revenue and 70,000 jobs in the previous four years.[47]

---

[45] J. Birger Christensen, [2002], p.4–5.

[46] D. Currie, [1997], p.3.

[47] www.euro.gov.uk.

The question of the social costs of not participating in the third stage of the EMU has been regarded also by the Danish government and business community. In spring 1999, the business newspaper, *Børsen*, argued that:

> Danish investors have lost 60 billions of kroner since the introduction of the euro due to the effect of high interest-rates on the stock market. (…) Danish stocks have a risk of becoming marginalised and overlooked by the foreign investors as long as we are outside the euro zone.[48]

In April 2000 the Trade Union Congress published a report on potential damage to the Danish labour market, which might be caused by rejection of the euro. First and foremost, it would cost 35,000 Danish jobs because higher interest rates would stop investment. The lost jobs would be split between three main sectors of the labour market, with 11,000 fewer people employed in the construction industry, 17,000 in the services sector and 6,500 in manufacturing.

As it was mentioned above, the main social concern connected with participation in the Eurozone, concerns the threatened existence of the Swedish and Danish models of welfare state. Economic analysts and observers predicted that establishment of the European single market as well as the Economic and Monetary Union would result in limiting or even erasing national social policies. However, it needs a substantial liberal justification for successfully introducing the Economic and Monetary Union. The liberal ideology, which is the main element of this task, could guide changes in corporate systems of establishing minimal pay, diminishing the role of trade unions, changes in relation between capital and labour, together with decreasing social benefits.[49] Most of these elements were presented in the debate on possible Swedish as well as Danish EMU membership. Nevertheless, one cannot forget that the European Central Bank does work in sustaining price stability, controlling the balance between the inflation level and levels of economic growth. Nor does the Stability and Growth

---

[48] H. Collet, [1999], p.11.

[49] M. Rhodes, 'Globalization, EMU and Welfare State Futures', in *Developments in West European Politics 2*, edited by P. Heywood, E. Jones, M. Rhodes, London, 2002, p.38–39.

Pact exclude the existence of welfare state. Its main goal is to be able to balance budgetary spending and revenues, as well as protecting national budgets from deficit caused by increased distributive politics. Development of welfare states is also supported by higher taxes, privatisation and low interest rates.

However, the main challenge for the Swedish and Danish welfare states is not the EMU membership itself but the negative demographic structure of the two countries, which is caused by a decrease in the birth rate, longer spans of life[50] and the emergence of ageing societies, that lead to an increase in the social and medical benefits paid for citizens. A falling European population could indirectly cause a decrease in aggregate demand, a decrease in the value of financial goods, and in the incomes of industrial companies, resulting from diminished efficiency of production and limited scale of production with a shaky balance of trade and national budget.[51] Furthermore, economic integration, which comprises liberalisation of trade, an increase in international commerce, and liberalisation of capital flow, causes differentiation of production and acting on economies of scale, together with intensification of international competitiveness. Accordingly, producers aspire to lower costs of production, which results in lower employment rates and payments.[52] Transnational corporations search for opportunities to lower costs of production, shifting production lines to less developed countries outside Europe, where such costs could be even half those of the EU member states. This trend causes increase in unemployment and differences in citizens' incomes, which in consequence leads to higher demand for national social programmes.

The Swedish model of welfare state is regarded as the biggest and the most expensive in Europe. Despite those facts, it is well prepared to face new challenges appearing in the world economy, connected with globalisation, growing societies, post-industrial employment and European economic integration. A range of minimal payment and qualification programmes protects citizens from poverty incurred from long periods of being unemployed.

---

[50] E. Huber, J. D. Stephens, *Welfare State and Production Regimes in the Era of Retrenchment*, University of North Carolina, 1999, p.12.

[51] M. Rhodes, 'Challenges to Welfare: External Constraints', in R. E. Goodin, B. Headey, R. Muffels, H-J. Dirven, [1999].

[52] T. M. Andersen, *European Integration and the Welfare State*, Aarhus, 2001.

Sweden, as well as the United Kingdom and Denmark, invests in educational programmes and workforce training, preparing people to face a competitive, highly specialised economy, based on knowledge. Bearing in mind changes in economic relations and budgetary spending connected with the Economic and Monetary Union, the Swedish welfare state can undergo modifications, but it will definitely not be abandoned. Therefore Swedish politicians and citizens should not worry about the survival of welfare programmes on joining the Eurozone. Social policy at the European level, written in the Stability and Growth Pact, resembles solutions introduced in Sweden at the beginning of the 1990s. It takes into consideration a certain level of inflation and economic growth in shaping the amount of payments, as well as balancing budgetary incomes and revenues.

When arguing for or against joining the EMU, costs of living must be analysed. Britain is generally a more expensive place to live than other European countries. The European Commission's report on car prices, published in July 2001, indicated that, 'prices in the United Kingdom were still much higher than in the Eurozone'. According to a survey by ECA International conducted in December 2000, London is the second most expensive city in the European Union. Only Copenhagen, which is also outside the Eurozone, was ranked higher. Furthermore, the Economist Intelligence Unit's latest worldwide cost of living survey shows that London was the eighth most expensive city in the world. The European Consumers' Association showed in February 1999 that the United Kingdom was the most expensive country in Europe, particularly for popular consumer goods. Prices in Britain were 30% higher than in Germany.[53]

Moreover, outside the Eurozone, Denmark, Britain and Sweden would not have any influence on European decisions on environmental and social issues, especially employment strategies, taken by the members of the Economic and Monetary Union.

Staying outside the Eurozone causes different consequences for the United Kingdom, Denmark and Sweden. They can be divided into two groups, with an emphasis on their positive and negative aspects. As was shown above, the positive ones are connected with economic and financial benefits the three analysed countries

---

[53] Ibid., p.5.

already have, despite being outside the EMU. Negative aspects concentrate on the debenefits Britain, Denmark and Sweden *could* experience if they were full members of the third stage of the EMU, enumerating especially the risks of currency fluctuations, lower inflow of FDI, lower productivity, higher transaction costs and lower quality.

VI: Prognoses on joining the Economic and Monetary Union

Introducing the euro into circulation on 1 January 2002, did not change the situation in the United Kingdom much. Nevertheless, the common currency managed to find its way there. The euro will soon become the second legal tender in Britain and then there will be only one step to winning the referendum on the European Monetary Union and replacing the pound with the euro. On the other hand, the EU Commissioner, Neil Kinnock, repeated that a positive result of the referendum was not evident, even though the euro actually functions in the United Kingdom. It would take approximately 34–40 months to prepare a referendum.[1] The procedure would encompass taking a decision on entering the Economic and Monetary Union and on organising a referendum on that question thoroughly (together with possible problems with approving the law on referenda in Parliament); and in the event of a positive result, establishing the euro and taking the pound sterling out of circulation.[2]

The economists from the City of London said that chances on successful preparations to a referendum on the membership in the Eurozone increased significantly after accepting the budget in April 2003. The government planned to introduce a restricted fiscal policy to enable the Bank of England to lower the interest rates and approve a more competitive exchange rate between the British pound and the euro. The Chancellor, Gordon Brown, outlined that according to the OECD report of June 2002, the British economy was closer to fulfilling the convergence criteria for joining the third phase of the EMU than several countries which are currently members of the Eurozone.[3]

---

[1] 'The Myth of Eurocreep', in *The Economist*, 5–11 January 2002; E. Pfanner, 'Euro Revives Membership Quandary Among British', in *International Herald Tribune*, Sweden, 5–6 January 2002.

[2] M. White, 'The Path to Euroland', in the *Guardian*, 30 January 2002.

[3] 'Continental drift', op. cit.

1. The United Kingdom

To become a member of the third stage of the EMU, the United Kingdom must meet economic requirements posed by the convergence criteria. Currently, Great Britain fulfils the conditions for price stability and interest rates as well as the fiscal criteria with regard to budget deficit and public debt. Moreover, the country is also expected to meet the inflation, interest and fiscal criteria in the years to come.

Regrettably, the United Kingdom has not yet complied with the exchange rate condition, which requires membership in the ERM2 with the euro. The inclusion of the pound sterling in ERM2 is exposed to deep psychological concerns existing in the British public and business community, given the experience of Black Wednesday in September 1992, when sterling was forced to leave the EMS.[4] Consequently, at the beginning of February 2003, the European Commission published a report on the condition of the British economy. It argued that that the United Kingdom did not necessarily have to cut spending or put up taxes to comply with the Stability and Growth Pact. Furthermore, the Commission agreed that Britain would not have to remain in the ERM2 for two years before joining the Eurozone, something the EMU member states had insisted on so far.[5]

The crucial problem is the determination of the appropriate central rate for the ERM2. According to the regulation of the ERM2, the rate has to be agreed with the ECB. The ERM2 entry rate does not have to be identical with the entry rate for the EMU, but it would give a strong signal about the possible EMU conversion rate for the pound. In any case, the United Kingdom should be able to maintain the rate without tensions before the convergence test.

---

[4] W. Becker, A. Järvbäck, [2002], p.4.

[5] *Brussels clearing the way for UK eurozone entry*, www.euobserver.com, 29 February 2003.

Table 6.1 *Fulfilment of convergence criteria in the United Kingdom*

	Inflation in %	Public Debt as % of GDP	Budget Deficit as % GDP	Nominal long-term interest rates
1992	4.7	41.0	-6.4	9.1
1993	3.0	47.6	-7.9	7.3
1994	2.4	49.6	-6.7	8.1
1995	2.8	51.8	-5.8	8.2
1996	2.9	52.3	-4.4	7.8
1997	2.8	50.8	-2.2	7.0
1998	2.7	47.6	0.4	5.5
1999	2.3	45.2	1.1	5.0
2000	2.1	42.4	4.3	5.3
2001	2.1	39.3	1.2	4.9
2002	2.0	37.2	0.4	4.9
2003*	1.8	34.8	0.5	4.7

*forecast

Source: *European Economy. The EU Economy: 2002, Review: Investing in the Future*, European Commission, Directorate-General for Economic and Financial Affairs, no.73/2002; IMF, OECD.

Before joining the EMU, the United Kingdom has not only to meet the convergence criteria but also needs to adjust its secondary legislation according to the introduction of an independent central bank, the banning of central bank credit to government, and preferential access of government to national financial markets. The independence of the Bank of England was strengthened by new legislation introduced by the Labour Party between 1997 and 2000. Nevertheless, there is need for action with regard to establishing full independence since it is the HM Treasury that sets an inflation target for the Bank of England.[6]

---

[6] W. Becker, A. Järvbäck, [2002], p.3.

It is expected that the Blair government and the Labour Party will continue to postpone the issue of meeting the five criteria until the continental economy recovers, and imbalances between business cycles and interest rates in the two regions will be reduced. By doing that, the government can also buy more time for continuing the ongoing trend of the public support for participation in the third stage of the EMU. This trend has been observed since mid-2001.[7] However, the biggest threat to calling a referendum is a continued weakening of the euro versus the pound, and an observed deterioration of the Eurozone economy.

Trends in public opinion would be the most important objective for the Blair government in choosing the right time for a popular plebiscite. Furthermore, possible referenda in Denmark or Sweden, which could lead to a shift in British public opinion, would also be crucial for the government's decision.[8]

At the beginning of March 2003, the British government concluded that the key economic conditions for euro entry had not yet been met, which could delay a referendum on entering the third stage of the EMU. The Chancellor of the Exchequer, Gordon Brown, has recently warned of the dangers of accepting 'rigid rules' to govern the British economy. A Treasury paper entitled 'Macro-economic Frameworks in the New Global Economy' published in December 2002, reported that if Britain wanted to join the monetary union 'the conditions that need to be met to minimise the risk of destabilising shocks are specific and demanding'. According to the report, the conditions consist of the following:

> The economy must be very open, with a high share of trade with the country to which it is pegged; the economic and financial system must already extensively rely on its partner's currency and the shocks it faces must be similar.

Observers say that Gordon Brown is unlikely to approve a European referendum in this parliament, but they also suggest that while Gordon Brown is Chancellor, Britain may never enter the euro.[9] In the meantime, Tony Blair has ruled out calling a euro

---

[7] J. Birger Christensen, [2002], p.9.

[8] Ibid., p.10.

[9] B. Russell, 'Report hints that Treasury will reject 2003 euro entry', in the *Independent*, 2 December 2002.

referendum on EMU membership, even if the five economic tests for joining the EMU are passed. The Prime Minister believes that public hostility to the single currency is so deep that it cannot be turned around in the four-month campaign envisaged in the National Changeover Plan. Tony Blair has decided to 'play it long' and wants a much longer campaign lasting between six months and a year to convince all doubters.[10] Moreover, a referendum on the EU Constitutional Treaty would be the first to be held in Great Britain.

2. Denmark

The new Danish government, following successful parliamentary elections in November 2001, confirmed its determination to plan economic policy, which included continuation of the fixed exchange rate policy. The Danish Prime Minister, Anders Fogh Rasmussen, announced in his New Year's speech that Denmark would be likely to hold a referendum on membership in the third stage of the EMU in 2004 or 2005. He stressed that exclusion from the Eurozone would reduce Danish authority and influence in crucial areas of European integration.[11] In March 2003 the Danish Finance Minister, Thor Pedersen, made it clear that there would be voting after 2004, when the project of the EU constitutional treaty would be known. Several months after, such a plebiscite would be more probable in Sweden.[12]

Nevertheless, Ditte Staun, spokesperson for the People's Movement Against EU, stressed that the proposal relating to the fact that in a future enlarged European Union, the small countries would not have a permanent representative in the European Central Bank, was not going to make the euro more acceptable to the Danes.[13]

---

[10] A. Grice, 'Blair rules out euro referendum in 2003 even if targets are met', in the *Independent*, 20 January 2003.

[11] 'Danish euro referendum puts pressure on Blair', www.euobserver.com, 2 January 2003.

[12] www.bbc.co.uk., 2 March 2003.

[13] The Governing Council of the ECB has presented unanimously a proposal for a new voting system inside the bank. According to the proposition, in the enlarged European Union, the number of votes would still be 15, as it is now. The six members of the Executive Board would maintain permanent voting rights, while the governors would share the remaining 15 voting rights on rotation among themselves.

It is not clear when a new referendum could take place in Denmark. According to the report of the European Commission on the state of Danish economy, the country meets all convergence criteria necessary for transition to join the third stage of the EMU. Moreover, it has been a member of the ERM2 since its introduction in 1999. Therefore the country is fully qualified to join the Eurozone.

Currently the most likely scenario is that the EMU membership would return to the political agenda once the United Kingdom and/or Sweden announce(s) a date of a referendum on their territory. Then Denmark would probably set a date for the second referendum on joining the Eurozone, provided that Danish polls continue to show rising support for the Economic and Monetary Union. Then the Danish government could wait for results of referenda in those two countries. If they were positive, a positive effect on Danish participation in the EMU seems the most likely. In the case of a 'yes' vote, Denmark can probably enter the EMU within two years' time, i.e. one year earlier than the United Kingdom and Sweden, since they are not members of the ERM2. However, there is still the risk of a second negative result in voting in Denmark. It is worth underlining that a Danish opinion poll on the euro issue does not necessarily mean a firm majority.[14]

The new system would be introduced in steps. First, there would be a division of members into two groups, when the European Monetary Union grows from 15 to 22 members. The first group would be composed of the five governors from the member states with the biggest shares in the euro area. They would share four votes. The second group would be composed of the rest of the governors – representing up to 17 countries, sharing 11 votes according to some EMU member states from time to time would be outside the votes; however, the bigger states not as often as the smaller states. When the number of governors reaches 22, they will be placed into three groups, with four voting rights given to the first group, eight to the second and three to the third. The division into groups would be based on two components: the share in the aggregate GDP at market prices of the EMU member states without a derogation, and the share in the total aggregated balance sheet of the monetary financial institutions of the EMU member states without a derogation. The EU heads of states and governments must approve the proposal unanimously. 'Three in four Danes against EU constitution', www.euobserver.com, 22 January 2003.

[14] W. Becker, A. Järvbäck, [2002], p.14–15.

Table 6.2   *Fulfilment of convergence criteria in Denmark*

	Inflation in %	Public Debt as % GDP	Budget Deficit as % GDP	Nominal long-term interest rates
1992	2.1	66.3	-2.2	10.1
1993	1.3	78.0	-2.9	7.2
1994	2.0	73.5	-2.4	7.9
1995	2.1	69.3	-2.3	8.3
1996	2.1	65.1	-1.0	7.2
1997	2.2	61.2	0.4	6.2
1998	1.8	55.6	1.1	4.9
1999	2.5	52.0	3.1	4.9
2000	2.9	46.1	2.5	5.6
2001	2.4	43.2	2.2	5.1
2002	2.4	42.5	1.6	5.1
2003*	2.0	40.0	2.0	5.0

*forecast

Source: *European Economy. The EU Economy: 2002, Review: Investing in the Future*, European Commission, Directorate-General for Economic and Financial Affairs, no.73/2002; IMF, OECD.

3.   Sweden

In sum, so far there has been no clear evidence that Swedish non-participation in the Economic and Monetary Union has resulted in major economic shortcomings. Interest rates are not significantly higher than in the Eurozone. Government finances and the labour market situation are even better than the EMU average. Moreover, in terms of economic growth, Sweden has surpassed the EMU countries' average in recent years, since there is no convincing argument that the choice of monetary policy and exchange rate systems are crucial for long-term economic development. Consequently, decisions on Swedish future relationship to the Eurozone will probably be based on political rather than economic considerations.[15] However, Mats Kinnwall argues that it seems unlikely that Sweden can remain as a full EU member without adopting the common currency in the long run. According to his view, Sweden will probably become a member of the Economic and Monetary Union, but later rather than sooner.[16]

According to the Convergence Report, 2002, of the European Commission, Sweden has to introduce secondary legislation. The Swedish central bank legislation is not yet compatible with requirements of the EC Treaty and the statute of the ECB in several respects. For instance, financial independence of the Riksbank is not fixed in a legally binding way. In particular, there are no clear legal provisions about the profit distribution to the government, and it is the government which could decide on the profit distribution of the Riksbank.[17] However, in March 2003, the European Parliament endorsed the report on the Swedish convergence programme for 2002. It stated that Sweden could join the Eurozone as soon as it fulfilled the criteria on independence of the Swedish Central Bank and on membership of the ERM2. Sweden already fulfils the remaining criteria for membership.[18]

The overall performance of the Swedish economy with regard to meeting the convergence criteria is more or less assured. Nevertheless, Sweden fails to meet the exchange rate criterion, since it is not a member of the ERM2 yet. The Swedish exchange rate regime can be described as relatively free-floating. Nevertheless, the exchange rate of the krona has shown considerable volatility so far. Membership in the ERM2 could also improve the macroeconomic environment because exchange rate fluctuations have been a major source of macroeconomic instability in the past. Thus, it would make sense to enter the ERM2, following the Danish example. This would mean that Sweden would fulfil one of the EMU membership conditions and would hence be expected to join the Economic and Monetary Union. But the Swedish government wants to be free with regard to EMU

---

[15] M. Kinnwall, [2002], p.11.

[16] M. Kinnwall, [2000], p.164.

[17] In 2002, the Riksbank reluctantly had to make an extraordinary contribution of €2.2 billion of its profit to the government budget. W. Becker, A. Järvbäck, [2002], p.11.

[18] 'Swedish euro camps gear up for crucial referendum', www.euobserver.com, 13 March 2003.

membership and will, therefore, participate in the ERM2 only after a final decision on that issue has been taken.[19]

Table 6.3   *Fulfilment of convergence criteria in Sweden*

	Inflation in %	Public Debt as % GDP	Budget Deficit as % GDP	Nominal long-term interest rates
1992	2.4	64.8	–	10.0
1993	4.7	75.1	-11.9	8.6
1994	2.2	77.7	-10.8	9.5
1995	2.5	76.6	-7.7	10.2
1996	0.5	76.0	-3.1	8.1
1997	0.7	73.1	-1.6	6.7
1998	-0.3	70.5	2.1	5.0
1999	0.5	65.0	1.7	5.0
2000	1.0	55.3	4.0	5.4
2001	2.4	52.3	3.8	5.1
2002	2.3	50.2	1.6	5.4
2003*	2.2	47.8	1.9	5.2

*forecast

Source: *European Economy. The EU Economy: 2002, Review: Investing in the Future*, European Commission, Directorate-General for Economic and Financial Affairs, no.73/2002; IMF, OECD.

All in all, the three countries in question fulfil the convergence criteria and their economic cycles are more or less synchronised with those of the EMU member states, which has been achieved with lower unemployment and inflation rates than in the Eurozone.

---

[19] W. Becker, A. Järvbäck, [2002], p.11–12.

VII: Conclusions

The aim of the book was to present British, Danish and Swedish approaches to the European Economic and Monetary Union. In relation to the EMU entry and membership in the Eurozone, these three countries show a great many reservations, together with an independent and critical attitude towards this European project.

First though, it must be stressed that the United Kingdom and Denmark have negotiated 'opt-out' clauses in the Treaty on European Union and they are 'countries with an exemption', which are to join the EMU when they declare their readiness and meet the convergence criteria. Sweden, however, is a 'country with derogation'. It is legally *obliged* to enter the Eurozone as soon as the convergence criteria.[1]

In making choices, Great Britain pays the most attention to her national interests and own profits. Therefore in many fields of European integration, including the Economic and Monetary Union, she has managed to have a special status, expressed in extraordinary regulations or opting-out clauses, according to which she can decide on her own if and when she undertakes cooperation in a certain sector. The United Kingdom has negative attitudes towards deepening European integration and postulates intergovernmental cooperation among the EU member states, having 'particular sympathy for such a reorganisation of Europe, which does not influence the British interests and rights in an unjustified way'.[2] Hence, she has abstained from membership in the euro area, pointing out several reasons for such an approach.

The reasons for Britain's restrained attitude to the European integration must be sought in the 1950s, when the first proposals of the creation of the European Coal and Steel Community were submitted. At that time Great Britain was convinced of her powerful position in international relations and her special relationship with the United States, having the same political and

---

[1] W. Becker, A. Järvbäck, [2002], p.3–4.

[2] T. Bainbridge, A. Teasdale, *Leksykon Unii Europejskiej*, Kraków, 1998, s. 369.

legal systems, a common history and a conviction of the US's leading role in guaranteeing European security after World War II. On the other hand, the British had strong contacts, mostly economic, with the countries from the Commonwealth. The general state of the British economy, especially regarding its low competitiveness in the manufacturing sectors of the economy, was against entering the European Communities. To make things worse, British citizens perceived relations with the European continent as necessary but risky.

After accession to the EC, the United Kingdom maintained her cautious attitude towards European integration, which is currently clearly seen in her approach to economic collaboration within the EMU. Opponents of British membership in the Eurozone emphasise the loss of national sovereignty and the lack of influence on monetary policy which is connected with participation in this European project. Moreover, they indicate several turbulences which could occur for the City of London as the main financial centre in Europe if Britain were to join the EMU, especially because of the low value of the single currency at the very first stage after introducing it into circulation, and threats for euro-offshore markets, which are developing in London. It has been argued that the pound was necessary for the EMU member states to maintain their position in financial relations, and without it, the euro was a weak and untrustworthy currency. Likewise, a serious argument against joining the third stage of the EMU is linked with differences in the business cycles between the United Kingdom and her continental counterparts. British economists stress that in that state of affairs the country would need specific economic solutions, especially interest rates to safeguard sound economy and, in the event of any economic crisis, to pursue its own independent fiscal and monetary policies, which would help her to overcome the crisis using tools specifically designed for her. Another argument against EMU membership concerns the so-called 'pension issue', according to which demographic pressures in the other EMU member states would also threaten Britain's ability to pay pensions, which was much greater than in the other countries thanks to the extraordinary development of the pension fund instrument. Eventually, opponents of participation in the Eurozone refer to the specific rules of the British financial system, where there are floating credit rates, while on the continent they are stable. In consequence, the aggregate demand in Britain is more susceptible to changes in the interest rates than in other European countries. And last but not least, there are also arguments associated with spending large amounts of money on preparations and the final switch to the single currency, which could be disastrous for the British budget.

Denmark joined the European Community together with the United Kingdom on 1 January 1973. It is argued that the main reason for such a move was close trading links and industrial relations between the two, and the Danish government was afraid of losing a potential big market for selling its products. Denmark is a small country, which is highly dependent on international trade. Despite these facts, the country has been rather unwilling to shift successive national policies and sectors of domestic influence to the supranational level. Like those in Great Britain, Danish politicians preferred to work for protection of the environment, social issues and decreasing levels of unemployment in Europe on an intergovernmental level. The same situation occurred when the Economic and Monetary Union was launched. Disregarding political and economic arguments, the Danish people rejected membership of the Eurozone twice. Once, during the referendum on Treaty on European Union in 1993, and a second time, when voting against the introduction of the common currency on their territory in 2000. It must be stressed that the arguments which the British hold against the EMU are also applicable to Danish opponents of the project. They point out a loss of national influence on interest and exchange rates, problems within the Eurozone connected with an apparent recession in the German economy, and restrictions originated from the Growth and Stability Pact.[3] They have emphasised the loss of national sovereignty and influence on mainly political European affairs, dependence on big European countries after accession to the third stage of the EMU, and the lack of democracy within the organisation, which could contribute to lessening the influence an ordinary Dane has on his or her life. Moreover, they also point out several specific problems, which

---

[3] The argument of weakness of the common currency is not relevant any more, but it was fiercely debated during preparations to the euro referendum in Denmark in September 2000.

influence their attitudes on prospects for joining the Eurozone. Those characteristic Danish reservations relate to domestic policy interplay, the economic condition of the country, preservation of the Danish model of welfare state, and maintaining high rates of employment in the country. Finally, Denmark expresses the need to offset Scandinavian relations and preserve a balance between the Nordic and the European integration.

For many years Sweden has stayed outside the mainstream of the process of European integration. Since the nineteenth century the country enjoyed sound political and socio-economic position as well as being involved in international trade and industrial relations. Its main economic partners were the United Kingdom, other Scandinavian countries (i.e. Norway and Denmark), the United States and Germany respectively. The country only joined the European Union on 1 January 1995. Like Denmark, Sweden is a small and open economy, specialising in the production of very competitive luxury hi-tech products. Even though the European continental markets were of major importance for Swedish companies, the country did well selling its manufactured goods on other continents also. This structure of the Swedish economy led to relative affluence of the country and its citizens. The process of European integration was something unknown and uncertain, which contributed to a rather hostile approach towards it, apart from being tied up with the European Community through the Free Trade Agreement and other documents on mutual cooperation.

Sweden, like the two countries mentioned above, preferred an intergovernmental level of collaboration, and therefore for decades was attached to the European Free Trade Area, trying to expand economic integration among the Nordic states as well. However, the most important element of the Swedish reservations towards the European Communities concerned its policy of neutrality, identified 'non-alignment in peacetime leading to neutrality in the event of war', according to which all EC proposals for establishing political union were unacceptable for Swedish governments. This is also the main reason for abstaining from the Economic and Monetary Union. Like the others, Sweden also holds arguments on different business cycles in comparison to the continental EMU members and the threat of asymmetric shock, which might appear in the Swedish economy after accession to the Eurozone. Moreover, joining it could also be risky for large welfare state programmes, and may contribute to tensions on the employment market. Likewise, for a while, there was also an argument on the weakness of the single currency. Nevertheless, in the Swedish case, it mainly concerned the low value of the krona in relation to the euro, which could have a major impact on Swedish exports and international trade when the country joined the third stage of the EMU.

This argument is connected with the one on fixed rates. Until the beginning of the 1990s Sweden held its national currency fixed to the US dollar during the whole period that the Bretton Woods system functioned, and after its collapse at the beginning of the 1970s, it used the German mark as an anchor. It proved to be disastrous for the Swedish economy. Introducing floating exchange rates in 1991 has been maintained so far, and has brought significant economic advantages in comparison to the previous system. On the other hand, political arguments point to disparities with the Swedish constitutional system, with its principle of open government and principle of public accountability, its developed notion of a local self-government and awareness of citizens' democratic rights, as well as possible loss of Swedish sovereignty after joining the Eurozone, which is not acceptable for Swedes.

The peculiarity and separateness of the United Kingdom, Denmark and Sweden are seen in all sectors of the cooperation within the European Union, not just in economic and monetary integration. It is, though, the most important European project right now. Thus, abstaining from it is seen by many as a negation of values and goals the European Community has created and developed for almost fifty years of its existence. The United Kingdom has always been regarded as an awkward partner by the continent. Now there are two more countries with such an unwilling attitude towards European integration, which could have important consequences on the whole process. It was aimed at changing the political and socio-economic conditions of European societies whose countries had been damaged during World War II. The idea was to improve standards of living across the continent, and the main objects of this activity were the ordinary citizens in Europe. Curiously, British, Danish and Swedish societies regard the Economic and Monetary Union as a project which could destroy their political and cultural identity, and they show a cautious attitude towards Europe. It is a very important sign for creators of the future shape of the European Union, something they should realise and take into account.

One must, however, understand that the approach towards the EMU in the three countries had been continuously changing, and its scope and features differ according to the internal situation and external factors. For example, during the first two years after introducing the single currency in 1999, the euro was very weak in comparison to the national currencies of the three countries in question. After its significant surge in value in 2001 and 2002, this argument is not so strong or relevant any more. Nevertheless, new ones have appeared, such as the issue of economic recession, which is apparent right now in the Eurozone, and is connected with the poor performance of the German economy as well as restrictions originating from the Stability and Growth Pact. Therefore Britain, together with Denmark and Sweden, call for intergovernmental cooperation, which could be more lucrative not only for their countries and societies but also for the other EU members and the organisation itself as well. It is also worth mentioning that the political and economic elites, as is the case in Sweden and recently in Denmark, are in favour of joining the Eurozone. The changes in their attitude were also noted in this analysis. In the United Kingdom they were connected with the shift of political power to the Labour Party, which is more friendly towards Europe. In fact, the new Labour government indicated that it supported joining the EMU in principle, if it were seen to benefit the British economy. However, it now argues that the differences between the United Kingdom and the other EMU member states, especially on interest rates and the economic cycle, are such that joining now is not reasonable.[4] Unfortunately, being in favour of the EMU in principle is not enough for successfully winning a Euro referendum and participating in the third stage of the EMU. The same is true for both Scandinavian countries.

The pleasant and simple way of handling money that Brits, Danes and Swedes travelling in the Eurozone experience following the successful physical introduction of the single currency helps to further strengthen the pro-euro camps in each country. This will be an important step towards calling for referenda on their

---

[4] C. Haskins, 'The Case for the Single Currency', in M. Baimbridge, B. Burkitt, P. Whyman, [2000], pp.166–167.

membership in the EMU, although public opinion in the countries is at least of equal importance. Sweden's more intensive debate on the EMU membership and scheduling a referendum on 14 September 2003 could have triggered a 'domino effect', influencing the results of both Danish and British referenda. This was regarded as being most important for the United Kingdom, where support for participation in the Eurozone expressed by the British people has been very low. A Swedish 'yes' in the referendum could have mobilised proponents of EMU membership in Britain to fix a date for a national plebiscite. The same could have happened in Denmark. At the same time, the Danish Prime Minister, Anders Fogh Rasmussen, stated that his country would hold a second referendum on the EMU entry in 2005 at the latest. However, the Swedish negative result postponed a decision on joining the Eurozone in both countries. Nevertheless, it is worth mentioning that in the case of Britain, the most important reason for calling an EMU referendum would be an assessment of the five economic self-imposed tests. The government has promised to assess these criteria until 7 May 2003. The answer was positive only in relation to the competitiveness test. Therefore there is no chance for a positive sentiment in Sweden and Denmark, or a significant shift towards the EMU membership in this main opposing country right now.

It must be mentioned though that it is more for political reasons rather than economic ones that the three countries have not introduced the single currency yet. The governments are in favour of membership of the Eurozone, but they cannot be assured of public support in referenda. Their citizens are concerned about the loss of national identity and monetary decision making. Opposition to the EMU entry is particularly strong in the United Kingdom. At the end of 2002, an opinion poll showed that more voters in Sweden and Denmark were in favour of the Economic and Monetary Union than were opposed. Even the euro-supporting camp in Great Britain has gained substantial ground. According to many social analysts, the reason for such a shift was the introduction of the single currency into circulation on 1 January 2002. Taking the deep hostility in the United Kingdom to EMU membership into account, it cannot be predicted, though, that those three countries will soon join the euro zone.[5]

---

[5] J. H. Bryson, [2002], p.3–4.

Table 7.1   *Support for the euro in the United Kingdom,*
Denmark and Sweden

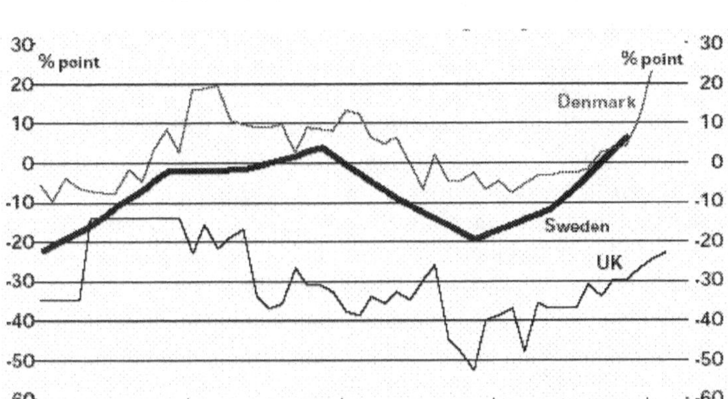

Source: Deutsche Bank Research.

For joining the Eurozone, Great Britain, Denmark and Sweden
have to fulfil the same convergence criteria as the twelve current
EMU member states. Denmark fulfils all of them, but the United
Kingdom and Sweden have not met the exchange rate criterion,
which is connected with participation in the ERM2. Denmark has
been a member of this system since the beginning of the EMU in
1999, while Great Britain and Sweden do not belong to it, and the
timing of their accession is still an open question. Furthermore,
Britain and Sweden have not yet met all the conditions with regard
to the so-called secondary legislation (e.g. independence of the
central banks).

The three countries have managed to stay outside the Eurozone
without experiencing noticeable disadvantages. However, they do not
enjoy the specific benefits of EMU membership, such as the fostering
of trade and FDI increased by the elimination of the exchange rate
risks among the EMU member states, the reduction of transaction costs
and participation in a large liquid financial market.[6]

However, changes in British, Danish and Swedish attitudes to
economic cooperation within the EMU are still possible. The other

---

[6] W. Becker, A. Järvbäck, [2002], p.1.

member states introduce changes, and are pursuing the agreed policy independently. They realised that Great Britain, Denmark and Sweden themselves needed to redefine their priorities, and no one could force them to do it. Oddly enough, external factors, especially good examples, can stimulate changes in the best way.

In conclusion, it must be stressed that the United Kingdom, Denmark and Sweden avoid participating in the Economic and Monetary Union primarily for political reasons. For many years it was only Britain which enjoyed a special position in the process of European integration and showed reservations towards the process. In the 1990s two other states, namely Denmark and Sweden received the name 'reluctant Europeans'. Denmark refused to join the third step of the EMU and negotiated an opt-out clause attached to the Maastricht Treaty. Furthermore, in September 2000, the Danes confirmed in the national referendum their negative attitude towards the single currency.

In an open letter, Swedish celebrities recently emphasised that their country should support Great Britain in her attitude towards the EMU, and repeated that 'as long as Britain – Europe's financial great power – stays outside, we have absolutely no reason to join the EMU. We are in good company, both politically and economically, with a country that has a better growth rather than the rest of the EU'.[7]

The group of the countries which are sceptical towards deepening European integration is becoming dangerously larger, and is headed by the United Kingdom herself. After some time, Europe may have to face the problem of internal tensions and separatist movements inside, which the EU by definition was supposed to erase.

---

[7] 'Keep Sweden out as long as Britain stays out', *Dagens Nyheter*, 2 July 2002.

Bibliography and Source Materials

Documents

Greenwood, S., *Britain and European Integration since the Second World War*, Documents in Contemporary History, Manchester, 1996

Plañavova-Latanowicz, J. [ed.], *Dokumenty dotyczące przystąpienia do Wspólnot Europejskich Danii, Irlandii i Wielkiej Brytanii oraz Grecji*, Documents of Accession, Warsaw University Centre for Europe, 1998, vol. I

Plañavova-Latanowicz, J. [ed.], *Dokumenty dotyczące przystąpienia do Unii Europejskiej Austrii, Finlandii i Szwecji*, Documents of Accession, Warsaw University Centre for Europe, 1998, vol. III

Przyborowska-Klimczak, A. and Skrzydło-Tefelska, E. [ed.], *Dokumenty Europejskie*, vol. I, Lublin, 1996

Przyborowska-Klimczak, A. and Skrzydło-Tefelska, E. [ed.], *Dokumenty Europejskie*, Lublin, 1999, vol. III

Weigall, D. and Stirk, P. [ed.], *The Origins and Development of the European Community – Documents*, Leicester, 1992

Statistical Reports etc.

Annual Report. The Danish Society of Financial Analysts, Copenhagen, 1998.

Bruhn, P. S., *Denmark – Inflation (CPI)*, LB Kiel Nordic Research, July 2002.

Economic Survey of Europe, No.1/2002, UN Economic Commission for Europe, United Nations, New York and Geneva, 2002.

Economic Survey of Denmark, 2002, *OECD Observer*, January 2002.

Economic Survey of Sweden, 2002, *OECD Observer*, July 2002

Eurobarometer. Public Opinion in the European Union, Report no.55, European Communities, 2001

European Economy. The EU Economy: 2002. Review: Investing in the Future, European Commission, Directorate-General for Economic and Financial Affairs, no.73/2002

Factsheet Denmark: Economy, The Royal Danish Ministry of Foreign Affairs, August 2001

Foreign Direct Investments in Denmark, Royal Danish Ministry of Foreign Affairs Facts, Invest in Denmark, June 2002

International Monetary Fund Public Information Notice no.02/55 on Denmark, May 2002

International Monetary Fund Country Report no.02/159 on Sweden, August 2002

Selected Retail Interest Rates from the Non-Euro Area EU Countries. Methodological Notes, European Central Bank, June 2002

The profile of the European countries and the EU in the international economy, List of Tables, 2002

UNCTAD Handbook of Statistics 2002, UN Conference on Trade and Development, United Nations, Geneva, 2002

World Investment Report 2002. Transnational Corporations and Export Competitiveness, UN Conference on Trade and Development, United Nations, New York and Geneva, 2002. http://www.unctad.org/wir

Books

Andersen, T. M., *European Integration and the Welfare State*, Aarhus, 2001

Andersson, T., *Dzieje Szwecji*, Warszawa, 1967

Austin, D., *The Commonwealth and Britain*, London, 1988

Baimbridge, M., Burkitt, B. and Whyman, P. [ed.], *The Impact of the Euro*, London, 2000

Bainbridge, T. and Teasdale, A., *Leksykon Unii Europejskiej*, Kraków, 1998

Baker, D. and Seawright, D. [ed.], *Britain For and Against Europe. British Politics and the Question of European Integration*, Oxford, 1998

Bartlett, C., *Konflikt globalny. Międzynarodowa rywalizacja wielkich mocarstw w latach 1880–1990*, Wrocław, 1997

Borchardt, K-D., *Integracja europejska. Powstanie i rozwój Unii Europejskiej*, Warszawa, 1996.

Bromhead, P., *Life in Modern Britain*, Manchester, 1991

Calleo, D. P., *Rethinking Europe's Future*, Princeton University Press, 2001.

Calvocoressi, P., *Polityka międzynarodowa po 1945 roku*, Warszawa, 1998

Chisholm, M., *Britain on the edge of Europe*, London, 1995

Ciamaga, L. et al [ed.], *Unia Europejska. Podręcznik akademicki*, Warszawa, 1999

Cieślak, T., *Zarys historii najnowszej krajów skandynawskich*, Warszawa, 1978.

Crouch, C. [ed.], *After the Euro. Shaping Institutions for Governance in the Wake of European Monetary Union*, Oxford University Press, 2000

Dutton, D., *British Politics Since 1945. The Rise and Fall of Consensus*, Blackwell, 1991

Dyson, K., Featherstone K., *The Road to Maastricht. Negotiating Economic and Monetary Union*, Oxford, 1999.

Fontaine, P., *10 lekcji o Europie*, Wspólnoty Europejskie, 1998

Fries, F., *Spór o Europę*, Warszawa, 1998

George, S., *Britain and European Integration since 1945*, Oxford, 1991

George, S., *Politics and Policy in the European Union*, Oxford, 1996

Gołembski, F., *Polityka zagraniczna Wielkiej Brytanii*, Warszawa, 2001

Goodin, R. E., Headey, B., Muffels, R., Dirven, H-J., *The Real World of Welfare Capitalism*, Cambridge, 1999

Grzybowski, M., *Systemy konstytucyjne państw skandynawskich*, Warszawa, 1998

Hadenius, S., *Swedish Politics during the 20th Century*, Swedish Institute, Stockholm, 1999

Hansen, P.[ed.], *How has Sweden managed outside the EMU?*, Stockholm, 2003

Heater, D., *Britain and the Outside World*, London, 1976

Heywood, P., Jones, E. and Rhodes, M. [ed.], *Developments in West European Politics 2*, London, 2002

Hirst, P., *Can the European Welfare State Survive Globalisation? Sweden, Denmark, and the Netherlands in Comparative Perspective*, London, 2000

Huber, E., Stephens, J. D., *Welfare State and Production Regimes in the Era of Retrenchment*, University of North Carolina, 1999

Kendle, J., *Federal Britain. A History*, London, 1997

Kennedy, P., *Mocarstwa Świata. Narodziny – Rozkwit – Upadek*, Warszawa, 1995

Kołodziejczyk, K., *Geneza wspólnotowej waluty – euro*, Warszawa, 2000

Leonard, D., *Przewodnik po Unii Europejskiej*, Warszawa, 1998

Lieber, R. J., *British Politics and European Unity. Parties, Elites, and Pressure Groups*, University of California Press, 1970

Matera, R., *Integracja ekonomiczna krajów nordyckich*, Toruń, 2001

McDonald, F. and Dearden, S. [ed.], *European Economic Integration*, Longman, 1999

Miles, L., *Sweden and European Integration*, Ashgate, 1997

Miles, L. [ed.], *Sweden and the European Union Evaluated*, London, 2000

Moravcsik, A., *The Choice for Europe. Social Purpose and State Power from Messina to Maastricht*, Cornell University Press, 1998

Muns, J. [ed.], *Spain and the Euro: Risks and Opportunities*, Barcelona, 1997

Noble, A., *Przewodnik po Unii Europejskiej. Od Rzymu do Maastricht i Amsterdamu*, Warszawa, 1998

Overturf, S. F., *Money and European Union*, London, 2000

Orędziak, L., *Euro – nowy pieniądz*, Warszawa, 1999

Parzymies, S., *Stosunki międzynarodowe w Europie 1945–1999*, Warszawa, 1999

Paxman, J., *The English. A Portrait of a People*, London, 1999

Petersson, O., *Swedish Government and Politics, Stockholm*, 1994

Popiuk-Rysińska, I., *Unia Europejska – geneza, kształt i konsekwencje integracji*, Warszawa, 1998

Robbins, K., *Zmierzch wielkiego mocarstwa. Wielka Brytania w latach 1870–1992*, Wrocław, 2000

Ruszkowski, J., Górnicz E., *Żurek M., Leksykon integracji europejskiej*, Warszawa, 1998

Sanders, D., *Losing an Empire, Finding a Role. British Foreign Policy since 1945*, London, 1990

Scharpf, F. W., *Governing in Europe: Effective and Democratic?*, Oxford, 1999

Spybey, T. [ed.], *Britain in Europe: An Introduction to Sociology*, London, 1997

Sverenius, T., *Krona eller Euro? Experternas argument för och emot EMU*, Rimbo, 2003

Thatcher, M., *Lata na Downing Street. Wspomnienia z okresu pelnienia funkcji premiera rządu Zjednoczonego Królestwa*, Gdansk, 2006

Tratt, J., *The Macmillan Government and Europe. A Study in the Process of Policy Development*, London, 1996

Weidenfeld, W., Wessels W., *Europa od A do Z. Podręcznik integracji europejskiej*, Gliwice, 1999

Woodward, E. L., *The Age of Reform 1815–1870*, Oxford, 1962

Young, H., *This Blessed Plot. Britain and Europe from Churchill to Blair*, London, 1999.

Articles and Reports

Andersson, M., 'EMU and Denmark', *Task Force on Economic and Monetary Union*, European Parliament, April 1998, PE 166.168/rev.2

Åström, S., 'Continuity or Change? Sweden appraises its security policy', *Current Sweden*, Swedish Institute, December 2001, no.434

Bäckström, U., 'Sweden's relations with the EMU', paper presented at the conference on the changing role of central banks, Lithuania, 3 October 1997

Bannock Consulting. An estimate of the one-off transition costs to the UK of joining the Euro', Bannock Consulting, July 2001

Barry, F., 'Does EMU Make Sense For Europe?' University College Dublin, September 1997

Becker, W., Järvbäck, A., 'EMU Watch. The United Kingdom, Sweden and Denmark on the Way to EMU', Deutsche Bank, August 2002, Research no.95

Belke, A., Gros, D., 'Estimating the Costs and Benefits of EMU: The Impact of External Shocks on Labour Markets', Tilburg University, Center for Economic Research, 1997, Discussion Paper no.95

Bergbom, L., 'Exchange Rate Variability Inside and Outside the EMU', Economic and Monetary Union Team, HM Treasury, December 1998

Birger Christensen, J. [ed.], 'Have debate – Need timetable', *Focus EMU*, Danske Bank Research, February 2002

Bjurulf, B., 'How did Sweden Manage the European Union?', Rheinische Friedrich Wilhelms-Universität Bonn, Centre for the European Integration Studies, Discussion Paper no.C96/2001, http://www.zei.de

Bryson, J. H., 'Special Report: Prospects for EMU Expansion', Wachovia Securities, Economic Group International, March 2002

Clinton-Davis, L., 'The Community and Britain: The Changing Relationship between London and Brussels', in *New Directions in British Politics? Essays on the Evolving Constitution*, edited by P. Norton, Hull, 1998

Collet, H., *On the Outside Looking In: Pragmatic Danes in Quick Reversal*, Yale University, November 1999

Collins, S., 'Wielka Brytania i Niemcy wobec rozszerzenia UE', *Sprawy Międzynarodowe*, 1997, no.4

'Co-ordination of economic policies in the EU: a presentation of key features of the main procedures', *Euro Papers*, July 2002, no.45

Currie, D., *The pros and cons*, HM Treasury, July 1997

Dalskov, J., *EMU and the markets*, Danske Bank Research, 2002

Edmonds, T., 'EMU: the approach to the Third Stage and the state of economic convergence', House of Commons Library, Economic Policy and Statistics Section, March 1998, Research Paper 98/35

Edmonds, T., 'The Euro-Zone: Year One', House of Commons Library, Economic Policy and Statistics Section, March 2000, Research Paper 00/34

Edmonds, T., 'The euro-zone: The early years & UK Convergence', House of Commons Library, Economic Policy and Statistics Section, July 2002, Research Paper 02/45

'The Euro area in the world's economy – developments in the first three years', July 2002, *Euro Papers* no.46

'Europe – The Future', HM Government, *Journal of Common Market Studies*, vol. 23, no. 1/1984

'Europe's Response to EMU', *4th Annual Report*, KPMG Consulting, January 2000

Ferguson, N., Kotlikoff, L. J., 'The Degeneration of EMU', *Foreign Affairs*, March/April 2000, vol. 72, no.2

Gamble, A., 'The European Issue in British Politics', in *Britain For and Against Europe. British Politics and the Question of European Integration*, edited by D. Baker and D. Seawright, Oxford, 1998

George, S., 'Great Britain and the European Community, The European Community: To Maastricht and Beyond', in *The Annals of the American Academy of Political and Social Science*, edited by R. D. Lambert, Philadelphia-Pennsylvania, 1994

Gołembski, F., 'Wielka Brytania wobec rozszerzenia Unii Europejskiej', *Sprawy Międzynarodowe*, 1998, no.2

Gottfries, N., 'Why is Sweden not in EMU?', Current Sweden, The Swedish Institute, January 2002, no.435

Grant, C., *Can Britain lead in Europe?*, Centre for European Reform, October 2002

Heathcoat-Amory, D., 'Why the United Kingdom must say "No"', *European Commission Economic Paper*, July 1994, no.108

Heikensten, L., 'Economic policy in EMU and Sweden', paper presented at the 2nd Seminar entitled 'EMU soon a reality – how is monetary policy affected?', Stockholm, 12 February 1998, *BIS Review* 9/1998

Hutchison, M. M., 'European Banking Distress and EMU: Institutional and Macroeconomic Risks', paper prepared for the workshop Structural Change and European Economic Integration, Denmark, Liseleje, 10–11 September 1999

Jackson K., 'Out of Europe: the Threat to Working People', *Britain in Europe*, London, 2000

Jenkins, A. K., 'The euro and public houses in the UK', *International Journal of Contemporary Hospitality Management*, 2000, 14/6

Jespersen, J., 'Why do Macroeconomists disagree on the Consequences of the Euro?', in *Money, macroeconomics and Keynes: volume one*, edited by S. C. Dow, P. Arestis, M. Desai, London, 2002

Johansson, K. M., *Sweden: another Awkward Partner?*, publication of the Forschungsinstitut für Politische Wissenschaft und Europäische Fragen der Universität zu Köln, http://www.politik.uni-koeln.de/wessels/de/publikationen/texte/TextMaurer/andreas/ Sweden.pdf

Karlsson, B., 'Neutrality and economy. Sweden and the European integration 1961–1972', *Svenska Nätverket för Europaforskning i Ekonomi*, http://www.snee.org/filer/papers/41.pdf

Kinnwall, M., 'How well has Sweden managed outside the EMU?', the article published in Swedish as 'Hur klarar sig Sverige utanför EMU?', *Journal of the Swedish Economic Association*, article published in English in *Svenska Nätverket för Europaforskning i Ekonomi*, 3/2002, http://www.snee.org/filer/papers/153.pdf

Klein, M. W., 'European Monetary Union', *New England Economic Review*, March/April 1998

Larsen, H., 'British and Danish European Policies on the 1990s: A Discourse Approach', *European Journal of International Relations*, London, 1999, vol. 5(4)

Laursen, F., *Denmark: in pursuit of influence and legitimacy*, publication of the Forschungsinstitut für Politische Wissenschaft und Europäische Fragen der Universität zu Köln, http://www.politik.uni-koeln.de/wessels/DE/PUBLIKATIONEN/texte/TextMaurer/andreas/ Denmark.pdf

Layard, R., Buiter, W., Currie, D., Huhne, C., Hutton, W., Kenen, P., Mundell, R., Turner, A., *The case for the euro, Britain in Europe Campaign Ltd.*, London, 2000

Lloyd, M., 'EMU: Relations between "ins" and "outs"', Directorate-General for Research, European Parliament, Working Paper, Economic Affairs Series, ECON-106, 10/98

Laursen, J., Høyer, H. D., and Jørgensen, K. E. [ed.], *Made in Denmark*, Jean Monet Center, University of Aarhus, http://www.jmc.au.dk/Made_in_Denmark.pdf

Matera, R., 'Droga Szwecji do Unii Europejskiej', *Sprawy Międzynarodowe*, 2000, no.4

Mathä, T., 'European Integration and Geographical Concentration of Swedish Multinationals', *SSE/EFI Working Paper Series in Economic and Finance*, February 1999, no.305

Miller, V., 'The Danish Referendum on Economic and Monetary Union', House of Commons Library, International Affairs and Defence Section, September 2000, Research Paper 00/78

Miller, V., 'EMU: Views in the other EU Member States', House of Commons Library, International Affairs and Defence Section, March 1998, Research Paper 98/39

Miles, L., 'Swedish Priorities For the IGC', *Current Sweden*, The Swedish Institute, March 1997, no.415

Nemichi, H., Marshall, L., Nicholson, B., FitzGerald N., *Out of Europe: the risk for business*, Britain in Europe Campaign Ltd., London, 2000

Parzymies, S., 'Konferencja Międzyrządowa 1996 państw Unii Europejskiej', *Sprawy Międzynarodowe*, 1995, no.4

Patterson, B., 'EMU and the United Kingdom', Task Force on Economic and Monetary Union, European Parliament, April 1998, PE 166.059/rev.3

Persson, K., 'Sweden, EMU and the krona', paper presented at the seminar at Svensk Handel, Stockholm, 16 November 2001, *BIS Review* 92/2001

Pickering, C., '"Sir Douglas in Euroland". Treasury Officials and the European Union, 1977–2001', *Public Administration*, 2000, vol. 80, no.3

Potton, E., Miller, V., Taylor, C., 'The Swedish Referendum on the Euro', House of Commons Library, Economic Policy and Statistics Section, International Affairs and Defence Section, 15 September 2003, Research Paper 03/68

Skjalm, K., *On the Outside... Denmark and the Euro*, Danish Institute of International Affairs, DUPI Report no.2000/8

Soltwedel, R., Dohse, D., Krieger-Boden, C., 'European Labour Markets and EMU Challenges Ahead', *Quarterly Magazine of the IMF*, June 2000, vol. 37, no.2

'Straight Bananas? 150 anti-European myths exploded', *Britain in Europe*, London, 2000

Ström Melin, A., 'Sweden's Presidency of the EU in Retrospect', *Current Sweden*, The Swedish Institute, November 2001, no.433

Suzuki, K., *Reform of British Competition Policy: Is European Integration the Only Major Factor?*, Stockholm School of Economics, 1999

Svensson, A. C., 'The Swedish Presidency, January-June 2001', *Current Sweden*, The Swedish Institute, December 2000, no.431

Svensson, L. E. O., 'Sweden and the Euro', *Briefing Paper for the Committee on Economic and Monetary Affairs of the European Parliament for the quarterly dialogue with the President of the European Central Bank*, January 2002

Srejber, E., 'Sweden and the European Integration', paper presented at the IBC Euroforum: Nordic Banking, Stockholm, 3 June 2002

Thomsen, J., 'Denmark and the Euro: A special relationship', paper presented at meeting at the Icelandic Central Bank, 10 March 2003

Tietmayer, Professor H, 'The Relationship between Economic Convergence and EMU', speech presented by the governor of the BundesbankBørsen Executive Club, *BIS Review* 30/1997

Trichet, J-C., 'The Euro after Two Years', *Journal of Common Market Studies*, March 2001, vol. 39

'Varför EU/EMU inte är ett vänster projekt?', *Nordisk Grön Vänster (GUE/NGL)*, 2002, European Parliament

'UK Membership of the Single Currency. An Assessment of Five Economic Tests', HM Treasury, October 1997

Ware, R., 'EMU: the constitutional implications', House of Commons Library, July 1998, Research Paper 98/78

Wojtyna, A., 'Rolnictwo brytyjskie wobec Wspólnej Polityki Rolnej EWG', *Sprawy Międzynarodowe*, 1974, no.2

Wynne, M. A., 'EMU: The End of the Beginning', presentation to the Board of Directors of the Federal Reserve Bank of Dallas, February 2002

Periodicals and Magazines

Forum, 2001, 2002, 2003, 2004

Gazeta Wyborcza, 2000, 2001, 2002, 2003, 2004

International Herald Tribune, 2002, 2003, 2004

Newsletter of the Danish Social-Liberal Party, 2000, 2001

Newsweek, 1999, 2000, 2001, 2002, 2003, 2004

Rocznik strategiczny, 1997/98, 1998/99, 1999/2000, 2000/01, 2001/02, 2002/03

Rzeczpospolita, 2000, 2001, 2002, 2003, 2004

The Economist, 2000, 2001, 2002, 2003, 2004

The Financial Times, 2001, 2002, 2003, 2004

The Guardian, 2000, 2001, 2002, 2003, 2004

The Independent, 2000, 2001, 2002, 2003, 2004

The Times, 2000, 2001, 2002, 2003, 2004

Time, 2000, 2001, 2002, 2003

Internet Sources

The Foreign and Commonwealth Office, http://www.fco.gov.uk

The UK Government Online, http://www.ukonline.gov.uk

The Prime Minister Online, http://www.number-10.gov.uk

The House of Commons, http://www.parliament.uk

Bank of England, http://www.bankofengland.co.uk

The Euro-Campaign of the Bank of England, http://www.euro.gov.uk

HM Treasury, http://www.hm-treasury.gov.uk

National Statistics Online, http://www.statistics.gov.uk

The Danish Ministry of Economic Affairs, http://www.oem.dk

Danish Ministry of Taxation, http://www.skat.dk

The Royal Danish Ministry of Foreign Affairs, http://www.um.dk

Danish Central Bank, http://www.nationalbanken.dk

The EU Information Centre in Denmark,
http://www.eu-oplysningen.dk

The Official Webpage about Denmark, http://www.denmark.dk

Danish Statistics Online, http://www.statbank.dk

Danmarks Statistik 2002, http://www.dst.dk

National Swedish Tax Board, http://www.rsv.se

Statistics Sweden, http:///www.scb.se

Swedish Ministry of Finance, http://finans.regeringen.se

The Swedish Government http://www.regeringen.se

The Swedish Ministry of Finance, http://finans.regeringen.se

The Swedish Ministry of Foreign Affairs,
http://ww.utrikes.regeringen.se

The Swedish Parliament, http://www.rikdagen.se

Swedish Central Bank, http://www.riksbank.se

National Institute for Economic Research Forecast, http://www.konj.se

Invest in Sweden Agency, http://www.isa.se

European Statistics Bureau 'Eurostat',
http://www.eu.int/comm/eurostat

European Central Bank, http://www.ecb.int

The European Union Online, http://europa.eu.int
US Foreign Commercial Service, http://www.export.com
US Department of State, http://www.state.gov
BBC News Online, http://news.bbc.co.uk
The EU Observer Online, http://www.euobserver.com.

www.ingramcontent.com/pod-product-compliance
Lightning Source LLC
Chambersburg PA
CBHW051441250726
48655CB00001B/178